Tropic of Cancer

CHINA

Beijing
Tianjin
Huang He
Wuhan
Chang Jiang
T'ai-pei
TAIWAN
Hong Kong
HONG KONG
Hanoi

GIA
AZERBAIJAN UZBEKISTAN KYRGYZSTAN
TURKMENISTAN TAJIKISTAN
Tehran AFGHANISTAN
Baghdad IRAN
ait
ARABIA PAKISTAN Lahore
QATAR Delhi NEPAL BHUTAN
U.A.E. Karachi Ganges
OMAN INDIA BANGLADESH
Calcutta BURMA
Bombay LAOS
Hyderabad
YMEN THAILAND VIETNAM
Bangalore Madras Bangkok CAMBODIA
Colombo SRI LANKA Ho Chi Minh
aba
PIA
MALIA Kuala Lumpur MALAYSIA
Singapore
BRUNEI
Manila
PHILIPPINES

0°

INDONESIA
PAPUA
NEW
GUINEA
SOLOMON
ISLANDS

alaam

St Augustine's Bay
Belamoty Mission
Benenitra
Ivahona
Bekofafa
Vangaindrano
MAURITIUS
RÉUNION

East MacDonnells
West MacDonnells
Haasts Bluff
Kintore
Lake Mac Donnell
Gibson Dessert

Carlo Station
Diamantina Lakes
National Park
Longreach
Barcaldine
Sapphire
Rockhampton

Tropic of Capricorn

Inhambane
Mavuma
Combumune Railhead
Bingo Boloi's Village
Baleni (Ivory Trail)
Ka Nkomo
Soekmekaar
Polokwane (Pietersberg)
Abbotspoort
Stockpoort

Ningaloo Reef
Capricorn Roadhouse
Jiggalong
Lake Disappointment

AUSTRALIA

Brisbane

Perth

Sydney
Canberra
Adelaide
Melbourne

40°

Indian

Hobart

Ocean

N

W E

S

OUR CAPRICORN JOURNEY ALONG
THE TROPIC OF CAPRICORN
THROUGH 10 COUNTRIES
AND THE CONTINENTS OF
FRICA, SOUTH AMERICA, AUSTRALIA
ND THE ISLAND OF MADAGASCAR—

Antarctic Circle

80° 120° 160°

FOLLOWING THE INVISIBLE LINE
CAPRICORN

Kingsley Holgate

MY FAMILY'S EPIC JOURNEY
AROUND THE WORLD

FOLLOWING THE INVISIBLE LINE
CAPRICORN

MY FAMILY'S EPIC JOURNEY AROUND THE WORLD

Kingsley Holgate

First published in 2003 by Struik Publishers
(a division of New Holland Publishing
(South Africa) (Pty) Ltd)

New Holland Publishing is a member of the
Johnnic Publishing Group

Garfield House
86–88 Edgware Road
W2 2EA London
United Kingdom
www.newhollandpublishers.com

Cornelis Struik House
80 McKenzie Street
Cape Town 8001
South Africa
www.struik.co.za

14 Aquatic Drive
Frenchs Forest
NSW 2086
Australia

218 Lake Road
Northcote
Auckland
New Zealand

ISBN 1 86872 781 5

1 3 5 7 9 10 8 6 4 2

Publishing manager: Dominique le Roux
Managing editor: Lesley Hay-Whitton
Designer: Alison Day
Editor: Monique Whitaker
Proofreader: Michelle Coburn
Cartographer: Steven Felmore
Illustrator: Fourie Ackerman

Reproduction by Hirt & Carter Cape (Pty) Ltd
Printed and bound by Tien Wah Press (Pte.) Ltd, Singapore

Visit us at **www.struik.co.za**
Log on to our photographic website
www.imagesofafrica.co.za
for an African experience.

A Capricorn Dedication

THESE HUMBLE SCRIBBLINGS FROM MY
CAPRICORN EXPEDITION JOURNAL ARE
WRITTEN FOR TWO VERY SPECIAL
PEOPLE, WITHOUT WHOM I COULD NEVER
HAVE SURVIVED THIS CRAZY ODYSSEY
AROUND THE WORLD

Gill I met when I was a young man, working
on the coast of Devon as a beach photographer.
She was on a working holiday from
Yorkshire and I was doing my 'rucksack on the back, kibbutz, German beerfest,
pokey flat in London' bit. We fell in love and Gill followed me back to Zululand. The
wedding took place in a little mission church, close to where King Shaka Zulu's great
military kraal of Kwabulawayo once stood. The Zulus named Gill 'Mashozi' (she who
wears shorts) and she was once heard to say, 'When I first met Kingsley he had a short
black beard and a rucksack full of dirty clothes. I fell in love twice, firstly with
Kingsley and then with Africa, my newly-adopted home.' That was 33 years ago
and we're still adventuring. Thanks, Mashozi!

Ross, now 30, is my best mate and only son – he's my right-hand man. Hopefully,
he and his son Tristan will continue to adventure well after the old 'Greybeard' has
turned up his toes. You who are fathers will understand this – to have been able to
adventure and have such wonderful shared experiences with your son, well, that's a
rare privilege, isn't it?

Siyabonga, Mashozi and Ross – I dedicate this Capricorn book to you both.
It was an unforgettable journey.

Kingsley Holgate

PLEASE NOTE – THE CAPRICORN EXPEDITION
TOOK 18 MONTHS TO COMPLETE, DURING WHICH
TIME THERE WERE CONSIDERABLE DELAYS!
CAUSED BY CLIMATIC CONDITIONS, BUREAUCRACY
AND THE SHIPPING OF LAND ROVERS, CHUMA
& SUCH BETWEEN THE CAPRICORN CONTINENTS

Dear Friend

Sawubona! Hi, bom dia, ja boet, dumelang, xav xirng, buenos dias, g'day cobber, bon jour and salaama. I greet you in just some of the many languages found along the Tropic of Capricorn, the line of latitude that joins our African Cradle of Humankind to Latin America, Australia and the island of Madagascar.

Please bear in mind that this is not an ordinary book, but one that's come together from the scribbled notes, pictures, sketches and maps taken from the battered and sweat-stained, leather-bound Capricorn Expedition journal. It's the true story of our world-first family adventure that has taken us around the globe in two South African Land Rovers, following the Tropic of Capricorn. With us we carried a Zulu calabash of seawater and a Capricorn Expedition Scroll of Peace and Goodwill.

Capricorn 23° 27' has been an amazing adventure. In Africa we dodged landmines and risked man-eating predators as we crossed the Kruger National Park on foot. We spent time experiencing fascinating African cultures and crossed the vast Kalahari and Namib deserts. In Brazil, the Guaranese Indians led us through the wet, tropical jungles of the Serra do Mar. In São Paulo we entered the largest concrete jungle along the Capricorn Line, before crossing the Rio Piranha, the Mato Grosso and the wilds of Paraguay, through which the Brazilians said we would never make it. There followed the volcanoes of the high Andes and the Atacama Desert, driest place on planet Earth. Then it was on to Australia, the largest Capricorn country. Here our expedition took us from the Great Barrier Reef in the east, across the Simpson Desert, which is the largest parallel sand dune desert in the world, the big red Gibson Desert, the Little Sandy Desert and lastly to the pristine marine beauty of Ningaloo in the west. Finally, there was Madagascar, a fascinating island lost in time, and one of the most difficult sections of the Expedition.

There were some days when the journey was incredibly tough and I was simply too tired to write even the date. At other times it was a joy to sit overlooking the Kalahari, the Namib or the Andes and scribble my notes in the expedition journal. I do hope that you enjoy the read - thank you for being part of our journey.

Siyabonga and Good Adventuring,

Kingsley Holgate

CAPRICORN SCROLL OF PEACE & GOODWILL

CAPRICORN CALABASH.

The Capricorn seed is sown

I first met Roger Gaisford in the early '70s, when he was an oddball geologist prospector type who panned for gold and lived in isolated tented camps in the wilds of Botswana and Zululand. Later, he guided me across the Kalahari in an old 4x4 called *Swaggies Breakfast*. All Roger carried was an old bedroll, a change of clothes, a three-legged pot, battered kettle, a near-empty food box and a bottle or two of booze. A hand-written sign on his Landie read: 'Society For The Preservation of Unpretentious Wines – Members Welcome.' We became great friends.

One night, years later, when Roger and I were seated around a fire with enamel mugs of Captain Morgan rum to fuel the imagination, he said in his rather schoolmasterly way, poking the fire with a stick as he did so: 'You know, Kingsley, you fellows should really think about following the line of the Tropic of Capricorn across Africa. It would be a great adventure and something of a world first.' I just stared into the coals and grunted.

At the time my family and I had just returned from a journey using an old 1873 map. We followed in the footsteps of Chuma and Susi, two unsung black heroes of exploration. It had been a fascinating journey for us and I must say that Capricorn sounded a bit staid by comparison, but I carried on listening as Roger enthused about Inhambane on the Mozambique coast and the many secrets and wonderful places along the Capricorn line. 'I bet you a bottle of the Captain's best that you can't do it,' he said. I laughed.

Later that night, after Roger had chugged off home in his antique Jeep, I lay in my Zulu beehive hut thinking about this imaginary line of Capricorn. I tossed and turned throughout the night and by breakfast my mind was firmly made up.

All great adventures commence with a vision; mine was now to cross the African continent along 23° 27' (it's actually 23° 26.5', to be exact), the Tropic of Capricorn. But could we make it, and in what vehicles? We'd need sponsors, money, maps and supplies. Once again there was that delightful feeling of commitment and nervous anticipation. It seemed that another great adventure was on the boil.

On getting back home to Zinkwazi, where we live in a sort of treehouse affair set amongst milkwoods, and overlooking the sea, I broke the news to Gill and Ross, my wife and son, who are the key members of all our family expeditions. Mashozi's first question was, 'Where will we get the money?' She is the expedition bursar and has learnt to keep our crazy ideas in check. Ross, the practical one, immediately went to our Africa Room and pulled out maps and charts. We spread them out on the floor and shooed the dogs away. Winston, the big male, looked on; he had seen it all before and probably thought to himself, 'Damn! They're going to leave home again!'

The name Capricorn is derived from the Latin words meaning 'goat horns', and Capricorn the tenth sign of the zodiac is symbolised by the mountain goat — oddly enough none of us are Capricorns; Mashozi is a Libra, Ross a Sagittarius and I'm Pisces: the fish!

GILL HOLGATE — HER NICKNAME IS 'MASHOZI' WE'VE BEEN MARRIED FOR 35 YEARS AND HAVE HAD SOME GREAT ADVENTURES TOGETHER — MASHOZI'S TASK IS THAT OF EXPEDITION BURSAR — SHE HAS TO LOOK AFTER THE CASH (THE LITTLE WE HAVE!) ALL THE PAPERWORK, VISAS PASSPORT AND ALL THE FOOD SUPPLIES' PLUS BEING THE 'MAMA' OF THIS CAPRICORN JOURNEY —— GOOD LUCK!

Capricorn line runs from just north of Inhambane on the Mozambique coast, through Mozambique, the Kruger National Park and South Africa's Limpopo Province, across Botswana's Kalahari, which is the greatest area of vegetated sand in the world, Namibia's giant, broken country of the Gramadoelas, the Namib Naukluft and then the Namib, most ancient desert on earth. 'The line' ends its journey across Africa on Namibia's Atlantic coast, to the south of Sandwich Bay.

But where does it go to from there, we wondered? I pulled out the huge National Geographic World Atlas and we found that after Africa the Tropic of Capricorn's journey continued to the coast of Brazil, some way below Rio de Janeiro, then across the mountains of the Serra do Mar, through the Brazilian city of São Paulo, across the huge Piranha Province, the Piranha River, the Motto Grosso, the wilds of Paraguay, the arid north of Argentina and then across the high Andes into Chile. Sandwiched between the Andes and the point on Chile's Pacific coast just north of Antofagasta where the Capricorn line meets the ocean, lies South America's final obstacle, the Atacama Desert – driest place on earth. Excitedly, we paged through to Australia. In Australia the line starts on Heron Island in the Great Barrier Reef and ends at Ningaloo. What a challenge that would be! Over 4 000 kilometres from east to west, across the great, red, untamed deserts of central Australia: the Simpson, Gibson and Little Sandy deserts, and also ancient Aboriginal lands. Last is Madagascar, where the line runs across the south of the island, through rainforest and semi-desert.

There are ten Capricorn countries in all: Mozambique, South Africa, Botswana, Namibia, Brazil, Paraguay, Argentina, Chile, Australia and the island of Madagascar, with its spiny forests, baobab trees and forest lemurs. Amazingly, millions of years ago, during the time of the super-continent of Gondwanaland, Africa, South America, Australia and Madagascar were all one. They then split, and are now joined only by the imaginary line of the Tropic of Capricorn.

We closed the atlas, laughed and looked at each other. I phoned Roger Gaisford; he was out and I left a message: 'Roger, the game is on. We are going to attempt a world first, following the Capricorn line around the globe by land.' The date was 12 November 2000.

Capricorn 23° 27' - Turning the vision into reality

Whilst the decision, and the vision, to get out and 'do it' is for some people the most difficult thing, for us that's always been the easiest. We have been privileged: our lives are full of wonderful ideas for great adventures that we'll never live long enough to be able

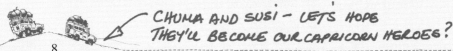

CHUMA AND SUSI — LET'S HOPE THEY'LL BECOME OUR CAPRICORN HEROES?

to complete. For us, the difficult phase is the one of raising the money and finding the sponsors. Once we knew that we wanted to circumnavigate the globe along the Capricorn line we had to find the means with which to succeed!

I once heard world-famous polar explorer Sir Ranulph Fiennes say in an interview that he had found that getting sponsors and money, and trying to get the bureaucrats along the way to buy into the expedition, was far more difficult than the expedition itself.

Arranging sponsorship generally means a flight from our coastal paradise to Johannesburg, South Africa's hub. For me it's another world, but Ross knows his way around the city, and soon the two of us were standing at reception in the smart, well-kept offices of Land Rover South Africa. I'd squeezed into a pair of khaki longs and combed my beard and Ross proceeded to tuck in his shirt. Father and son were at it again! We were there to see Paul Melhuish, Land Rover's Marketing Director, and were ushered into a really smart boardroom. It was late afternoon and beers were offered. Phew! Nice and relaxed.

We showed a video clip of our recent successful Livingstone's Footsteps Expedition, which Ross had produced for the National Geographic Channel. Fortunately for us, Paul knew of our family's history and background, and like us he had been born and brought up in South Africa's KwaZulu-Natal Province. He knew the Nkwaleni Valley, where Ross had been born and where Gill and I'd begun married life running a remote trading post. We'd been the only white family surrounded by thousands of Zulu people. Paul saw value in the project. 'I think we should go for it,' he said. 'Exploration and adventure is synonymous with Land Rover – I really like the idea.'

Outside the building Ross and I bumped into Moira Moses, popular Managing Director of Land Rover SA. Land Rovers aren't new to Moira: she was born on the slopes of Mount Kilimanjaro and is a great adventurer at heart, so she instantly warmed to our planned adventure. The expedition would be managed, from a Land Rover point of view, by Lesley Sutton, their Media Affairs Co-ordinator. We soon found she too had a love for the African bush, a great sense of adventure and a pleasant, straightforward attitude towards marketing. We had used Land Rovers in the past and they were our expedition vehicles of choice, as they are ideal for incredibly rough conditions. We are also romantics at heart, and there is no doubt that Land Rover pioneered early 4x4 exploration in Africa. The designer of Porsche once

ROSS HOLGATE – HE'S A GREAT ADVENTURER AND IS MY RIGHT HAND MAN – HE'LL HANDLE ALL THE TECHNICAL SIDE AND THE DIFFICULT TASK OF EXPEDITION NAVIGATOR – WHILST WE'LL HAVE A CAMERAMAN FOR EACH LEG OF THE JOURNEY – THE DOCUMENTARY OF THIS CRAZY ADVENTURE WILL BE ROSS'S RESPONSIBILITY – I'M PRIVILEGED AS A FATHER TO BE ABLE TO DO A JOURNEY LIKE THIS WITH MY SON – WE'RE ALSO GREAT MATES!

SUSI

said, 'There is only one vehicle you can bolt anything onto and it still looks pretty – that's a Land Rover!' And so with time and more discussions we were offered two brand new Land Rover Td5 Defender Station Wagons. Needless to say we were overjoyed!

And what would we do without good old Captain Morgan rum? Rum supported the sailors of the Royal Navy for generations, and Captain Morgan, with their spirit of freedom and adventure, has been our most loyal sponsor – not only with their fine product, but also with funding numerous past expeditions. We always have the Captain Morgan decals stuck to the expedition vehicles. Part of the logo is the Buccaneer Captain Morgan himself complete with long hair and beard; not surprising, therefore, that at Zambian roadblocks I have often been saluted with the words, 'Good morning Captain!' The Captain has also helped us across a number of border posts and through some sticky situations. It is great to use for flambéeing steak on a spade and makes wonderful renoster coffee and mosquito repellent! As expected, the marketing team was delighted with the idea of Capricorn 23° 27', 'Around the World by Land', and pledged stock and some funding. Of course we drank a toast to their unfailing spirit of adventure!

So, we now had Land Rovers, Captain Morgan rum and some funding. What we really needed was a fuel sponsor. One company kept us on a string, then let us down at the last moment due to a change of staff, leaving us no time to approach anyone else. Once again we were forced to dip into the family pension fund. At this rate we'd better not live too long! It's always an interesting debate: do you enjoy life now (and risk an impoverished old age) or seek a life of security and retire wealthy, but possibly too old to do the things you really should be doing *now*? We decided that, come what may, we were going to tackle the Tropic of Capricorn.

But how would we move between Capricorn countries? Then came a stroke of good luck: through old friend Dave Oxlee we got an introduction to Flight Centre's Marketing Director, Barry Robinson-Butler. What a great organisation – not only do they offer guaranteed lowest airfares, but they are a young, dynamic team who specialise in getting adventurers to their destinations. Barry pulled out all the stops for us and agreed to cover the air links between Africa, South America, Australia and Madagascar. In return we'd carry the Flight Centre decals on the Land Rovers and mention them in all media coverage. At last, after six months, we had wings.

Continental Tyres agreed to supply us with their wide Contitrack tyres, which we believed would be ideal for all the deserts we had to navigate. Ernst Spaans from African Satellite Corporation in Johannesburg would supply a satellite phone. From past adventures, Ernst had become a good friend, once even visiting us whilst we circumnavigated the Makgadikgadi salt pans in Central Botswana using land yachts, and his satellite phone communications had on several occasions saved our lives. Robertsons Spices agreed to supply us with soups, Aromat, Bovril, Marmite and Rajah Curry powder; those little things that South Africans cannot do without.

A number of potential sponsors wished us well but had to turn us down for various reasons. Some had insufficient budgets and others said, 'Great idea Kingsley, but it doesn't fit our profile,' or, 'Sorry, the Marketing Director is still on leave / in a meeting / at a conference / out of the office / sick in bed / simply doesn't give a damn about a crazy family that wants to circumnavigate the world by land along the Tropic of Capricorn!' That's life, and we've learnt to take it. At least we had a departure date: 16 May 2001.

But can we beat the red tape?

However much time one has to plan, the crunch still comes near departure date. Just two weeks before we were due to leave we still didn't have permission to jump the fence from Mozambique into the Kruger National Park, and then walk the Capricorn line across the park itself. Likewise, permission from Namibia's Ministry of Environment and Tourism still hadn't been given for us to cross the massive Namib-Naukluft, or the Namib Desert itself. I started to have nightmares. After all the talk, imagine if we couldn't stick to the line. Land Rover had pledged the vehicles, but couldn't find stock. And after Namibia we still had no clue how we were going to get the vehicles to South America and beyond.

Luckily, my friend Duncan Davis stepped in here. I don't know where he got the name 'Drunken Duncan', but I had met him a few times and realised that it took an enormous amount of booze to fill his massive frame. He owns Phoenix Shipping, and when I phoned him for shipping contacts in Durban to find out about getting the vehicles to South America, he didn't hesitate. 'I'm your man,' he said. 'I've got a ship leaving for Montevideo in Uruguay. It is a bit south of the Capricorn line, but feel free to put them aboard. Be my guest!' I am always humbled by the incredible support we get. I think it's that natural spirit of adventure in people, especially in South Africans.

Then, with just 12 days left to our departure date, disaster struck. We got a telephone call from Namibia's Ministry of Environment to say, 'Mr Holgate, your application to follow the Tropic of Capricorn across the Namib Desert has been rejected.'

Damn it! I felt powerless. Faxes and emails are never as good as meeting people face to face. I knew I should have flown to Windhoek, but as always it had been too expensive. I slammed the door in frustration and, whistling for the dogs, ducked out through the trees and onto the beach. The spring tide had washed the beach clean and a fresh north-easterly blew off the Indian Ocean. It's all so timeless, not a human being in sight, not a footprint. I walked south towards Nonoti Lagoon, the sun on my back, and our dogs Winston, Edward and Baker running and barking for sticks. Why, when I had all this, did I want to carry on adventuring? Especially now that I'm a grandfather. The beard's grey, the right knee's damaged from the Zambezi Expedition, the lower back stiff from thousands of kilometres of inflatable boat journeys on the rivers and lakes of Africa, my liver's tired from all the malaria and I've got a useless right shoulder after a bad fall on the Tugela River. But I laugh at the thought of giving it up. What would life be without that feeling of excitement before the start of another great journey, not knowing what's around the next corner, who you are going to meet, where you are going to sleep – the sheer joy of the adventure? I wouldn't change it for anything.

And so I enlisted Taryn Stoddart's help. She is my old friend Gary Prentice's delightful girlfriend. They live down the road from us and Taryn is to provide back-up for the Capricorn Journey. Tall and blonde, I think she might have Viking blood in her, and she is a real lifeline for a grey-beard adventurer who still doesn't have a

THE BLESSING OF THE CAPRICORN CALABASH

cellphone or a watch, let alone a computer. I dictated an appeal to Maria Kapere, Namibia's Director of Parks and Wildlife, and Taryn's fingers raced across the keyboard. I begged for her support for this world-first endeavour, and followed this up with a phone call to her secretary. I know not to try to push these things too quickly. Over many years I've learnt that, while the Swiss may have developed the clock, it is Africa that owns the time.

With three days to go, the expedition vehicles arrived. Two brand, spanking new white Land Rover Defender Td5 station wagons. Ross leapt to work organising long-range fuel tanks, water carriers, bullbars, winches, spare wheels, roof-racks and high-lift jacks. In the meantime Gill quietly organised food boxes, medical supplies and all our personal gear. Friends dropped around to say goodbye, the telephone kept ringing, and Radio 702 wanted an interview. We knew that one of our biggest challenges was going to be crossing the Namib Desert, so we packed extra sand ladders and 'roll-out' corrugated rubber mats.

As on all our expeditions I decided to keep a leather-bound journal, to record our adventure, as it unfolded. I knew there would be a minefield of obstacles, and also exciting, frustrating and sometimes dangerous times. I hoped we would make it, and I hope now that you will enjoy sharing these pages of the Capricorn Expedition journal with us.

Day 1: A Zulu mvalalisa - what a send-off

It's Wednesday 16 May 2001. We sent off invitations several weeks ago, urging friends to wear their favourite bush hat and come along to Shakaland for a bit of merry-making and a Capricorn farewell. Shakaland was started by my crazy anthropologist friend Barry Leitch, the Zulus from the nearby Nkwaleni Valley and me, after the filming of the international television series depicting the life-story of the great King Shaka Zulu. In 1983 we turned the film set into an oddball Zulu cultural attraction. It soon outgrew our laid-back management, mostly conducted while sitting on cow dung floors, cross-legged on grass mats and goat skins, eating with our hands from *izingqoko* (handcarved wooden platters for meat), and drinking copious quantities of Zulu beer. The guests wondered if they'd ever survive the endless hours of Zulu drumming and dancing, the leaking beehive huts and the goats in the rooms. But all that has changed now. Shakaland is managed by Protea Hotels, has a beautiful thatched dome restaurant and is one of the finest cultural attractions in Africa – but to us it remains our spiritual home.

Ross was born here in the Nkwaleni Valley and we feel at home amongst our Zulu friends, whom we've known for years. For us this is the ideal place to kick off our crazy Capricorn adventure. The farewell festivities commence in the old historic bar just before sunset, by which time most of the guests are red-faced and talking loudly. Most of them aren't averse to taking a shandy on a hot afternoon, so to speak, and now there's free Captain Morgan rum. Barry Leitch, dressed in a leopard skin headdress and brightly decorated Zulu trousers, gets the *mvalalisa*, or farewell ceremony, going by leaping into a frenzied *giya*, whilst the Zulus shout out his praise names as he dances.

Zulu people in ceremonial beadwork and skins escort the guests up to the entrance of the great kraal, where Ross has just stuck the last Capricorn decals onto the two expedition Landies. A Zulu *sangoma* (diviner) and her white clay-faced, bare-breasted initiate bless the vehicles with a swish of a wildebeest tail fly-whisk. The Zulus chant to the drum beat and

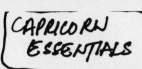

CAPRICORN ESSENTIALS

CAPTAIN MORGAN EXPEDITION RUM

ENAMEL MUG A BIG ONE FOR SPECIAL OCCASIONS! AND RENOSTER COFFEE —

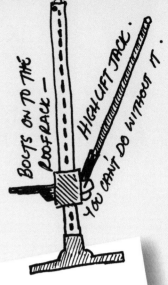

BOLTS ON TO THE ROOFRACK —
HIGH LIFT JACK.
YOU CAN'T DO WITHOUT IT.

GOOD OLD MAG-LITE —
SPARE BATTERIES & GLOBES

LEATHERMAN

RUBBER SAND MATS — YOU ROLL THEM OUT UNDER THE WHEELS!

TRADITIONAL AFFIARS
CUSTOMS AND CULTURE

BIRTH CERTIFICATE

460228 0000 00

ID NO :

MPUNGOSE

SURNAME :

NONDWAYISO KINGSLEY RALPH HOLGATE

FIRST NAMES :

1946-02-28

DATE OF BIRTH :

MALE

SEX :

SOUTH AFRICA

COUNTRY OF BIRTH :

WHITE BY BIRTH ZULU BY CHOICE

RACE :

THIS WILL CONFUSE THE AUSSIES!

2001-05-16

DATE ISSUED :

SHAKALAND

PLACE :

HIS WORSHIP THE MAYOR ALDERMAN STAN LARKAN

BY :

AS A BIT OF A FAREWELL JOKE THE MAYOR AND THE LOCAL CHIEF PRESENT ME WITH A NEW BIRTH CERTIFICATE

the sound of the *sangoma*'s pebble-filled cocoon ankle rattles. A type of wild heather called *imphephu* smoulders in a broken pot shard. The guests are asked to inhale the smoke so as to call up the ancestral spirits. Land Rover's Moira Moses hands over the keys to Ross, Gill and me. Cameras click and we are filmed for the television actuality programme *Carte Blanche*. At last we have an expedition!

I tell the story of David Livingstone's two loyal companions, Chuma and Susi. Dr Livingstone died a lonely death kneeling in prayer in an African hut in Chief Chitambo's village. Chuma and Susi cut his heart out and buried it in a biscuit tin under a giant mapundu tree. They then salt-dried his corpse, placed it in a hollow bark cylinder, wrapped it in sail cloth and strung it to a pole. There followed the longest and bravest funeral march in African history, a journey of over 1 600 kilometres to Bagamoyo and Zanzibar. In honour of these two brave, unsung heroes of African exploration, we christen the two Capricorn Expedition Land Rovers *Chuma* and *Susi*.

Well over 100 people fit into the hut of the ancestral spirits at the top end of the kraal. The sponsors make farewell speeches. The mayor, Alderman Stan Larken, and our local chief, Mrs Mpungoze, sign the Capricorn Scroll of Peace and Goodwill that we plan to carry around the world. With much humour I'm presented with a birth certificate making me a member of the local Zulu community and giving me the surname Mpungoze. The *isigenyana* hunting dance has the dancers leaping into the air, using their animal-tail sticks as imaginary spears to perform the ancient rituals of the hunt to the rhythmic throbbing of two massive rawhide drums. Moira Moses bids us *bon voyage* and Paul Raphaely from Captain Morgan suggests we continue the revelry around the fire down at the bar – the same fire where Roger Gaisford and I sat, giving birth to the Capricorn idea, just six months ago. Roger's here tonight, wearing his old leather bush hat and laughing his head off. I overhear him saying to our local bank manager, 'Bloody crazy idea this Capricorn Expedition, don't you think?'

Day 2: Hangovers in the Place of Heaven

KwaZulu, Place of Heaven! Generally, being woken gently by the sound of a Zulu guitar outside your beehive hut bedroom at 7 o'clock in the morning would be romantic. But not when you only got to bed at 4 am. Still, this is the stuff that grand expedition farewells are made of, so we stagger out of bed for one of Shakaland's great specialities: coffee and a full English breakfast.

The big night is over and now, in expedition mode, Lesley Sutton from Land Rover leads us out of Shakaland in a cavalcade of Land Rovers and journalists. Everybody is in a jolly mood as they join us for the first day of our journey, heading north to meet the Tropic of Capricorn. The dirt track out of Shakaland winds over the historic Elangeni Hills, high above the Nkwaleni Valley. It was in the Mzule River Valley below us that the beautiful Nandi was courted by Zulu King Senzangakhona, in the late 18th century. The two got carried away and some time later, when Nandi told Senzangakhona she was pregnant, he brushed her aside saying, '*Hambani*, you only have a *shaka* in your stomach.' (An *ishaka* is an intestinal beetle that is said to disrupt a woman's menstrual cycle.) Well, some months later, Nandi turned up again at Senzangakhona's palace, this time with the baby Shaka in her arms. Little did Nandi know then that southern Africa would reverberate to the name of Shaka, and that her son was to become the greatest king the Zulu nation would ever know.

Down in the Mfule Valley, near Barry Leitch's old homestead at Simunye, we're invited to attend an *icece* or coming of age ceremony. It's a sort of debutantes' ball in the bush, in which a Zulu girl who has come of age is shown off to the community after having been fattened up for several months. She performs a dance, during which money is pinned to her hair by the men of the area, a beast is slaughtered and it's a great party. We are made most welcome, goat skins and mats are put out for us to sit on and we're offered giant clay pots of sorghum beer. Will we ever get to the Capricorn line to start our journey officially?

Day 3: Our final goodbyes and hambani kahle

What a beautiful morning. We overnighted at Simunye Bush Camp on the Mfule River, chatted to the visiting journalists and had a great evening. It's an emotional time for Ross as he says goodbye to his girlfriend Geraldine and their baby son Tristan Kingsley. This is the first time Ross has had to leave the *umfanyan* (little boy). Father and son go off for a while on horseback, the little fella clutching the saddle. Hopefully one day our grandchild will read this expedition journal and get to adventure in his father's footsteps.

We're eager to get going, so after final goodbyes we splash Land Rovers *Chuma* and *Susi* across the Mfule River and, with engines roaring, race up to the trading store at the top of the hill. Gill and I travel in *Chuma*, Ross and Mike Yelseth in *Susi*, both vehicles loaded to the hilt with maps, supplies, tents, Captain Morgan and camera equipment. It's great to have Mike along; he's one of South Africa's finest cameramen and an old partner in adventure. We completed a Zambezi mouth-to-source together, the Madgadikgadi salt pans by land yacht, and a circumnavigation of Lake Turkana (the world's largest desert lake). We all get on well: he's really professional and a good laugh around the fire, so we're lucky he's coming along; especially as we are filming the expedition, not only for *Carte Blanche*, but also for a National Geographic documentary.

We have been travelling with Mike for years, but we've never seen him so absolutely infatuated before.

MIKE YELSETH — HE'S LIKE A FAMILY MEMBER — I GUESS IT'S BECAUSE OF ALL THE SHARED ADVENTURES THAT WE'RE SUCH KINDRED SPIRITS — MIKE'S ONE OF SOUTH AFRICA'S MOST ACCOMPLISHED ADVENTURE CAMERAMEN. WHAT'S BETTER STILL IS THAT HE'S USED TO EXPEDITION LIFE AND KNOWS HOW TO FILM 'ON THE RUN'. HE LOVES A GOOD YARN AND IS GREAT FUN AROUND THE CAMPFIRE AT NIGHT — MIKE'S DOING AFRICA

I believe the poor fellow's love sick! Vanessa is an old mate of ours and the two of them met at our house at Christmas. We pull his leg about it: normally he's only got tropical diseases and sunburn to worry about, now it's a more serious malady and one that appears to be permanent. Every time there's a cellphone signal he's on the phone to her.

Day 4: To Maputaland and beyond

In the early colonial days the area was known as Tongaland. Now this coastal strip of Northern Zululand to the south of the Mozambican border is known as Maputaland, a delightful wetland of lakes, estuaries and coral reefs, inhabited by the friendly and laid-back Tonga people who enjoy the local *njomani* wine tapped from the thousands of ilala palm trees.

Our spirits soar as we race north. The Land Rover has that new-car smell, and as I watch the gauges and the revs I'm reminded that we are used to the earlier Tdi four-cylinder, slow-revving plodders, and are still getting used to these new, high-tech, five-cylinder machines. We've taken the precaution of waterproofing the electronics boxes under the front passenger seats. In the areas we're going to there will be no fancy mechanics. The new Landies handle beautifully, and the sand track north of Mbazwana soon delivers us to the bustling market town of Kwa-Ngwanase where we stock up with diesel and supplies before crossing into Mozambique.

The Capricorn team is in great spirits as we reach the border. The South African police conduct careful checks here, as this bush outpost at Ponta do Ouro is a great favourite with cross-border car thieves. The red, green, black and yellow Mozambican flag, complete with a star set behind a hoe and an AK47 rifle crossed over an open book, flutters above a small shack on the Mozambican side. Here it's all smiles and *bom dia*'s as we hand over the vehicle papers and Portuguese letters of introduction. In the days before border posts the Tonga people wandered freely across this area; then came the European Scramble for Africa, in which the continent was carved up like a cake. Now we have English newspapers, bacon and eggs and Castle beer on the one side, and flat chicken, *pão* bread and Laurentina *cerveja* (beer) on the other. The Mozambican border officials, having spied the expedition decals, call me Captain Morgan. They have never heard of the Tropic of Capricorn, so with maps spread out on the Land Rover bonnet, we have an impromptu geography lesson.

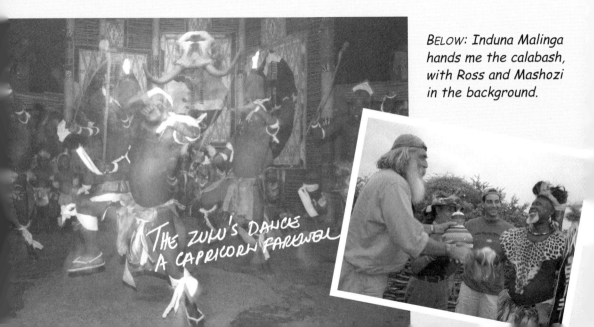

BELOW: *Induna Malinga hands me the calabash, with Ross and Mashozi in the background.*

THE ZULU'S DANCE A CAPRICORN FAREWELL

uMLALAZI

IHHOVISI LIKAMEYA : MAYORAL OFFICE : KANTOOR VAN DIE BURGEMEESTER

HUTCHINSON ROAD/WEG ESHOWE : KWAZULU-NATAL

☎ 37, 3815   ☎ +27 (0)35 4741141 : 4741373 : 4741375   FAX: 035 4744733

Mr K Holgate
Capricorn Expedition
Eshowe
3815

Dear Kingsley, Gill and Ross

It is with pleasure that I write this letter and convey to you my best wishes, and those of the uMlalazi Council, from the people of this Municipality of uMlalazi in the Province of KwaZulu-Natal, South Africa.

We in the uMlalazi Municipality recognise and acknowledge the challenge of this World First Capricorn Expedition which will foster sound relationships and peace with all peoples.

On behalf of the citizens and Councillors of the uMlalazi Municipality we hope that you will extend to those that you meet our message of goodwill, peace and friendship.

We wish all the adventurous members of the World First Capricorn Expedition Bon Voyage for a safe and eventful passage around the World.

May your forthcoming endeavours be blessed with success and happiness.

My thoughts go with you,

Stan Larkan
Mayor

Mozambique

Our planned Tropic of Capricorn journey will take us from 23°27' on the coast of Mozambique – just north of the ancient city of Inhambane, then west into the setting sun, across the provinces of Inhambare and Gaza. We'll have to cross the flooded Rio Limpopo and follow the Tropic to the Kruger National Park fence – we don't know quite what to expect!

Day 5: Casa Lisa and Pineshine

Mike films the Land Rovers ploughing through the deep muddy water. The large Betacam camera on his shoulder seems like part of his body and, in true Mike fashion, there's a cigarette dangling from the corner of his mouth. Our past shared adventures on the Zambezi, in Angola and the Congo, have made him part of our family; it's not like having a film crew around, and Mike is quick enough to film things as they happen, on the move. The only problem is that Ross and Mike are dangerous company for each other, especially if left alone near the rum pots.

We turn a corner and to the north of us, across the bay, lies Maputo, capital of Mozambique and once the grand old lady Lourenço Marques. Sadly she's only a faded shadow of her former colonial self. How things change – a few years ago we were the enemy, now Nelson Mandela is married to Graça Machel, the revolution is over, at last peace has come to South Africa and Mozambique, and we are welcome.

There is wild confusion at the Catembe Ferry: money changers, hawkers selling fish, bananas, boiled eggs, sweet potatoes, colourful cloth, woven baskets, cold beer, Coca-Cola and cigarettes. Overloaded trucks, hooters blaring, line up to get onto the ferry. It's the weekend, and people are shouting and laughing over the loud music. Out of the confusion steps Custodio Manhica, ex-Frelimo soldier and old friend. 'Señor King,' he shouts and comes rushing forward, a huge smile lighting up his face. He's wearing a great, big, straw hat and a rucksack over his shoulder. We embrace warmly, the Portuguese way. Custodio is to be our guide across Mozambique. It's wonderful to see him and I am hugely relieved he's made it.

I like to spend some time in Mozambique
The sunny sky is aqua blue
And all the couples dancing cheek to cheek
It's very nice to stay a week or two

Bob Dylan wrote the words to this song in 1975 and, although the country has been left desperately poor after the ravages of socialism and war, the people in Maputo still have a zest for life and living. Custodio is certainly no exception to the rule. We met years ago, when we employed him as our guide and risked landmines and bandits to travel to Pemba and on to the island of Ibo. It was a wild adventure. With us travelled dear old friend Paul Hallowes, a Kenyan-born eccentric who fell in love with the challenge of war-torn Mozambique. Years later, with Custodio as his partner, they hacked a rustic tourist camp, pub and restaurant out of the bush some 50 kilometres north

EAST
WEST

INDIAN OCEAN
23°27'

TROPIC OF CAPRICORN
COAST OF MOCAMBIQUE

WE FILL THE CAPRICORN CALABASH WITH INDIAN OCEAN SEA-WATER

FRIENDLY CAPRICORN VILLAGERS OF TERRA DA BOA GENTE

MBANGENI
BEAUTIFUL SAND FOREST – BUT!

DANGER OF LANDMINES

COMBUMUNE RAILHEAD .

FLOODED Limpopo

BY BICYCLE WITH EX-FRELIMO MATAIS NGONYAMA

INADVERTENTLY WE'RE FOLLOWING 'JOMPA JOZZ' TO JUMP THE FENCE TO JO'BURG - THE ILLEGAL IMMIGRANT TRAIL

FENCE LINE . NO SEX!
23°27' R.S.A.
KRUGER NATIONAL PARK

Paul and his pineshine

CUSTODIO MANHIKA: HE'S AGREED TO LEAVE ROSSIE AND THE CHILDREN BEHIND FOR A FEW WEEKS TO JOIN THIS CRAZY CAPRICORN ADVENTURE! WE'RE OLD FRIENDS AND IT'LL BE GOOD TO TRAVEL AGAIN TOGETHER - CUSTODIO WITH HIS FLOPPY HAT AND EASY GOING MANNER, SOON GETS EVERYBODY ON HIS SIDE - WE'LL RELY ON HIM TO TRANSLATE & FOR HIS KNOWLEDGE OF THE AREA —

of Maputo on the Xai-Xai Road. Not surprisingly, it's called Casa Lisa after Lizzie, Paul's wife, the driving force behind the restaurant, which is famous for its charcoal-grilled flat chicken.

Having crossed into Maputo on the ferry, Casa Lisa is our next destination, and we arrive just before sunset. Paul is a legend at the bar, his constant cries of 'Next round!' competing with the cranked up noise of his old jazz, blues and rock'n'roll tapes. Many a fisherman intent on travelling north has taken a day or two to recover from his Fawlty Towers-like 'hospitality'. Apart from running the camp Paul also grows pineapples, and from a copper still on his bar counter produces a spirit he calls pineshine. It's got a kick like an angry ostrich, and I'm convinced he runs his tractor on it! Towards midnight, Mike takes up the challenge to drink one-for-one with old Paul, but soon our daredevil cameraman crumples to the floor as if shot by a sniper. Quite incoherent and with saliva dribbling from the corner of his mouth he slurs just one word: 'pineshine', before falling deeply unconscious.

Custodio

Day 6: Terra da Boa Gente - The Land of Good People

Gill is terrified of old sailing dhows. We once had a frightening experience during which we nearly drowned and she's never got over it. Her eyes widen as a wave washes over the gunnels and the skipper grunts to the sole crew member to ease off on the main sheet.

To the creaking and groaning of the dhow's mangrove ribs and hand-sawn planks, we sail with the wind across the Bay of Inhambane to the ancient city of Inhambane, with old friend Erwin Jakes. We asked him to put together a meeting with the Governor of Inhambane Province to request a letter to carry with us through Capricorn's unknown bush country, and since Inhambane is the closest town to the start of our journey along the Tropic of Capricorn, we really want the Governor to endorse the Capricorn Scroll of Peace and Goodwill we are carrying around the world.

At times travelling in Africa can be a really humbling experience. Outside the governor's office the heads of police, education, tourism, the military and the governor of Inhambane Province, Mr Aires Ali, Dave Law (the colourful owner of Barra Lodge), together with the mayor of the city, are patiently waiting. They emerge from the old faded Portuguese colonial building that serves as their headquarters and everybody stands to attention. A busy little man representing the local TV station aims his minute camera, the man from the radio station presses play and waves his old-fashioned microphone at everybody and anybody who opens their mouth. Not to be outdone, 'the man from protocol' (as he is introduced to us) orders us around smartly, and the local newspaper man scribbles wildly in his notebook. We didn't expect anything like this, and here we are in wet shorts, sandals and T-shirts.

Just as the proceedings are about to commence, a little old lady runs up and switches on the town's fountain, resulting in a trickle of water that tries desperately to defy gravity.

His Excellency the Governor of the Province of Inhambane is a fine looking man. Dressed in a smart West African print shirt, he speaks of the pride with which he, his councillors and the people of Inhambane welcome our Capricorn Expedition. He explains that Inhambane has a long maritime history throughout which it has welcomed adventurers and pioneers such as ourselves. In January 1498, the great Portuguese explorer Vasco da Gama anchored in this very bay and was so well received that he called it Terra da Boa Gente, 'The Land of Good People'. The governor endorses our Capricorn Scroll of Peace and Goodwill, we all shake hands and, like an idiot (not realising he is Muslim), I present him with a bottle of Captain Morgan rum. With a smile he graciously accepts the gift, before passing it on to the mayor, who grins with delight – the crowd roars with laughter. The sun is fast setting in the west as the little old lady switches off the fountain. We all shake hands again and then the man from protocol walks us down to the jetty.

The wooden prow of our handmade boat cuts slowly through the Indian Ocean, turned golden by the setting sun. It feels so timeless, making me think of the tens of thousands of slaves whose hearts were filled with terror as they were loaded into boats like these to be taken across to Inhambane. Similar boats have been crossing this bay over the centuries, carrying slaves, ivory, gold, mangrove poles and coconuts, but this is the first time that a family, intent on travelling around the world along the Capricorn line, is being ferried across the Baia de Inhambane. Like Vasco da

The governor of Inhambane, Mr Aires Ali, signs the Scroll, as Erwin Jakes and the Mayor look on.

Gama before us, we are touched by the welcome we've received from the people of Terra da Boa Gente. It feels like a good omen for the journey that lies ahead.

Day 7: 23° 27' - We Reach Trópico de Capricórnio

North of Inhambane we search for the Tropic of Capricorn and the start of our expedition using a GPS (global positioning system) and somewhat outdated survey maps (the most recent we could get were printed in the '70s). We squeeze the Land Rovers through thick bush as we make our way from village to village, asking directions as we go. It's late afternoon and many of the local people are exceedingly merry on palm wine, directions are somewhat garbled and erratic hand signals point us in a variety of different directions.

With deflated tyres and engines roaring, we plough through deep, soft white sand, zigzagging between the palm trees. Fishermen walking off the beach with their catch are amazed to find strange white people in the middle of nowhere, looking for an imaginary line called the Trópico de Capricórnio. They've never heard of it and gather wide-eyed to watch Ross spread out a survey map on the bonnet of the Land Rover. The friendly fishermen point

23°27'

out a gap in the sand dunes that takes us down onto a deserted, unspoilt stretch of Mozambican beach. The wind is blowing up white horses from the south-east, and it's almost dark by the time we pitch camp exactly on 23° 27', where the Tropic of Capricorn leaves the coral-clad shallows of the Indian Ocean to begin its journey across Africa.

Everyone is jolly and there is a wonderful feeling of excitement. A fisherman offers us a fair-sized rock cod. Our camp table is a massive squared-off log that conveniently washed off a cargo ship to land on our Capricorn beach. We gather driftwood and soon have a bright yellow blaze blowing sparks into the starlit sky. With our hands we pick the succulent flesh from the rock cod, throwing the scales down on the glowing coals, and then enjoy chunks of beef skewered on sticks and eaten with coarse salt. Our camp is a simple affair: grub boxes, an old smoke-blackened camp kettle, enamel mugs and plates, lightweight tents and old canvas camp chairs. The breeze keeps the mosquitoes at bay as we sit barefoot in the sand.

One of the locals, Señor Zaire, has been hired as camp security for the night. He has shared our camp meal and is now wrapped up in his blanket next to the fire. Mashozi, Ross and Mike are also off to bed early. Custodio and I sit up drinking Captain Morgan rum and discussing Mozambique's turbulent history. From Custodio I learn that, once Vasco da Gama had 'discovered' what is now Mozambique, the Portuguese set up fortified trading posts along this coastline, as they needed refreshment stations to resupply their ships on the way from Europe to India. Apart from reprovisioning their ships, they traded in gold from the ancient kingdom of Monomatapa. Then ivory became the sought-after commodity, followed in the 1700s by 'black gold', that despicable trade in human beings. It is estimated that over a million Mozambican people were sold into slavery. In the 1800s the Scramble for Africa led to Portugal being granted ownership of Mozambique. How generous of Britain, France and Germany to give away a huge piece of Africa, as world powers divided up the continent, with hardly a thought for the native inhabitants. The Portuguese called the area Portuguese East Africa. Later it was called Mozambique and was run as a province of Portugal. The central government remained in Portugal and very little social investment was put into Mozambique. Adult males were encouraged to work on the South African gold mines, a contract that South Africa paid for in gold. So now, in Mozambique, we are able to communicate with the local people in 'Fanagalo', the old Zulu-based lingua franca of southern Africa's mine workers.

The rest is history: a change to a socialist government in Portugal, the revolution in Mozambique and the destruction of this country in a long, drawn-out and bloody civil war between the Marxist-backed Frelimo and the (at one time) Rhodesian- and South African-backed Renamo. As always, it was the ordinary people like Custodio who suffered.

During the evening the south-easterly picks up, the tents flap and waves crash onto the beach just metres from our little camp, squeezed between the highwater mark and the dunes. I lie awake wondering what adventures, fears and challenges lie ahead of us along Capricorn. Señor Zaire coughs occasionally and stokes the fire. Later I hear him snoring. Soon the sun will be up and we'll commence one of the greatest adventures of our lives. *Boa noite.*

Day 8: Coral reefs, calabashes and coconuts

It's up before sunrise for our first morning on the Capricorn line. Señor Zaire blows life into last night's coals, and by the time the kettle has boiled the dark clouds over the sea are lit up

THE JOURNEY ALONG THE INVISIBLE LINE IS ABOUT TO BEGIN

with the sun's rays. Just 50 metres or so north of our camp, fresh water bubbles out of a pool on the beach. Crystal clear, it comes from under the dunes and is filtered by the fine white sand. The local women arrive to fill their water containers, using open calabashes tied to long sticks, and are amazed to find us leaping about in the waves, filling our beaded Zulu calabash with Indian Ocean seawater. Yes, I know it's crazy, but we're going to carry this symbolic calabash around the world along the Capricorn line. We plan to fill it at the beginning and empty it at the end of each of the Capricorn continents. Indian Ocean seawater from here on the Tropic of Capricorn will be carried across Mozambique, South Africa, Botswana and Namibia to be emptied into the Atlantic, where the giant red sand dunes of the ancient Namib Desert fall into the sea. Then it will be South America, Australia, Madagascar and finally back to this very point where we are now for the end of the expedition in about a year's time. How strange it feels knowing that we will head west from here, around the globe, to return to this very same spot. I hope we make it!

It's quite an emotional time for us as a family. Gill, Ross and I hug each other as we emerge from the waves with our calabash. We've worked hard for this moment, and here at last our vision is becoming a reality and we are about to set off. We could not have hoped for a more favourable start to the expedition and the Capricorn team is in high spirits. After loading our kit, we fire up *Chuma* and *Susi*.

We enter a beautiful belt of high palm trees and neat reed-walled villages, thatched with woven coconut palm leaves. The people who live here are Matsua and speak Chitsue. We stop to fill our water containers at a village well. Gill is always fussy about getting water at the first available opportunity, and since she's in charge of supplies, we bow to her wisdom. Because of our slack attitude she's had many a night in the bush without cooking or bathing water. The

THE "CAPRICORN GREYBEARD" WRITING UP THIS EXPEDITION JOURNAL ON THE COAST OF MOCAMBIQUE

"CAPRICORN EXPEDITION."

women at the well are shy at first. The children hide behind their mothers and shriek at the sight of my large frame and bushy beard, but soon the colourfully dressed village mamas are laughing and smiling as they fill up our water containers. The entire village rushes out to gawk at the strangers. A young boy shins up a tall coconut palm. The villagers shout '*tivonele*!' ('watch out') as a fat green missile falls from the sky, and soon we are drinking fresh coconut milk.

It's slow going as we follow the GPS through hundreds of square kilometres of tall palm trees, grinding along in first and second gear. Towards nightfall we stop a group of locals in a battered old pick-up truck. 'Are we on the right track and is it safe to camp here for the night?' we ask. More importantly, 'Are there landmines?' Fortunately the answer is, '*Nada*, no landmines here.' Soon the land owner, Señor Joakim, arrives. He's a slightly built man with an open, honest face and a shy smile. He urges us to spend the night at his home, which once belonged to a Portuguese family before they fled the country. They promised Señor Joakim that they would one day return to Africa. They never did, and now only the old bullet-ridden house, broken down Mercedes Benz truck and the lemon and cashew nut trees remind one of those former Portuguese colonial times.

What a kind man Señor Joakim is. He gives us dry coconut husks for our fire and gifts of groundnuts, oranges, lemons and bananas. We roast a chicken in our three-legged cast-iron pot and Ross even does roast potatoes, rice and gravy. Custodio is excellent company and Señor Joakim is delighted to have such unusual guests camp out under his giant cashew nut trees. He's an educated man and knows about the Trópico de Capricórnio.

During the night I wake up to Gill's crying and groaning. She is having a nightmare. Is it fear of landmines or the journey ahead? She's a seasoned campaigner and will tell me if she is worried. I shake her gently and ask if she's okay. 'I'm not bloody snoring,' she says and goes back to sleep. She's only recently started snoring a bit, but tells me that it's only when she's under canvas – aided, might I add, by a drink or two. We have been married for nearly 35 years, and there're no secrets!

Day 9: Pencil boxes and landmines

It's midday when we leave the coastal plain of coconut palms and villages behind us. Heading due west we struggle to navigate through increasingly thick bush, which tears at the Landies. We spend a great deal of time at villages asking the way forward. They all think we're bloody crazy. Everybody knows there's a road to the south, so why do we have to follow this imaginary *Trópico do Capricórnio*? It just confirms what they already know: nothing's changed, white people are mad.

Land Rover gave us a number of plastic pencil boxes to hand out at rural schools. Can you imagine the delight with which the young kids receive us at a tiny bush school constructed from forest poles and thatch in a little village on the Capricorn line? Trunks of pencil boxes are off-loaded from the Land Rovers' roofracks. Every smiling kid gets one and I give an impromptu geography lesson about the Trópico do Capricórnio and teach the entire school to count from one to five in English. The amazed teachers sign our Capricorn Scroll of Peace and Goodwill and the sound of the children's song of farewell carries us west into the setting sun. There's loud music and a party atmosphere at the next village. We stop to buy a few supplies, but Gill turns down the offer of smoked cane rat, saying she would rather starve.

We set up camp in an old maize field, believing that where maize is growing, there's less chance of landmines. Señor Americo, the owner of the maize field, shares our simple meal. He tells us of the war years and how his people were all moved out of their villages to the Frelimo-protected towns. Only now are they returning to the bush and planting the land again. With a grave expression he warns us that we should be careful ahead as there are many unexploded landmines that have not yet been cleared, and we should ask at each village. Inquiries made before we left led us to believe that most of the mines had been lifted. This is obviously not the case, and the danger of landmines immediately adds a frightening dimension to our journey.

Day 10: 23° 27' lost and found

Señor Americo arrives in time to share breakfast with us and bum a few batteries for his transistor radio. Our tents are wet from a heavy dew, and we sit facing the morning sun like baboons on a cliff top, except that, in addition to scratching ourselves, we're holding steaming enamel mugs of coffee and condensed milk, and Mike and Custodio are already

puffing on their first cigarettes of the day. We leave Señor Americo with some malarial treatment for his sick wife. His radio, now full of new energy, blares forth music, news and football results. We have reconnected Señor Americo to the world.

Down the track, and somewhat lost again, we come across an old East German drilling rig, sinking a Red Cross-funded borehole, all part of a scheme to get people back into the bush. The drilling rig crew is intrigued but concerned by our Capricorn journey. We put all the survey maps for this region together, using their mugs, pots and an old camp kettle as paperweights. The rigger, Señor Abilio, is adamant that we should not continue further than the village of Mavuma, as the area ahead was 'very hot' during the war and there are many unexploded landmines. He strongly suggests that from Mavuma we should leave the Capricorn line and head north to the old Portuguese Administrative Centre of Funhalouro. There we must get advice from the administrator.

Mavuma turns out to be a tired, bombed-out, bullet-holed, one-time Portuguese trading post that sells cigarettes, smoked bushmeat (mostly warthog, impala and duiker), soap, coffee, sugar, salt and home-brewed sorghum beer. We groan as Gill purchases a traditional earthenware pot: we know that each time we pack or unpack the Land Rover we're going to have to worry about not breaking it. Still, I must concede that our home is full of beautiful crafts from all over Africa thanks to Gill. What's really bothering us, however, is not just that we might break Gill's pot, but the danger of us all being blown to smithereens by landmines.

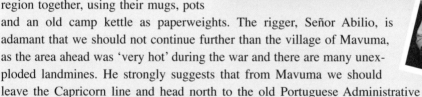

IN PORTUGUESE IT'S 'THE TRÓPICO DO CAPRICÓRNIO'

25

23°27'

In Funhalouro the design of the administrator's whitewashed house and offices is frozen in Portuguese colonial times. The administrator is away in Maputo, but we meet with his assistant, who arrives and agrees to sign our Scroll of Peace and Goodwill. He is amazed by our Capricorn journey and clearly impressed by our letter from the Governor of Inhambane. He says that the only way we can take is a detour, way north of the Capricorn line, which will take us on a 'safer road', he says, and bring us back to the Tropic of Capricorn closer to the Rio Limpopo. 'Señors, don't continue west from Mavuma. It's too dangerous!' we are earnestly warned.

This is a real blow. Our objective is to average no more than 50 kilometres from the Tropic of Capricorn and wherever possible to stick exactly on or as close to 23° 27' as humanly possible. This other road the administrator's assistant wants us to take is 200 kilometres north of the line. It's a disaster. Surely there's another way?

We drive into town in search of cold *cerveja* and a solution. It's Saturday afternoon, music is blaring and the bars are full in this fly-blown, Wild West town. It really is a difficult situation. Only this morning we interviewed two legless landmine victims who crawled from their villages to sit near the roadside, desperately poor and with no artificial limbs or wheelchairs. Now another reminder – a young girl on crutches with one leg missing hobbles past. From Custodio I learn that she was blown up just two months ago.

Leaving the Capricorn team on the verandah of the friendly bar, Custodio and I go walk-about. A tough-looking fella in an old Toyota truck with South African number plates offers to lead us along a closer route that is currently being cleared by a Zimbabwe de-mining team. Red-eyed and smelling of grog, he demands R2 000 for the favour. Sitting in the back of his truck drinking beer and eyeing us through sunglasses are three of his henchmen. Custodio continues to negotiate, but I've got an uneasy feeling. I suggest to Custodio we turn down their offer and tell them we're giving up and going back to Maputo. He agrees, and they laugh as we walk away. If they've got AK47s hidden in their vehicle we'll be at their mercy. They will simply lead us to our possible deaths in the middle of nowhere and rob us of everything. If we fork out R2 000 they will know we have money, and judging by their looks they will want everything, including the Land Rovers.

We stop a lorry driver, his vehicle groaning under the weight of massive trunks of hardwood timber, raped from the indigenous forests. He looks at us suspiciously, as if we have 'Greenpeace' written across our foreheads. 'Take the administrator's road to the north. It's the only one,' he says, before lurching off in his diesel-belching truck. The war and land-mines have given this giant piece of African bush time to recover, but now, with peace, humans are back with a vengeance.

Hugely disappointed, Custodio and I walk back towards the bar. A serious young man comes over and addresses Custodio in Portuguese. He points back down the Mavuma road and starts drawing with his finger in the sand. 'Señor King! I think we have a solution,' says Custodio excitedly. I feel comfortable relying on Custodio's ability to translate. His English and Portuguese are good and he has a quiet confidence about him that people respect. He's never in a hurry and has completely bought into our Capricorn Expedition. Dressed in his old T-shirt, shorts and sandals, a cigarette stuck in the corner of his mouth as always and an old straw hat on his head, he looks very laid-back, but he too is desperate to find a solution to the landmine problem and a way forward along the Capricorn line.

Our new friend, a plain-clothes policeman, explains there's a recently-made track that turns west just north of Mavuma. 'It's been cut by poachers and illegal loggers. Follow it carefully making sure you're following old vehicle and animal tracks. At times the track is very sandy and narrow and the bush thick. You'll have to keep asking along the way, but if you're careful I think it can take you to the Rio Limpopo. Good luck my friends and be careful!'

'Custodio, you've got your wife Rossie and young children at home. Are you prepared to risk it?' I ask. He turns to me with a smile in his eyes. 'Let's go and tell the others the good news,' he says. Gill, Ross and Mike are overjoyed. I explain there are risks and that our policeman informant has not travelled the entire track to the Rio Limpopo, so there is no guarantee the way is safe.

It's a fiercely hot day as we push on through the dust. Sure enough, there's a small track just outside Mavuma heading west along Capricorn. What's even better are the numerous cattle tracks, pock-marking the surface of the sand. With our hearts in our mouths Gill and I lead and Ross, Mike and Custodio follow. At times it strikes me how ridiculous it is that we've got caught up in sticking to this imaginary line, with its many challenges and difficulties. It would be easy enough to cheat, but we'd only be fooling ourselves.

Making sure to keep the other Land Rover in sight in our rear-view mirror, we twist and turn through an area of beautiful sand forest, the canopies of the tall trees spreading above us. We come across a team of strongly muscled men carrying saws and axes. Yes, we are on the right track towards a place called Kupu, which we have located on the map. The GPS mounted on the dashboard of the Land Rover confirms our good fortune, as we follow some fairly recent vehicle tracks through the sand. At sunset, feeling bolder now, we take a chance and turn off the track into a beautiful clearing of fine white sand surrounded by trees.

This small inland beach paradise immediately becomes our home for the night, and the Capricorn team sets up camp with ease. Custodio has mastered the art of putting up his light-weight tent, and for Mike, Ross, Gill and me it's second nature. Ross is the roofrack man. He passes down the dented camp table, and strong East African-type canvas chairs. Gill is already fiddling in the grub box. The 'bar' is open and the fire is a merry blaze already, while a lamp off the battery throws a light over the cooking area, where the last of the fresh meat disappears into the stew pot. The horrible feeling of dodging landmines has made everybody a bit tense and the enamel mugs of Captain Morgan seem to empty more rapidly than usual.

Day 11: Monkey apples and a booby-trapped fridge

Ahead of us lies the Limpopo River and we have a deadline by which we have to reach the Kruger National Park fence. Johann Oelofse, a senior park ranger, is waiting to escort us along the Capricorn line on foot (it's never been done before, and it has been a minefield of negotiation to get permission for this section of the trip alone).

With all this in mind, there is a rush to pack and get going. But first I unscrew the spade from the roofrack and step gingerly through the bush to execute 'morning ablutions'. On the way back I can't resist dressing my beard and hair with a mass of a wispy, fern-like

23°27' IS THIS INVISIBLE LINE WORTH DYING FOR?

creeper, commonly known as Grandfather's Beard, pulled from a tree, and a long stick adds to the 'Father Time' look. In my other hand I carry two round monkey apples, each the size of a cricket ball. With a bent back and using the stick for support I hobble into camp and explain in an ancient voice that yes, indeed, this great journey of discovery is taking many years. Weighing the monkey apples in my hand, I look at Ross with a maniacal stare (it's becoming easier these days!): 'Young man, you'll need 'big balls' to complete this Capricorn Odyssey!' I proclaim. There are roars of laughter and Ross so enjoys the ridiculous stunt that I have to do a replay for Mike's camera, which of course delays the packing. In Africa it is difficult to rush a good journey.

Once we pass Kupu the bush thickens, and sometimes we need to stop to cut away low branches. The windscreen protectors (two cables that run diagonally from either end of the bullbar to the front corners of the roofrack) manage to deflect branches from the windscreen, but we can't avoid the tearing of the rooftop tarpaulins and the constant scratching of the bush against the sides of *Chuma* and *Susi*. Made for bush use, the side mirrors fold back with a click against the body. Still, it's slow going and takes a lot of concentration. It's the Limpopo or bust!

We reach the remains of an old cattle ranch and follow a broken fence line for kilometre after kilometre. The faint track now travels through tall elephant grass, and a fallen tree blocks the way, so I follow Ross as he makes a detour through the high grass. I am careful to keep in his tracks, but quite frankly I'd rather be in front leading the way. How would I feel at the sight of his Land Rover being torn apart and hurled into the sky? Here, miles from nowhere, there are no hospitals and virtually no roads. Imagine the desperate satellite phone call for help. It's a terrifying thought – and all for an imaginary line called Capricorn.

We leave the fence line behind. Now the track is hardly discernible and at times we travel blind. The recent floods have left large pans filled with crystal clear water, decorated with water lilies and dry fish eagle trees, all surrounded by white, sandy beaches. Custodio and Ross walk ahead, testing the deep water before we plough through in the Landies. We find a section of the track again, but no vehicle tracks. There's a piece of an old stone and concrete bridge that has been blown apart, and Ross walks towards it, but I shout, 'Come back!' We've been warned to stay clear of the approaches to bridges and culverts. A little further on I get stuck coming out of one of the pans and have to be winched forward. Mike's filming, Custodio chainsmokes, Ross studies maps and the GPS with a frown, and Gill goes quiet. We're all getting a bit tense.

Then we meet a lone barbel fisherman. *Halala!* We hear we're on the right track and our spirits soar. I take this opportunity to have a chat with Ross. He's young, and has a girlfriend and a baby son, while Gill and I are over 55 and have had a great innings, so we should lead the way, I tell him. We all laugh and I pull off down the track to Kubo Village. It's marked on the 1972 map as a sizeable settlement, but that was a long time ago. Now the wind whistles through the bullet-ridden walls of the derelict Portuguese colonial outpost, complete with underground water storage tanks, giant bedrooms, terracotta tiled roofs, workshops, warehouses, cattle dip tanks, and an old trading store. In its time this must have been one of the finest cattle ranches in Mozambique. Now the only meat on offer is some smoked impala and warthog being sold by the local poacher from under a tree to a few wide-eyed locals who've arrived in an old beaten up truck.

"THE FRIDGE PARTY"

The road ahead, they say, is free of landmines. What a relief! I wander off to explore the ruins and, in what must once have been a beautiful high-ceilinged room, find an old, rusty fridge. Sneaking back to the Land Rovers I grab some booze, put it in the old fridge and close the door, shouting for the others to come and look around the old house. Ross comes in and stands looking at the fridge. I look up from where I am sitting on an old concrete block on the floor. 'Might be booby trapped,' I warn, 'don't touch it.' Jumping up, I say, 'Let me, I've lived my life.' I jerk open the fridge door and with a shout jump backwards. The look on their faces when they see a fridge full of booze! We all feel relieved that we've escaped the landmines, and we sit on the floor of the old hacienda and celebrate.

Back on the winding track, we push on into the dark. A lady on a donkey confirms that we are on the track to Dindinza. In the night, at a crossing, we find a lone white man, Señor Almeida. We're amazed to hear that he has survived the war and is hanging on amidst the ruins of his old homestead, with no lights and hundreds of cooing pigeons roosting in the rafters. Señor Almeida has gone 'bush'; he's taken a local wife and, judging by the number of blue-eyed, chocolate-coloured kids, he has kept himself reasonably busy. At first he's nervous to see us strangers, but after chatting to Custodio and reading the governor's letter he signs the Capricorn Scroll with a flourish and shows us the *buraco*, the hole in his verandah wall where Renamo attempted to dynamite his house. Nowadays he trades and runs cattle. 'It's a hard and lonely life,' he says, 'but at least the war is over and I'm alive and free.' His sons give us directions and we move on into the night.

We camp in the thick bush with not a person in sight, but in the distance we hear jackal and hyena as we eat the last of yesterday's stew. Mike and Ross sit up around the fire. *Boa noite* fellow travellers of the Capricorn line.

Day 12: Combumune railway and the Rio Limpopo

Progress is painfully slow. We set up the satellite phone and get through to Johann Oelofse, first chatting to his wife Jocelyn. They fully understand our predicament, all the frustrating delays and problems, and they ask us to contact them again once we have crossed the Limpopo and are closer to the Kruger National Park fence line. I immediately sense a kindred adventurer spirit in Johann that has me looking forward to meeting him. Ross rigs up the canvas bucket shower on a tree, and we're each allowed five litres of water (Gill a little more). Back in *Chuma* and *Susi* we bounce west, with pristine African sandforest surrounding us for as far as the eye can see.

23°27'

We reach a thatched kraal, where the owner has an ox-drawn wagon and fields of maize, millet, cassava and pumpkins. Hanging from a tree are some massive fish hooks and thick line. 'In the nearby swamp you catch *vundu* as big as a man,' he says as he signs the Capricorn Scroll. He tells us of the horrific war years and how he had to leave this village. Now he's old and it's difficult to start again. I notice, however, that he has several young wives all hard at work grinding corn and shelling groundnuts.

Closer to Combumune the destruction of the forests is noticeable. We see and smell the smoke from countless charcoal pits. In the villages woodcutters and carpenters are turning the tropical hardwoods into furniture and planks. The town of Combumune is on the railway line that carries people, chickens, goats, bushmeat, firewood, charcoal, planks, handmade furniture and trade goods through the bush to the markets of Maputo. The surly administrator signs the Capricorn Scroll and gives us fresh drinking water from his well. Many of the people here speak Tsonga. Hopeful travellers wait listlessly, sitting or sleeping on the station platform, and patient mothers breastfeed their wailing infants. Everybody is seated on or next to their pile of worldly belongings. Some, I know, will be travelling south to Maputo in search of a better life. But I'm sure many are unaware of the poverty, AIDS, crime and high unemployment there. They've got a contact in the city and there's the lure of the 'bright lights'. Some will make it – most won't. And the train is three days late.

If we were Victorian explorers we would have written, 'After a long and difficult journey from the coast, we finally arrive at our great geographic prize – the mighty Limpopo.' We have made it, but to our astonishment and dismay, and despite the fact that we are now into the dry season, the Rio Limpopo is still running high and wide after the recent devastating floods. The river banks are fringed with dark green, wild fig trees. It's late afternoon and colourful Nguni cattle come down to drink. This is the largest number of cattle we have seen along Mozambique's Capricorn line. The national herd was killed off and eaten during the civil war. Tsonga girls, who've come down to the river to bathe, wash clothes, collect water and flirt with the herd boys, gather with excitement around the Land Rovers. They tell us that it's impossible to cross the river here by vehicle, and even further up at Mapai the river is too high to cross to Pafuri and the Kruger National Park.

Nevertheless, we try to cross and get hopelessly stuck on a sandbank halfway out in the Limpopo. It takes an hour of digging and pushing, but finally by sunset we're camped on the sandbank. We swim in the cool river and wash the mud from our bodies. Later we are told, 'Yes, there are some crocodiles, but not too many.' Ross wades and swims across the remainder of the river. 'It's impossible by vehicle, we'll have to find another solution,' he says. It's a clear night and the river gurgles next to our tent.

Day 13: Señor Matais Ngonyama and his uncle's bicycle

We've been up since sunrise hatching a plot. Local ex-Frelimo soldier Señor Matais Ngonyama has borrowed his uncle's bicycle and for a fee is going to guide Ross and me to Chief Boloi's village, about 80 kilometres away on the other side of the Limpopo, and then on to the Kruger National Park. He claims to have done the journey before, but when I ask, 'Is this the route the illegal immigrants take to jump the fence into South Africa?' he and his uncle laugh and change the subject.

Gill, with Custodio and Mike, will take the Land Rovers and detour 250 kilometres around to the south to cross the Limpopo by bridge, and then work her way back to rendezvous with us at Chief Bingo Boloi's village, but she is unhappy that the party is splitting up. Obviously, she is concerned about malaria, wild animals, the danger of landmines and her husband and only son taking off into the bush with a total stranger. We unload our mountain bikes, oil the chains and pump the tyres. Into our rucksacks we load packets of soup, tins of bully beef, beans, sugar, salt, rice and tea. We take all the drinking water we can carry and check the medical kit. I slip in some Captain Morgan (in a plastic bottle), biscuits and processed cheese, but I don't take a tent; we'll sleep under the stars. The GPS goes into a sealed plastic bag and I draw a rough map by hand from the drawings we made in the sand whilst questioning Matais Ngonyama's uncle.

What a sight! Matais Ngonyama arrives, in a baseball cap and faded Frelimo camouflage fatigues, with his uncle's old balloon-tyred bicycle, which is loaded to the hilt. Ross and I load up our modern mountain bikes and, at the last minute, I add some sachets of *Rehydrat* and a plastic jar of crunchy peanut butter for energy. The Land Rover tyre inner tube that we pump up to help float the bicycles across the Limpopo develops a hernia in the hot sun and bursts, giving us the fright of our lives. As we are about to cross the Limpopo we are called back by the vehicle party who are up to their axles in soft black mud. It takes over two hours of pushing, winching and finally finding an alternative route to get them out of the mud. Then a last farewell and they're off, Custodio driving one Land Rover and Mashozi the other. Custodio waves his grass hat out of the window. As always we have scribbled two identical notes, each with 'Plan A' and emergency 'Plan B'. Mashozi has the one note, Ross and I the other.

Fortunately, the crocodiles don't get us as we swim and wade with the bicycles across the river. In one deep section the current is quite strong, but we finally make it. We take a well-worn footpath out of the valley and up to a village. Two mamas motion for us to come inside. They are baking fresh Portuguese bread, *pão*, in an outside clay oven fired with hardwood coals. It smells wonderful and we buy 20 big rolls for the journey. They put us on the right path (hey, I thought the guide was supposed to know the way!), and we're soon pedalling into the afternoon sun, pushing on

PLAN A.

GO DIRECTLY TO VILLAGE OF CHIEF BINGO BALOI AND WAIT FOR OUR ARRIVAL – IF WE SEND YOU NEWS IT WILL BE IN MY WRITING OR ROSS – IF NO NEWS JUST WAIT AND DON'T MOVE – CUT OFF TIME IS WEDNESDAY AT 12 NOON

PLAN B

IF NO NEWS FROM ROSS OR ME BY 12 NOON WEDNESDAY GO BACK TO LIMPOPO RIVER AND ORGANIZE A SEARCH PARTY – WITH ADMINISTRATOR AT COMBUMUNE AND MATAIS UNCLE – IF NOTHING BY SUNSET OF FRIDAY – CALL CASA LISA AND ORGANIZE AIR SEARCH – USE SAT PHONE. GOOD LUCK !

DOWN THE JOMPA JOZZ TRACK TO THE K.N.P. FENCE

BLOODY HELL ! WE'LL HAVE TO DO IT BY BICYCLE !

well into the night. When we finally stop we light a small fire to cook up some beans, which we have with bread and sweet tea that I 'power up' with the contents of my secret waterbottle.

Matais Ngonyama, who was very reserved initially, starts to brighten up after the doctored tea and a few cigarettes. We communicate in Fanagalo slang, with some choice Zulu and Tsonga words thrown in. Yes, he's come this way before and there are no landmines here, but we should be careful of illegal poachers. This area, close to the Kruger National Park, still has a lot of wildlife and we are aware of the conservationists' grand plan to incorporate it into Kruger, turning it into a massive trans-frontier peace park. During the night the sound of gun shots has all three of us sitting bolt upright. '*Ba dubula izinyamazana*' ('They are shooting wild animals'), says Matais with a grin, as if it is quite normal. Not wanting to add to the poachers' bounty, we extinguish our small fire, preferring to remain hidden for the night. The ground is hard and there is a heavy dew. Ross has brought only a light sheet sleeping bag and complains that he's absolutely freezing.

Day 14: Poachers, no sex, and the track to Jompa Jozz

We wake early and it only takes our good man Matais a few minutes of walking around to realise that we are utterly and completely lost. He admits to having tried to take a short cut in the dark. We have to backtrack all the way to the 'bread village' before heading west again along a well-worn path. Matais soon puts us to shame: sitting upright on his antique bicycle, he out-pedals our multi-geared mountain bikes and has us sweating and panting for dear life. To make things worse the sand just gets softer and softer as the day becomes hotter, and we soon find it easier to get off our bikes and push. As the hours tick by we pass through exquisite countryside, with not a person or village in sight. We wade into a grassy swamp and push the waterbottles into the grass to fill them with brown-coloured water. We add purification tabs and a sachet or two of *Rehydrat*. Matais loves the taste, especially when I tell him it is strong *muthi*, or medicine. However, this turns out to be a mistake, as he swallows bottle after bottle.

Ross is worried about our direction. There's a fork in the path and we stop to scrutinise our hand-drawn map. Matais shouts in alarm as a man crashes through the nearby bush, running away from us. We've disturbed a poacher who obviously thinks we work for the Mozambican Game Department and runs for his life. He has a bag over his shoulder and is carrying an old 303 rifle. Earlier this morning we came across a lot of snares and Matais demonstrated to us how they are set and the animals caught. Needless to say we broke them up and threw them into the bush, which had Matais looking around nervously.

Ross wants to go left and Matais favours right. We decide to follow the GPS, explaining to Matais that this little black plastic machine never lies and that if he hadn't got us lost last night we'd be more inclined to believe him. He looks rather annoyed, but it's nothing a bit more from my precious waterbottle won't sort out. We all take a sip, he grins, and we move forward.

Just a short way further along the path we run into a man with a mean look, a rasta hairstyle and an AK47 over his shoulder. I don't know who gets the bigger fright, him or us. '*Boa tarde*,' I stammer, sliding to a halt with my brakes locked.

CAPRICORN EXPEDITION

I DON'T KNOW WHO GOT THE BIGGEST FRIGHT– HIM OR US!!

Matais is equally surprised by this rather nasty-looking character. He utters just a few words of greeting, then urges us forward. It is all over in a few seconds, but we only stop, quite out of breath, after 10 minutes or so. Matais looks back down the path and drawing his finger across his throat says, 'If I hadn't been with *mlungus* (white people), he would have killed me for the bicycle, which he would use for transporting the venison. The vultures would have found my body in the bush. He's bad that one. He hires the AK from government officials in Combumune and repays them with venison and skins.' As we pedal off I think to myself that the new peace park will indeed be an interesting challenge.

Throughout our bicycle journey, Ross and I have noticed that all the footprints on the paths head west and that there are countless extinguished camp fires beside the track. Somewhat sheepishly Matais gives credit to the rumours we've heard. He tells us that we are inadvertently following the illegal Mozambican immigrants' trail known as Jompa Jozz (to 'jump to Johannesburg', meaning to jump over the Kruger National Park fence, cross the park into South Africa and head on to Johannesburg). We've heard that a number of unfortunate young men who take this trail get eaten by lions as they cross the Kruger Park. Matais leans his bicycle against a tree and explains it this way: 'You see, for generations my people have been encouraged to work on the South African gold mines. It became an *mtethu*, a sort of rite of passage. My grandfather, my father and my uncles and older brothers all worked on the mines. They were important men in our village and brought home bicycles, radios, treadmill sewing machines, corrugated iron, rainwater tanks, fish-hooks, ploughs and colourful blankets. They were wealthy and had many wives. Then the war came. The white people left and things changed. Now it is very difficult to get a visa to work in South Africa. But still the *mtethu* remains, and even when a little boy is crying in our village and does not want to eat his food, his mother says, "Eat up *umfanyan* or you will not be strong enough to Jompa Jozz".'

'But what about the man-eating lions?' I ask. 'Sure, there are many accidents,' he says seriously, 'but that is because the young men think they are clever and don't listen to the *sangomas*. Before you leave to Jompa Jozz you must not have sex for five days, so that your blood will be hot!' Matais lifts up his hand and stretches out his five fingers to emphasise the point. 'Then you must drink the good luck medicines they give you, and when you get to your first elephant footprint you must do like this.' He demonstrates by making a thick circle of grass and placing it carefully on the ground. 'You put the grass around the elephant footprint and then step over it carefully. That way you will survive the lions and elephants, and bring gifts home for your wives and children.''Have you tried it Matais?' He is about to answer my question, then he laughs, picks up his bicycle and pushes on through the sand following the footprints west along Jompa Jozz.Suddenly, from around a corner and pedalling furiously, comes Richman Boloi, Chief Boloi's son. His face breaks into a huge smile at the sight of the Capricorn travellers, and he pulls a note from his pocket: 'The Land Rover party has arrived safely at Chief Bingo Boloi's and is awaiting your arrival.' I scribble this note back to Gill: 'Hi Luv, glad you've made it! Well done! Please don't move from Bingo Boloi. We should arrive by noon tomorrow. Don't move; just wait! Tough going – got lost. Wild, unbelievably beautiful country, but difficult conditions and soft sand. No people, just two poachers. Drinking swamp water but 100 percent okay. Very tired. Love, King and Ross.' Richman Boloi pedals off with the message. He'll ride through the night to deliver it to Mashozi.

23°27'

After he's gone we find a dead warthog in the path with the wire snare so tight around its snout that, once it escaped from the trap, it was unable to open its mouth. It must have died a slow, agonising death from thirst and starvation. I know that people are starving, but what terrible pain and suffering for the wildlife. I wish I had the answer.

We spend the night in a mopani forest with some big logs burning to keep us warm, as Ross is not taking any chances with the cold. We eat the last of the grub and empty the special waterbottle. Matais and I are now able to communicate quite well. He tells me of his Frelimo war days and the fight against Renamo. '*Mnandi kakhulu,*' ('Very tasty') he says, dipping his spoon again and again into the jar of peanut butter. We use the last of the tea bags to make up a Captain's brew: tea, rum and condensed milk. There's a cool breeze blowing and the three Capricornians huddle close to the fire.

Day 15: Cars for cattle and sangomas in the night

We cross the Shingwedzi River and pedal on through maize fields to our destination. What a welcome! The village children sing us in and the chief receives us in the shade of a large tree. All the members of the Expedition are delighted to meet up again. Mashozi prepares us a real egg and bacon breakfast, which we wash down with mugs of sweet tea. Bloody luxury!

Chief Boloi signs the Capricorn Scroll and Mike and Custodio tell us the story of how, whilst they were waiting for us, a stolen pickup truck arrived from South Africa to a great welcoming ceremony, at which it had been delivered in exchange for 20 head of cattle – proof that South Africa's 're-distribution of wealth' extends beyond her borders. We also learn that young men from this village lead the Jompa Jozz recruits over the Kruger Park fence and across the park for a fee. We have indeed followed the illegal immigrants' trail across Mozambique. For us it has been a wonderful and exciting journey along the Tropic of Capricorn, but I wonder what it is really like for those young fellows who jump the fence to brave the lions of the Kruger Park and the dangers of the concrete jungle of Johannesburg.

We drive some distance and then walk through the bush to touch the Kruger National Park fence on the Capricorn line. When we asked the South African authorities to allow us to Jompa Jozz, the request was turned down. We now have to detour north up the fence line up to Pafuri to enter South Africa legally.

We drop our good friend Matais off at the village of Makandezulu. He insists on taking a different route back to the Limpopo for fear of being killed by the poaching man. We pay him well for his services but his last words are, 'Won't you take me to South Africa?'

'Why don't you just jump the fence?' I ask. He laughs out loud and pedals off on his uncle's bicycle with a full jar of peanut butter in his rucksack. At sunset we pitch camp under a massive fig tree on a sandbank overlooking the Shingwedzi River. The recent floods have left behind plenty of driftwood for a fire, and we bathe in a cold, shallow pool in the river. From a nearby village a *sangoma* and her initiates keep up a rhythmic chant throughout the night. With all the wailing and drumming, Custodio believes she's removing a demon from a patient.

Day 16: Obrigado to Custodio and adeus to Mozambique

We find a safari hunting camp close to the Kruger National Park fence line, with green tents overlooking the river and a well-maintained airstrip. The manager, Don Petterson, eyes us suspiciously, and only when we explain our mission does he relax. Don is an interesting 'old Africa hand' slightly deaf from all the shooting. We share a cup of coffee and a chat, explaining that we're off to meet Johann Oelofse who is going to escort us on foot along the Tropic of Capricorn through the Kruger Park. Don taps the stone coffee table with his knuckles. 'He's a hard-headed man that one,' he says. Don is reluctant to let us use his road up the fence line, but finally agrees. He signs the Capricorn Scroll with a conservation message and waves us goodbye, a lone figure in the middle of nowhere. The track that takes us up the fence line is truly spectacular, especially where it runs along the top of the Lebombo Mountains before joining the dusty potholed track that leads through countless baobabs, now silhouetted against the setting sun. I think back on our Capricorn journey through Mozambique, the beautiful palm-frond coastline, the friendliness and hospitality of the people, the fear of landmines, the unspoilt sand forests, Matais Ngonyama and the Jompa Jozz trail by bicycle, and the joy of finally reaching the Kruger Park fence.

At Pafuri the Mozambican Customs and Immigration have stayed open for us, thanks to a request from the South African border guards, whom we managed to contact by satellite phone earlier in the day (when we realised we wouldn't make it by sunset). Sadly, the time has come to say goodbye to Custodio. We hug warmly, and there are tears in our eyes as we watch him walk away down the Pafuri-Mapai road, then turn back to wave his straw hat, a rucksack on his back and the ever-present cigarette stuck in the corner of his mouth. We would never have made it along the Capricorn line across Mozambique without him. The Governor of Inhambane, Señor Aires Ali, was correct when he said that Mozambique's finest asset was its people. Like Vasco da Gama, we've found this to be true. Custodio Manhica is certainly no exception. He truly is a citizen of *Terra da Boa Gente*, 'The Land of Good People'.

With Custodio we finally make it to the Kruger Park fence.

The ancient salt works at Baleni

South Africa

It's been a huge task to get permission to cross the Kruger National Park on foot — and having followed the Jomparozz trail we're nervous as all hell about predators — then it's the Lenpopo Province, with its variety of colourful cultures — all part of our crazy journey along this imaginary line what links our Cradle of Humankind to the other Capricorn countries

Day 17: Hot baths and cold beer

I feel somewhat strange, but also secure, to be back in the country of my birth. Morné, a young Afrikaans police sergeant, ushers us through South African Immigration and Customs at Pafuri in the far north-eastern corner of the Kruger National Park. It's way past closing time for this small border post but they've stayed open for the tired Capricorn adventurers, thanks to a message received from Johann Oelofse, the senior Parks Warden, who is waiting for us further south.

What a jolly evening. We overnight with Chris and Betty Morris at the old Kwa Teba Camp. Morné and his wife Marlize join us and soon we're having a *lekker* braai (barbecue). They're fascinated by our journey, and we're fascinated by their life here at this old, colourful outpost. This old Teba Camp, with its thatched roofs, beautiful gardens, wide mosquito-screened verandahs and old ceiling fans, was in its day the entry point into South Africa for tens of thousands of black Mozambican mine workers. In those early days it wasn't necessary to Jompa Jozz over the fence. Young, strong, Mozambican men would be recruited in the bush and then make their way to Pafuri to be processed and signed on. A resident doctor would check for diseases. They'd be given their jabs, fed and housed and then moved south to the next station at Soekmekaar (on the Tropic of Capricorn), from where they would travel by train or lorry to the various mines in what was then the Transvaal and Orange Free State.

The Kwa Teba Camp has now been turned into accommodation for visitors to Kruger. With Chris and Betty, our knowledgeable and hospitable hosts, we learn about the days of the old hunters, poachers and Black Birders (Native Recruiting Officers), and the carryings on that led to this area being known as 'Crooks Corner'. Morné explains that most of the problems are with poachers, who come across from Mozambique. He asks if we came through a safari hunting camp on our way up the Kruger fence line, and comments that: 'The big fellow, Johann Oelofse, who's waiting for you at Mopani Camp, well, he's

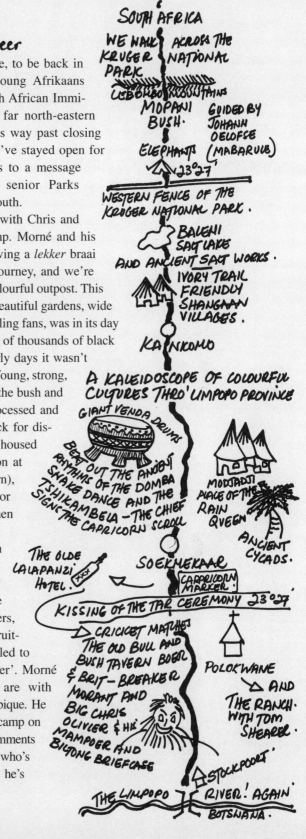

SOUTH AFRICA

WE WALK ACROSS THE KRUGER NATIONAL PARK

LEBOMBO MOUNTAINS

MOPANI BUSH.   GUIDED BY JOHANN OELOFSE (MABARULE)

ELEPHANTS 23°27'

WESTERN FENCE OF THE KRUGER NATIONAL PARK.

BALENI SALT LAKE AND ANCIENT SALT WORKS.

IVORY TRAIL FRIENDLY SHANGAAN VILLAGES.

KA NKOMO

A KALEIDOSCOPE OF COLOURFUL CULTURES THRO' LIMPOPO PROVINCE

GIANT VENDA DRUMS

BEAT OUT THE ANCIENT RHYTHMS OF THE DOMBA SNAKE DANCE AND THE TSHIKAMBELA — THE CHIEF SIGNS THE CAPRICORN SCROLL

MODJADJI PLACE OF THE RAIN QUEEN

ANCIENT CYCADS.

THE OLDE LALAPANZI HOTEL.   SOEKMEKAAR   CAPRICORN MARKER.

KISSING OF THE TAR CEREMONY 23°27'

CRICKET MATCHES THE OLD BULL AND BUSH TAVERN BOER & BRIT-BREAKER MORANT AND BIG CHRIS OLIVIER & HIS MAMPOER AND BILTONG BRIEFCASE

POLOKWANE AND THE RANCH WITH TOM SHEARER.

STOCKPOORT.

THE LIMPOPO RIVER! AGAIN

BOTSWANA.

MOZAMBIQUE

23°27'

△ SHIBAVASENGELE BEACON

- - - - - - - - - - - -
BORDER FENCE
KRUGER/NATIONAL PARK
R.S.A.
/\/\/\/\/\/\ LEBOMBO MOUNTAINS

MOPANI CAMP

ACROSS THE PARK ON FOOT WITH JOHANN OELOFSE- "MABARULE"

WESTERN BOUNDARY

SOUTINI

BALENI SALT LAKE AND ANCIENT SALT WORKS

IVORY TRAIL CAMP

KANKOMO

(WEST ACROSS THE LIMPOPO PROVINCE)

GA KORANTA

SOEK- MEKAAR

BANDOLIERSKOP
LALAPANZI HOTEL
N1 NORTH

CAPRICORN MARKER

SOUTH ← N1 HIGHWAY → N

having a bloody war with those blokes on the other side of the fence. He claims that they're cutting the fences and using bait to entice the lions over to the Mozambican side. Once they've got them that side, they call in the foreign big game hunters, who fly in to a bush airstrip, and bang! There goes another Kruger Park lion.' He claims it happens all the time. 'My investigation docket's several inches thick, but to prove it we'll actually have to catch them in the act, and that's difficult, especially as it's happening across the border.'

'Morné, what about the problem with the illegal immigrants?' I ask. 'You know the power lines you crossed as you come up the fence? Well, some of them cross there because the bush is cleared and it makes it easier to walk. But the lions are bloody clever things you know. They know that these blokes cross here and they lie and wait. For them it's a soft target and easy meat. The police, army and Parks Board do patrols, but still they come. The poor blokes are starving in Mozambique.'

And so the evening wears on. A celebratory bottle of Captain Morgan is produced, more boerewors, steaks and chops thrown on the coals, and there's even fresh salad and ice. Betty Morris lets Mashozi use her bath, foamies and all. The Capricorn lads take turns for a hot shower. Mike and Ross spend a good deal of time on the phone and come back smiling. Little Tristan Kingsley is growing by the day and the women on the other end of the line send their love.

Ahead of us lies one of the greatest challenges of our journey: to cross the Kruger National Park on foot along the Tropic of Capricorn. To our knowledge it has never been done before, and now there're man-eating lions to worry about. Welcome to South Africa!

Day 18: Kruger National Park

Johann Oelofse turns out to be a gentle giant of a man. Over 6'6" tall, he wears a large, Australian broad-brimmed Bushwacker's hat, khaki shirt and shorts, and size 14 kudu-skin boots. His .458 'elephant gun' seems small in his huge hands. The local people call him Mabarule after a famous local chief.

Such is the nature of our Capricorn Expedition that we have to go back to the eastern fence line and touch the Jompa Jozz fence, but this time on the South African side, before setting off again. Our base for this part of the expedition is Mopani Camp, below the hill where Johann and his wife

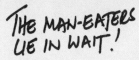

Jocelyn live, overlooking one of the greatest wildlife sanctuaries in the world. We leave our scratched and abused Landies here and take off with Mabarule back to the Mozambican fence line and the Tropic of Capricorn. Our camp for the night is at his secret place high on top of the Lebombo Mountains. We pitch our tents and make a small hardwood fire amongst the giant rocks that give the place a homely African Stonehenge feel. Mike films the huge orange sun disappearing in the west. We all go quiet, even the birds, as we look out across the mopani plains. A small herd of elephant moves slowly across the setting sun. 'In Africa we get paid in sunsets and sunrises,' says Mabarule. The mopani bush seems to stretch forever. Ahead of us lies the rest of our Capricorn journey, behind us is the fence line and the thousands of square kilometres of Mozambique we have just crossed. It's as if the Capricorn journey past, present and future is all around us.

Mabarule points down the fence line, only just visible in the last light. His face hardens as he squints into his well-worn binoculars. 'It's those bastards on the other side that are stealing my lions, opening the fence and baiting them for foreign hunters. I'll get them!' he says. I catch the look in Ross and Mashozi's eyes, but we say nothing. We're just travellers passing through and will have our own battles to fight down this imaginary Capricorn line.

Our small yellow camp fire lights up the massive rocks that shield us from the cool evening breeze. Mabarule loves a Captain or three and we have a wonderful bushveld evening, swapping yarns and pulling legs.

'You're not the first bunch of buggers to go down there,' he says pointing backwards over his shoulder with his thumb towards Mozambique. 'But not all have been so lucky. In the late 19th century the Voortrekker leader Lang Hans van Rensburg, with his wife and entire family, crossed here at Shalowe Poort and went along the Tropic of Capricorn line into Mozambique, his creaking ox-wagons loaded high with elephant tusks. Lang Hans was determined to navigate a way down to the coast, in the hope of finding a Portuguese ship that would turn his ivory into gold. The Tsonga, greedy for his ivory and cattle, attacked them at night when the wagons were arranged one behind the other. The front wagon had got stuck whilst crossing the river, which prevented the Voortrekkers from building a laager that evening. It took many weeks for news of the disaster to filter back via the bush telegraph and still more time for the celebrated Boer Commander Andries Potgieter to get a search party together. Armed with their Martini Henry rifles they rode their horses down to the wagons near Combumune, but the Tsonga hopelessly outnumbered them and they were forced to retreat, although not before hearing the cries for help from Lang Hans van Rensburg's daughters, held captive in the Tsonga villages and never seen again. 'Recently,' says Mabarule, 'an expedition like yours went down that way to search for facts. They found the remains of the old wagons and the locals presented them with Lang Hans van Rensburg's blacksmith's anvil that had been taken from the wagons, but, as for Lang Hans's offspring, they found nothing.'

Mike is by this time into his cups and keeps on referring to Lang Arm van Rensburg, with much bending of his own elbow – it is a night to remember.

Days 19–22: Man-eaters

Mabarule, in his massive size 14s, leads the way west with giant, confident strides; cradled in his arms is his well-worn .458 'elephant gun' capable of stopping a charging lion, elephant or buffalo. Mashozi, fit and tough in her khaki shorts and old bush hat, with her water-bottle and binoculars, and her little feet in worn velskoene with red laces, is second in line. Ross's punishment for being lean and mean is to carry the largest rucksack. I follow, old Nondwayiza, the slightly overweight lilytrotter. Right now I wish I'd drunk a bit less last night. Last in line is Mike, old 'Lang Arm' himself, whose spindly legs effortlessly carry the Betacam camera, slung at the ready over his shoulder.

We come across an old village site – there is a circle of stone walls and some broken pot shards, which indicate that we're not the first people to admire this incredible view from up here on the Lebombo Mountains. Long before white people came through here with their guns and wagons in search of ivory for billiard balls and piano keys, and long before Paul Kruger, the burly President of the then Transvaal Republic, proclaimed this area a wildlife reserve in the latter half of the 1800s, black tribespeople lived here. Children laughed, played and gathered wild honey. The women gossiped as they stitched hand-tanned skin garments, using animal sinew as thread. Searching for game, the men must have gazed out across these vast plains whilst they sharpened their arrows and discussed the strategy of the hunt. To the north of us, at a place called Thulamela, archaeologists have discovered a pure gold rhinoceros statue and the ruins of a sophisticated ancient empire. I am sure that the spirits of these ancient ones will be happy to know that the great herds of wild animals still roam here today.

Next to the old village stands an ancient baobab. The Bushmen believe that God, in a fit of anger, pulled the baobab tree from the ground and when he threw it back it landed upside down with the roots in the air. This turned out to be a blessing, though, as very often rain water is trapped in the trunk, providing drinking water in an extremely arid land. As a sign of respect Mabarule asks us all to place our hands on the pulpy grey trunk and rest them there in silence as we look up into the timeless branches that tower above us.

Using our GPS to guide us we plod on through the thick mopani veld. Mabarule explains that the shorter bonsai mopanis have been stunted by poor soil and rock, and the bigger trees stand in better soil and old river courses. He did his Master's degree on the grasses of the park, and he begins a detailed explanation. But, seeing the dumb looks on our faces, he says, 'Think of it this way: here there are three main types of grasses. For the animals this grass here is like steak, over there we have the hamburgers and, whilst the grass over there looks pretty tasty, it's only hotdogs.' Put like that it's easy to understand.

A giant bull elephant gives us a warning shake of his massive tusks and ears, and in the distance a herd of giraffe, long necks bent forward, ambles across the plain. We pass the heat of the day under a giant leadwood tree that, even in death, still stands straight and tall. A beacon of age, these leadwood trees have been carbon dated back to before the time of Christ. These trees, like the African elephant, are Mabarule's favourite.

Trudge, trudge... hours become days as this fascinating stretch of African bush comes alive through Mabarule's lifetime of experiences. Fresh lion spoor across a dry riverbed gets us talking about the danger of a lion attack. The terrible truth of the area we are walking through is that because of the soft targets the Jompa Jozz immigrants provide, some of the lions have become man-eaters and we have to be extremely careful. Here, on the Tropic of Capricorn, a number of these man-eaters have become used to stalking and killing humans, and Mabarule's rangers once found a sole Jompa Jozz survivor in a tree, screaming like a maniac. At the base of the tree were just the bones of his companions who had been attacked and eaten by a pride of lions. The sad part about this is that the rangers have to hunt down the man-eaters and kill them or they themselves will become the soft targets. Mabarule's life here in the park has had its share of action and the scars on his neck are a reminder of the time he was attacked by a leopard, but lived to tell the tale.

Grass seeds stick to our socks, my feet, more used to sandals than boots, have blisters on the heels and ticks have climbed up our legs, but finally we reach the western boundary of the park. For us it has been an amazing experience, the wide open spaces, the herds of game and the shared journey with Mabarule, who despite his personal situation keeps his head high, sharing his great knowledge with us and standing out like an ancient ironwood on these vast plains. We shake hands warmly. Fortunately, unlike those poor Mozambicans, we've lived to tell the tale and made it to exactly 23° 27' on the western fence line.

Reunited with our Landies (they've been driven round for us by Mabarule's game scouts) we meet Arrie Horn and Klaas Boonzaaier, who are involved with the Limpopo Province government in setting up a cultural tourism venture known as the Ivory Trail. We follow them down a winding, dusty trail to our camp for the night, a Tsonga village known as Baleni, virtually on the Capricorn line. Klaas has a Clint Eastwood cowboy look and Arrie is a jovial round-faced fellow – both are true men of the bush, dedicated to assisting the local communities. We throw some fresh meat on the coals, tell a few yarns and are soon in bed.

Day 23: Ancient salt works and Nwmilambu the snake

Near the camp we find an ancient lake where the Tsonga people have come every winter for the past 150 years or so to scrape away the salt-laden dry earth crust from the overflow of the hot springs near Baleni Lake. All this is the work of the women, and the salt scrapings are carried off on their heads to an historic salt works on the banks of the Klein Letaba River, known as eSoutini. These Tsonga people came from their motherland initially as traders between the east coast and the interior, and eventually in greater numbers as refugees, a result of the Zulu wars under Shoshangane, one of Shaka's generals. It appears that the Tsonga here are the last people to maintain this centuries-old practice of extracting salt in the area around the hot springs. Before them came the Sotho, Venda and the Lemba. The technical practice at this ancient salt works has not changed much in over 2 000 years.

The Tsonga people here at eSoutini understand our Zulu, and their wonderfully friendly welcome soon makes us feel at home. A big Tsonga mama with a great sense of humour, surrounded by her daughters, scrapes the dark, charcoal-coloured salt into a mound to be loaded into containers and carried on their heads down to the river. There, in a tree-shaded clearing, the fascinating ancient practice begins. First, traditional gifts have to be presented to the ancestral spirits – small pinches of maize meal, snuff, a bundle of sticks, beads, some traditional cloth, tobacco and salt – all placed at the base of an ancient leadwood tree. The ancestral spirits are satisfied and the salt-making process begins. Sand and water from the Letaba River are added to the salt-encrusted soil and slowly filtered through mud, leaves and branches to produce clear, salty water, which is then boiled off in large containers over open fires to produce small cones of large-grained salt. This Baleni salt is greatly sought after by traditional healers and diviners who use it in their *muthi*, believing that it has supernatural properties.

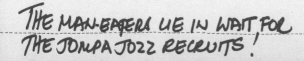

THE MAN-EATERS LIE IN WAIT FOR
THE JOMPA JOZZ RECRUITS!

23° 27'

Many taboos are linked to this salt-making process: no salt must come into contact with open wounds and initiates who have been recently circumcised may not eat the salt. The salt must not be brought close to a potter as it will cause their pots to crack while firing. Pregnant women are not allowed near eSoutini, and when a child is born the people have to appease the spirits by giving details of the newborn baby and making further peace offerings to their ancestral spirits under the ancient leadwood tree.

The local people claim that in the hot springs the noise of drums, the roaring of a lion and humming can be heard at night. A big snake, Nwmilambu, is said to live in the spring that feeds the lake. All these supernatural things have an effect on the whiteness and strength of the salt. The people sing the praises of those ancestors who have worked here before them, and at mid-day we are offered thick maize meal porridge and fried mopani worms as we sit around the cooking fire in the shade of a wild fig tree.

The diviners and traditional healers believe that if they burn a mixture containing the spiritual salt outside their homesteads it will attract patients and customers. And so it happens that late this evening we find ourselves sitting on a cow dung-smeared floor as a fascinating old crone of a diviner, dressed in skins, beads and an old sports jacket, throws her bones and professes that we will have a tough and difficult journey and one that she cannot guarantee we will complete. With a sneeze she claims that one of us is a diviner! We all look at Mashozi, who is that way inclined. Mashozi grins and gives the diviner a seashell taken from the Capricorn coast of Mozambique. In return we are presented with some small pieces of eSoutini salt, which Mashozi wraps up carefully and places in each Land Rover.

Day 24: Slaves to 23° 27' and the GPS

Back in *Chuma* and *Susi* we zigzag as best we can down the Capricorn line. The constant travelling is wearing us down a bit. Everything, including my hair and beard, is covered in thick red dust as we travel west through the land of the Tsonga, with their beautifully decorated, thatched, conical villages. Still, our spirits remain high – we somehow feel inexorably linked to wherever 23° 27' takes us. This area is proving to be a wonderful mix of traditional African-, Afrikaans- and English-speaking cultures – reflecting the real diversity of our newly democratic country. For our Capricorn team from KwaZulu-Natal it is proving something of a rediscovery of our own land, complete with all its growing pains. At times we detour off 'the line' to observe something special and then, feeling like naughty school kids playing truant, we come back to 23° 27' at the exact spot we left and continue slowly west. The late afternoons find us squinting from behind the Land Rovers' sun visors into the golden, orange-red, dust-fed sunsets of South Africa's Limpopo Province. We've become slaves to the survey map and the GPS, and it's proving tiring. I guess we need a rest day.

Day 25: Modjadji the Rain Queen

Albert Mudau and Lazarus Mokoena welcome us to the Ivory Trail Camp set amongst the ancient Modjadji cycads on the hills overlooking the Rain Queen's palace, east of Polokwane in the Ga-Modjadji district. The huts are beautifully decorated with grey, white and brown geometric designs, hand-painted from natural dyes and cow dung. All around us are these giant, prehistoric cycads, with massive trunks, bright green leaves and orange, pineapple-like cones.

A couple of impala and a shy grey duiker scamper off into the undergrowth. There's a feeling of mystery to the place of the Lobedu Clan, who are now integrated with the Pedi. Amazingly, charcoal-coloured storm clouds begin to gather and the thousands of cycads are silhouetted black against the grey sky. During the night, around the fire, the bush babies in the trees scream like scalded children – this then is the land of Modjadji.

The Rain Queen is much revered to this day, and we are told how Nelson Mandela once tried to make a last-minute impromptu visit to her but was turned down because he had not made an appointment. On a subsequent visit the heavens opened and the road to her thatched palace turned into an impassable quagmire. President Mandela was airlifted out by helicopter, but today travellers up the steep hill to Modjadji take a new macadamised road, a gift from the former president.

Sadly, Modjadji is ill and has been for some time. Around the palace there is a feeling of gloom and despair, not surprising when one understands that every mood and feeling of the Queen can affect the very survival of her people, who in this dry area close to the Capricorn line rely on the rain for their crops and grazing for their livestock. We are told that in the old days the rain queens were never allowed to die a natural death, and commited suicide by taking a deadly potion of human parts, crocodile, baboons' brains and snake. Even to this day they are not allowed to marry. Their lovers are chosen from royal blood and the Queen's oldest daughter becomes the next rain queen. Hundreds of devotees begin arriving to pray, in an all-night vigil for the Queen's health. She is too ill for us to see her, but we meet with her soft-spoken daughter. There is a great sadness to this place, and when night comes we attend the ceremony at the camp, where the singing is mournful and slow. We present her Induna-elect (tribal representative) with a colourful blanket, a gift to the Rain Queen from our Capricorn Expedition.

Day 26–27: Shoot straight, you bastards!

The Lalapanzi Hotel, owned by the Gilfillans, turns out to be a fascinating spot where Boer meets Brit along the Capricorn Line. The hotel once hosted an international cricket match, between South Africa and what was then Rhodesia, and was well known for its fun-filled cattle sales and carnivals. In the Bull and Bush Pub we meet Chris Olivier, who's huge and round with a massive beard, and entertains us with stories about his adventures on the Capricorn line. In his briefcase, cocooned in sponge rubber, is a bottle of peach mampoer and some shot glasses, not the ideal thing for my malarial liver!

Rolling his r's in his guttural, Afrikaans-accented English, and between sips of mampoer and the slicing of kudu biltong with a worn penknife, he says: 'Ja-nee, ou Kingsley! How bleddy long has it taken you to grow that great big ugly bearrrd of yourrrs?' The pub erupts with laughter and he continues, 'I understand that Australia is the world's largest Capricorn country? Well, here's a bit of local history that links our Capricorn line to the worrrld Down Under.' And Chris proceeds to tell us the story of Australian 'Breaker' Morant. Apart from being a daredevil, hard-drinking ladies' man, he was extremely talented at breaking-in wild horses, earning him the nickname of 'The Breaker'. The start of the Anglo-Boer War in 1899 gave him the ideal gap to dodge bad debt and love affairs, so he sailed to South Africa, along with over 2 000 Australians. Morant's amazing ability to handle horses soon caught the attention of his South Australian

Hi Taryn

How are you? Can you believe it, we survived Mozambique and the hike across Kruger. With all the obstacles and trying to keep to this damn imaginary line it's taking a lot of time and effort, but it's all worth while. It's proving a great adventure and despite a bit of wear and tear we're fit and well. How are the dogs? I am missing Winston.

Today we were invited to attend a domba dance just north of the Capricorn line. It was a sort of initiation training at which the colourfully-dressed married women teach the young, near-naked Venda maidens the sinuous, rhythmic snake dance. With hands holding their elbows they mime the movements of a giant python said to live in the sacred lake of Fundudzi. It was mesmerizing: the sound of the singing, the shake of the ankle rattles and the resounding beat of the giant rawhide drums. All this happened in the light of a massive fire. Dressed in wild animal skins and ostrich feathers, Malungwane, the dance leader, was the only male dancer amongst more than 50 women and girls.

The entire village turned out to see the ceremony and we were invited to sit on mats on the ground with the chief and the elders. Instead of the customary clay pots of millet beer, we were offered a terrific selection of dry white wines poured with great ceremony into delicate wine glasses. We finished an entire case. Who would have thought that Venda Chief Madzivhandila would be a wine connoisseur? Africa is never as you expect it. The Chief endorsed our Capricorn Scroll with a flourish, and after much hand-shaking and laughter we turned Chuma and Suzi towards the old Lalapanzi Hotel, one of the oldest and closest pubs to the Tropic of Capricorn.
Will phone you from Polokwane. Thanks for everything.
All our love, the Capricorn Team

MONDAY
15th –
THE
DOMBA
DANCE
CARRIES ON
WAY INTO THE
NIGHT

Colonel, who suggested him as a dispatch rider to the *Daily Telegraph* war correspondent.

Breaker Morant then became a lieutenant in the Bushveldt Carbineers – a mostly-Australian force, which came to South Africa to fight the Boers. 'Believe me,' said Chris between more biltong and mampoer, 'No unit was more bloody fearrrred by the Boers than the Bushveldt Carbineers.' In August 1901 Captain Hunt, a close friend of Morant's and his fiancée's brother, and 17 Carbineers rushed a Boer farmhouse, only to find far more Boers than expected. During the attack Morant's father-in-law and a sergeant were killed.

Captain Hunt – initially only wounded – was later killed, mutilated and stripped of his uniform. Morant went berserk with anger and killed Visser, a Boer found wearing Hunt's uniform, in revenge. Boer prisoners-of-war and a German missionary called Hesse were also killed by Morant and his men. 'You see, Kingsley, the rrreason that Morant had the Gerrrman missionary shot,' explains Chris, 'was that he was scared he would "spill the beans" about the illegal killing of Boer prisoners-of-war.' Unfortunately for Morant, his killing of the missionary led to an international incident. So, to try to ease tensions with Germany, the British charged him and some of his men with war crimes. Morant was a bloody tough character and showed nothing but contempt for the court. He admitted that he shot the Boers – justifying his actions by saying that Lord Kitchener had instructed that no prisoners were to be taken. Still, he and his men were found guilty of murder. Next morning they took Breaker Morant out to be executed first, but he never lost his nerve. Before he was shot he had a cigarette, he refused a blindfold and then famously said to the firing squad: 'Shoot straight, you bastards, and don't make a mess of it.'

A hundred years on and Morant's become something of a cult figure to the Australians. Some go to South Africa to visit his grave, and many claim he was simply following British orders to take no prisoners and landed up a scapegoat, executed to appease the Germans. So the question is still asked: Was the shooting of Breaker Morant justice or murder?

'Forrr us Boerrrs,' says Chris, 'Breaker Morant remains a scoundrel. You see, Kingsley, some of those people he killed were my rrrelatives.'

Our Capricorn Expedition is made more fascinating by the characters we meet along the Tropic and after many more strange stories, and much biltong and mampoer, we say goodbye to big Chris Olivier and head down the Capricorn line to Bandolierskop, near where the missionary Hesse and some of the Boer prisoners were shot just a hundred years ago.

Days 28–30: R&R at the Ranch

Just north of Polokwane, capital of Limpopo Province, we reach the N1 heading north towards Zimbabwe. This is the first major highway we have crossed since leaving the coast of Mozambique. The passing motorists are amazed to see the dusty Capricorn team having a kissing-of-the-tar ceremony. Sadly, the Tropic of Capricorn monument situated here is covered in graffiti and peppered with bullet holes. I guess not everybody has grown to respect the Capricorn line as we have.

The Land Rover dealer and his workshop foreman in Polokwane gaze in horror at our two new Landies. It's only their first service and already they have done a lifetime's worth of work, crossing rivers, fighting their way through thick bush and grinding over soft sand and rocks, and through tall elephant grass and swamps – bless their hearts! *Chuma* and *Susi* certainly weren't born into the world of boulevard cruising. With our Landies in the pits, we finally have

In 1958 Basil Shearer conducted some unusual research on the great north road. As each vehicle passed a stone was placed in the appropriate drum – the result warranted the building of the Ranch Motel!

the break we need, and our old friend Tom Shearer, owner of The Ranch Hotel, helps us out. Mashozi and I even get a room with a jacuzzi, as well as a chance to relax, wash clothes and plan the next section of our Capricorn adventure.

Day 31: Africa, Cradle of Humankind

Tom Shearer continues to entertain us royally. Last night he held a dinner party for us and local Limpopo Province tourism officials, and of course our bearded friend Chris was part of it all, complete with briefcase and mampoer.

This morning Tom's gone out of his way to show us the area. With Mandy and Kevin, archaeologists from Wits University, we take off to explore the nearby cave of Makapansgat. The historic cave, reached through an ancient limeworks, has fossilised bones, teeth and skulls embedded in its floor. There are even fossils of the dung balls made by an ancient species of dung beetle, as well as fossils of predators like sabre-toothed cats, and huge dassies – as big as large dogs – and enormous porcupines.

In these vast chambers Mandy and Kevin point out many other ancient life forms. We can see the fossilised remains of blue-green algae, which flourished here some 2 500 million years ago, when the area was under the sea. The next cave we visit is named the Cave of Hearths, where we get to see a Stone Age hearth – the earliest evidence of the deliberate use of fire in Africa. There are even remnants of a meal eaten here by Stone Age people, so many thousands of years ago. Compared to all this our expedition is a mere grain of sand in time, but I do have the feeling that our journey somehow links Africa's Cradle of Humankind to the other Capricorn countries around the world; after all, this is where it all began.

I am struggling to comprehend the full significance of a place whose life is measured in millions of years, and so it is the more recent story of the cave of Mokopane that really touches me. Over a thousand Ba-tlou people, under Chief Mokopane, died of thirst and starvation in this huge cave in 1854 – trapped here, under seige from the Boers.

A Boer hunting party had been attacked by the Ba-tlou and everyone in it killed outright, apart from the Boer leader Hermanus Potgieter who was dragged to the top of a hill and flayed alive. The Ba-tlou also killed a number of Boer men, women and children at a place now known as Moorddrift ('ford of murder') – smashing their skulls against two camel thorn trees. What brought on these attacks was the abduction of young Ba-tlou orphans as slaves and the murder of Chief Mokopane's brother by Potgieter. The Boers had also stolen much of the Ba-tlou's best land, and with it the grazing and game it afforded.

In retaliation for the resulting Ba-tlou attacks, the Boers launched their own attack – and the Ba-tlou fled to the cave for safety, taking along their cattle and provisions. They barricaded the

cave entrance and shot at any Boers who came near. Hermanus Potgieter's nephew Piet was killed in this way, and it was Paul Kruger (later to become President of the Transvaal Republic) who retrieved his body. The seige lasted 25 days, during which time the Boers tried unsuccessfully to force the Ba-tlou out by pounding the entrance to the cave with a field cannon and by rolling smouldering logs into the cave mouth. In their turn the Ba-tlou tried to escape under cover of a stampede of their cattle, but although Chief Mokopane managed to get away, tied underneath an ox, most of the Ba-tlou remained trapped in the cave. Finally, their food and water ran out, and they all died of dehydration or starvation.

Mandy stops speaking and we stand there in silence, wearing our silly-looking blue, plastic helmets in case of a rock fall. The cave is still littered with utensils, human skulls and bones, and you can see small living spaces amongst the rocks where almost an entire Ndebele clan lived and died during the siege. The hairs on my arms tingle; I look across at Ross and Gill, who are standing wide-eyed and still.

Day 32: A new arrival - will he make it?

We say our goodbyes to Tom Shearer. I'm probably going to write this time and time again, but one of the most fascinating and satisfying things about this around-the-world Tropic of Capricorn Expedition is the wonderful people we meet along the way. The Tropic, it appears, is a line of human kindness that links the people of Capricorn together, and Tom is a great link in the chain. At the Polokwane Land Rover dealership we find *Chuma* and *Susi* washed, cleaned, greased and serviced – they look perky and ready to roll.

Today a new member is joining our Capricorn team, thanks to Captain Morgan. They've helped sponsor this expedition; their logos are on the Land Rover doors, and they assist us with funding and with a bottle or two of their product. The rum eases the difficult parts of the journey and, as you can well imagine, brings good cheer to the fireside each evening.

About a year ago Captain Morgan ran a photographic competition in a student magazine, the winner of which would get to go on an expedition with the Holgate family. Well, we never gave another thought to it, but then, out of the blue, we get a telephone call: the winner is Troy Wade, a young advertising executive from Cape Town. So, here we are racing to the local airport to pick up an expedition member we don't know and have never seen before. What if he doesn't fit in? What if he doesn't like the bush? Gill, Ross, Mike and I are a tight-knit bunch, so it will be hard for the newcomer to find his place in the group.

There's no chance of missing Troy – tall and lanky, with his safari gear and rucksack, pale city skin, short-cropped black hair and, can you believe it, a ring though one of his eyebrows. I overhear Ross mumbling, 'How come the winner isn't blonde and beautiful with a name like Celeste or Stephanie?' 'We've got eyebrow Troy instead,' we laugh! He jumps in with Ross and Mike, and we head out west along Capricorn to Masebe, in the beautiful Waterberg Mountains. Here we sleep under canvas at the Ivory Trail Camp. The Ivory Trail blokes and Limpopo Province tourism have been incredibly supportive of our expedition and this is our last night with them. The fire crackles, we swap yarns, fill our enamel mugs and throw meat on the coals, while a hyaena cackles in the distance. Troy is doing his best to fit in – he's young, cheerful and eager to help. 'You know, Kingsley,' he tells me, 'I've dreamt about doing something like this all my life.' Time will tell how he fares with our group.

Botswana

Our Capricorn journey across Botswana will take us from cattle post to cattle post across the immense Kalahari desert. We'll have to watch out for lions at night. The Landies will have to churn endless soft sand, in this wide open expanse with few recognisable landmarks — and what about all the veterinary cordon fences?!

Day 33: Brandy for breakfast

The bridge is indeed closed to vehicles. The police inspector on the South African side is trying to be helpful: sure, he'll stamp our passports out of South Africa, but he can't open the bridge, because that belongs to Botswana. He radios across the river and the Botswanan officials meet us on the bridge. They are keen to help, but their telephone is not working and they will have to get clearance from the head of immigration at Serowe. So we take out our satellite phone and make the call whilst sitting cross-legged in the middle of the closed Limpopo bridge. The border officials look down at us suspiciously.

'So sorry, sir,' says the man from Serowe, 'but this is not a matter for immigration; this problem is for the Chief Engineer of Roads in Gaborone.' There's a tunnel-like echo on the line, which certainly doesn't make things any easier. The man in Gaborone refers us to his counterpart in South Africa, who, he says, was responsible for closing the bridge. The South Africans in turn refer us back to Botswana. Says the friendly Botswanan Immigration Officer, with a big smile, 'How can you open something when you don't know who closed it?' No one is prepared to make a decision and the buck gets passed from one department to another, and the border authorities get bored and go back to their respective posts. We're left standing in the middle of the bridge.

Finally, we hit on a solution. Mike, Troy and I will walk across the bridge, and Ross and Gill will have to make a long detour in the Land Rovers to cross the river at Groblersbrug, meeting us later on in the day at Parrs Halt. Once we are across the Limpopo bridge in Botswana our passports are stamped with a flourish. Armed with a small rucksack of oranges, water and the Expedition Scroll now stamped by the Botswanan authorities, we step out west along the dirt road that leads to Parrs Halt.

The closure of the Limpopo bridge has turned Parrs Halt into a dusty ghost town of two houses, some sheds, a filling station, a closed bottle store and a few cattle pens, all surrounded by thornbush. We make our way towards a ramshackle old house, with the year 1902 written on the wall. A Toyota *bakkie* with its bonnet up is parked in front of the mosquito-gauzed

BOTSWANA

SUPERB HOSPITALITY FROM OLD MAN DOEP!

PARRS HALT

RAIL
ROAD

GABS

TROPIC OF CAPRICORN SIGN

FRANCISTOWN

23°27'

INTO THE KALAHARI FOLLOWING A GPS

VET FENCES A PROBLEM

SOFT SAND LOST CATTLE POST TO CATTLE POST

KHUTSE GAME RESERVE WE TRACK CHEETAH ALONG CAPRICORN

CAPRICORN SIGN

TSETSENG

KANG FOR DIESEL THEN BACK ONTO CAPRICORN

SALT PANS

PANS UKWI (LUCKY RED ROOSTER)

OLD SAN BUCHMEN ENDORSE CAPRICORN SCROLL OF PEACE & GOODWILL WITH A SIMPLE X THEY'D NEVER HELD A PEN BEFORE

verandah. An elderly white man dressed in shorts appears in the doorway, amazed to find three people walking through the bush towards him. As a greeting I raise my old straw hat that is shielding me from the Capricorn sun. 'Where the hell are you okes from?' he asks in a broad Afrikaans accent. 'We're following the Tropic of Capricorn around the world,' we offer in reply. Without hesitation he invites us in.

The verandah is packed with old junk, including an old mannequin with half its face shot away (target practice, I suppose). The sitting room doubles as a bedroom, office and pub. The dusty, patched, powder blue ceiling sags with age. Old man Du Plessis is a delightful codger. He tells us he's 'only' 82. His wrinkled old cook has a wizened little bushman-like face. She's a mere 97 years old. 'Oom Doep' is a cattle trader and the old lady has been with him for over 40 years. The many photographs on the walls tell a story. Anneline Kriel, a former Miss South Africa (who went on to become Miss World), is pictured posing with a leopard next to his daughter ('They were at university together,' says Doep proudly). Old family portraits, cattle medicines, dip and syringes line the walls.

He tells us how he escaped from a prisoner-of-war camp in Italy during the Second World War – Rommel's artillery left Oom Doep a bit deaf and we have to shout at the top of our voices to communicate with him – and how he survives out here in the bush selling cattle. 'My children want to put me in an old age home, but how would I cope after all this freedom?' The old mama keeps a stream of cold beers coming from the kitchen. I ask old Doep about his withered hand. He points to the corner of the room and says, 'It was on that bed that it happened – I was sleeping in Adam's pyjamas and woke up screaming. A cobra had me by the hand. I pulled the snake's teeth from my body and threw it, wriggling, out the window. Using an old sock I tied a tourniquet around my upper arm, then with one hand drove my *bakkie* to the Limpopo, woke up the border guards, and made it through the night to Nylstroom. I was in hospital for a long time and as you can see I lost a finger, but the new skin that they grafted off my backside saved my hand. The doctor said it was the wrong thing to have used a tourniquet and it would have been better to have allowed the poison to move through my body.' With a toothless grin the old mama calls us through into the kitchen, where a shelf of brandy bottles, some painted elephants and an ancient fridge make up the décor. Breakfast is steak, boerewors, thick slices of bread and brandy. By the time Gill and Ross arrive in the Land Rovers, Mike, Troy and I are red-faced and rowdy. Oom Doep calls for more brandy. 'You'll need strength for your Capricorn journey,' he shouts.

Ross and Gill bundle us into the Land Rovers and Oom Doep waves from the verandah. There's a foot-and-mouth disease scare on and Gill tells me that all our fresh meat, dairy products and bully beef have been confiscated at the border. Later, we swerve to avoid a flock of guinea fowl in the road, but one doesn't make it and ends up in the evening's pot, as we camp out in the Kalahari on the Tropic of Capricorn, just west of the Gaborone–Francistown road.

Days 34-36: Cattle post to cattle post

I love the Kalahari and the feeling of freedom one gets travelling along narrow sand tracks guided by only a GPS and survey maps. From cattle post to cattle post we go: asking questions and directions; sometimes getting tired, frustrated and completely lost; using hand signals and making drawings in the sand; spending nights under the stars, the sounds of lions, hyaenas and jackals around us, as we sit at smouldering hardwood fires; and listening to the early morning bird calls while we rake last night's coals for breakfast coffee. This is what we came for. What hassles us are the controversial, veterinary-cordon cattle fences that criss-cross the country. Botswana has a proud conservation record, but many of its inhabitants would love to see less game reserve land and more grazing for cattle – let's hope good sense prevails.

Ross does an incredible job of navigating between cattle posts. At each lonely post are cattlemen, who look like Bushmen and live in grass huts around the boreholes. There are ancient Lister engines, blowing plumes of black diesel smoke as they pump life-giving underground water into leaking reservoirs and cattle troughs. And despite living in this dry, bush country the cattle look fat and healthy. When there's no drought it's a good living for the owners, who come in every now and again from the towns to count their cattle and bring diesel and supplies.

Jack Fritz is a colourful character of Herero, German and Bushman descent. Originally from Namibia, he now manages a dilapidated, fly-infested, dusty and hot cattle post close to the Capricorn line. Some of his men bring in a dead beast. They have chased off the lions and brought the leftovers into camp for a feast. In the compound stands a completely burnt-out Toyota Landcruiser. 'Can you believe it,' laughs Jack Fritz, 'some bloody mechanic: the silly bugger had a cigarette in his mouth while he was pouring petrol into the carburettor – whoosh! Somehow he survived. I fired the bastard, but now we've got no transport to get to the bottle store, and the lions are killing our livestock.' We move off down the cattle fence, following Jack Fritz's directions, west, along Capricorn.

Days 37-40: Kalahari stories

Ostriches race alongside the Land Rovers as we find a cut-line, made through the bush for mapping, that brings us to the Khutse Game Reserve, a small piece of wilderness tacked onto the bottom of the vast Central Kalahari Game Reserve. For us it's paradise. We see a leopard in the late afternoon and camp under a lone acacia tree, with the setting sun, an orange-yellow ball in the west. This is the 'Africa of Old', an area that is still home to hunter-gatherer Bushmen, and yesterday 22 lions were sighted in the area. Soon we have all the tents up – no bedrolls under the stars tonight – we don't want to become lion-fodder! The fire

TROY GOES BUSH

ENAMEL MUG A BIG
ONE FOR SPECIAL OCCASIONS
AND RENOSTER COFFEE –

is lit and the renoster coffee on the boil. We establish a small base camp here, our intention being to photograph wildlife in the area of the Tropic of Capricorn. It's an idyllic break in the journey. We watch the sun rise and sip our coffee, clasping our enamel mugs with both hands to keep our fingers warm. We pack our food away from maurading hyaenas, zip up the tents and move off slowly across the dawn in *Chuma* and *Susi*. It's a cold, crisp Kalahari morning.

Proud oryx plod by with determination across sunburned pans that fill with water in the wet season. These amazing animals are built to survive in this harsh Kalahari thirstland, where athletic springbok *pronk* and a small herd of giraffe follows the gemsbok over the horizon. Feeling a bit laid-back, we stop on a ridge overlooking a waterhole. A few springbok amble down to drink, and in the distance we spot a male lion, but it moves off and we continue our journey. Following the GPS we find, in the middle of nowhere alongside the sand track, a small, green, wooden sign marking the Capricorn line.

Mike and Ross set up a camera on the roof of *Susi*, while Troy drives, and Mashozi and I follow in *Chuma*. Ross has got eyes like a hawk and he's the first to see them: a pair of hunting cheetahs making their way roughly along the line of Capricorn. They attempt to stalk springbok and then a small herd of wildebeest, but as hunters their hit rate is appalling. Their prey soon get their scent and race off, dust flying. It appears there are no free meals along Capricorn – we have better luck with Mashozi's grub box.

We know never to travel or leave camp without adequate drinking water supplies. Out here in the Kalahari one can die of thirst in no time at all, and yet the Bushman people survive well. They store water in ostrich shells and bury them in the sand. They also grind up seeds of the cucumber-like tsama melon to make a coarse flour, and extract the moisture from the succulent flesh of the melon, which is more than 90 percent fluid and can keep a person alive for weeks on end. Locating a damp place in the sand, old Bushman women will often dig a small hole with their hands. A hollow reed is placed in this 'sipping well' and the lower end of the depression is packed with a filter of fine grass. The sand is replaced around the reed and tramped down firmly. After some time the women return to suck at the protruding reed. This they do for an hour or more before the reduction in atmospheric pressure draws the groundwater up the hollow reed. By sipping though a thinner reed, which they insert into the first, the women then transfer the water into an empty ostrich shell. The life of the missionary explorer Dr David Livingstone was saved by Bushman women in this way on one of his journeys across the Kalahari.

And so our journey along Capricorn continues. We leave Khutse behind and soon arrive at a small village. It's early evening, music blares from a bottle store and customers shuffle cards in a dingy pub. The massive pile of empty beer cans is impressive; the money comes from diamond mining and cattle. Red dust hangs in the air. We expected to find diesel here, but there is none, so we siphon from our emergency rooftop jerry cans and push on through the night in the direction of Kang, the closest place where we can buy diesel. At 3 am we call it a day and lay our bedrolls on the side of the track. Without knowing it we've camped next to a village. Livestock tramps through our camp and, as if on cue, every time someone wakes up to complain the donkeys bray, 'Aagghh-phew, aagghh-phew,' in chorus.

We wake just a few hours later and push through to Kang, situated on the Trans-Kalahari Highway that runs across the Tropic of Capricorn. Here we fuel up and re-supply for the journey west. A bumper sticker from Hukuntsi Store in the Western Kalahari reads: 'A man's paradise and a woman and vehicle's hell!' The sand is soft here and it's tough going for the Land Rovers. At Ukwe we meet an elderly Bushman couple: Xhaka Moneke and her companion Xhwake Hise. They've come to the village to get water from the government lorry. Old and wrinkled, and dressed in cast-off Western clothes, all they own are a few tattered blankets, a pipe for tobacco and a small puppy. Through an interpreter, who speaks in their click language, I learn that both of them were born in the early 1920s. Slowly, I show them how to hold a pen, so they can endorse our Capricorn Scroll of Peace and Goodwill with a shaky cross. They might be illiterate but these two delightful little characters once lived as proud hunter-gatherers using their incredible bush skills to survive in the desert. Sadly, they now exist on handouts, such as this water from the government lorry. Much of their old ancestral hunting lands have been taken over for game reserves and cattle ranches, and they are being forced to adapt to moden society.

But, deeper in the Kalahari, Bushman still hunt with bows and poisoned arrows. They use poison from larvae of the leaf-cutting beetle *Diamphidia simplex*. Once the larvae pupate they bury themselves in small cocoons below ground. The Bushman carry these small cocoons around with them and, when they need to poison an arrow, the small grub inside the cocoon is carefully removed and rolled between thumb and forefinger until the innards become liquid. The head is then pulled off and the fluid spread on the arrowhead. Eight to ten grubs are required for one arrowhead. There is no known antidote for this poison and all large creatures, including humans, will die from a full dose within 10 to 20 hours.

As shown in their rock paintings, the myths and legends of the Bushman are many and varied. Legend has it that a young girl, wishing for a little light so that her family might see to return home in the dark, reached down and threw some wood ash into the night sky. And so the Milky Way was born. Some Bushman attribute the great Kalahari storms to a giant mythical leopard who, when angry, flashes its 'lightning' eyes and roars thunderously.

Days 41-42: A fortunate red rooster

Our Capricorn Kalahari journey has an amazing sense of freedom to it. The continuous onward journey and not knowing what lies around the next corner; that's the bug that's bitten us. I once read that the difference between a tourist and a traveller is that the former has an itinerary – we never know what on earth will happen next! Troy, with eager youthfulness, has really become part of this journey. He's scribbling a rough journal and is enjoying every moment. Wherever possible he rides on top of the Land Rover, taking in the

23°27' THREATENS TO BREAK US!

vastness and freedom of it all. He's burnt brown by the sun and has developed such an enormous appetite that I've given him the Zulu name Mahlafuna, 'he who eats often and with relish'. Plates of stew and rice disappear down the hatch and in the morning the leftovers are turned into bubble and squeak, which he wolfs down. We don't mind because he has the job of cleaning the old three-legged cast-iron pot. This is a very different Troy from the pale-looking city dude we picked up at Polokwane Airport a week or so ago.

At times Ross is very quiet. Of course he misses his girlfriend Geraldine and their little boy Tristan Kingsley. We know cameraman Mike is smitten with Vanessa, and he disappears every now and then from camp with the satellite phone (it's supposed to be for emergencies only!) and reappears with a broad grin. We've never seen him like this before, and naturally he gets his leg pulled. For Gill and me it's easier; we've got each other's company and understanding. Sure we miss home occasionally, especially our dogs, but like Ross we are adventure addicts and, whilst the thought of the long, tough journey ahead is daunting, we wouldn't change this lifestyle for anything. One day rolls into the next: we load the grub boxes, put out the fire, tie the old camp chairs and water containers onto the roof, spread the survey maps out on the bonnet of the Land Rover, mark the morning's GPS points, check oil and water, crack a few jokes and move off west. *Chuma* and *Susi* growl along in low gear, as they zig-zag between trees and bushes, with their tyres reduced to one bar so that they can churn through the endless soft Kalahari sand. Stretched behind the back row of seats in *Susi* is a thin strand of wire, from which hang several slices of thick salted beef, with a margin of yellow fat. It dries quickly in the winter heat, and, much to Mahlafuna's delight, these thick slices of biltong are served with maizemeal porridge, mixed with sugar and butter. It's a delicacy for the Capricorn travellers.

Botswana is a peaceful country. Each village has a central boma or *kgotla*, an enclosure fenced with indigenous tree poles, and a gong to summon the villagers. This is where the Botswana flag flies and the chief and village elders meet. It is here that criminals are tried and punished in the traditional way. If they are found guilty they're given a public beating and are fined cattle or money.

We pitch camp on a large salt pan near Ukwe. Snow white in colour, it is surrounded by Kalahari bush. Botswanan tinsmiths make great utensils, and in a village outside Kang we buy Mashozi one of those old-fashioned galvanised baths as a bit of a joke – she woke up this morning and said, 'I'd kill for a bath!' – and loaded it onto the Land Rover roofrack. Well, tonight's my turn. I drag the bath out into the middle of the pan, heat up the old enamel kettle and soon give my fellow Capricornians a rendition of, 'Singing in the bathtub, singing for joy. Singing the song lifebuoy can't help singing, 'cause I know I'm a lifebuoy safe from head to toe...'. People do really ridiculous things in the bush! It's a merry evening indeed as we have an 'End of the Kalahari' party. We buy a beautiful, big, red rooster from a nearby village, but when we get back to camp Mashozi refuses to

Botswana is a wildlife paradise, with elephant and cheetah.

let Ross slaughter it and locks it up, with food and water, in *Chuma*. With Mashozi it's always a problem: whenever we find a bit of live protein she adopts it and gives it a name.

I'm woken by the crowing of our red rooster, who's shat all over the Land Rover seats and is now loudly heralding the new dawn. Mashozi giggles and chuckles, and when we return to the village the locals look shocked and horrified, thinking we will want our money back. But we don't, and the delighted red rooster chases after a clucking hen. Our journey across Botswana's Kalahari is complete: a boundary fence separates Botswana from Namibia and we are forced to travel north to the border post of Mamuno. The cowbell hanging from *Chuma*'s bushbar tinkles merrily. Our eyes squint into the setting sun and the dust: Namibia, here we come!

SINGING IN THE BATHTUB
— UKWE PAN IN THE
KALAHARI — .

THEY CAN'T BELIEVE IT
WHEN WE GIVE BACK THE
BIG RED ROOSTER!

WHAT IDIOTS WOULD BATTLE ACROSS THE DESERT CARRYING A BICYCLE AND A BATHTUB

Namibia

Sandwiched between the Kalahari and the Atlantic, Namibia could prove the most difficult part of our cross-Africa challenge — Ahead of us lie the rocky Granadoelas, the winding vlaktes of the Namib-Naukluft and the high sand dunes of the ancient Namib. I'm nervous as hell! And we still don't have final permission to tackle the desert.

Day 43: A night in Little Texas

The border post seems out of place after the wide open freedom and space of the Kalahari. Official buildings, a wide tarred road, a modern filling station, a white ceramic toilet that flushes and water out of a tap. Ross and Mike immediately touch base with their 'lovies', and even young Troy seems to be rekindling an old Cape Town love affair. I suppose a long journey gives one time to reflect on things. The Botswanan border officials at Mamuno are relaxed and friendly, and there are anti-corruption posters pasted up on the walls. This is somewhat easier than our crossing into the country over the 'closed' Limpopo bridge. A busload of elderly South African tourists crowds around the Land Rovers. These tourists all look so clean and tidy, as if from another world. They've seen part of our journey on the South African TV programme *Carte Blanche* and are full of questions: 'Where do you sleep?' 'What do you eat?' 'How are the Land Rovers going?' 'What about the wild animals?' Of course we exaggerate a bit and tell them a few yarns.

The Namibian border post is called *buitepos,* a flashback to the days when Namibia's official language was Afrikaans, following a League of Nations mandate that took the country away from the Germans after the First World War and gave South Africa control over South West Africa (as it was then called). Namibia finally gained full independence from South Africa in 1990.

It's already late afternoon, so we decide to push on to the town of Gobabis for a bit of 'R and R', and to plan our crossing of Namibia along the Tropic of Capricorn. The name Gobabis is said to be derived from the Nama word *goabbes*, meaning 'the place of elephants', but these animals have gone now and today Gobabis is a busy cattle ranching centre. The local white people are mostly Afrikaans speaking. They wear khaki shorts, long socks velskoene and wide-brimmed hats, drive 4x4 pick-up trucks, and proudly call the area 'Little Texas'. A statue of a massive Brahman bull welcomes us into this friendly Wild West frontier town. Outside the Old Central Hotel a cattle rancher invites us to come to his place for a '*lekker* kudu *braai*', but we've already booked into the old colonial hotel, on the walls of which are signs written in giant letters: 'STEAK SEAFOOD HAVEN AND BAR.' What more could the Capricornians wish for?

There're some thirsty customers at the bar and the Capricorn team is soon filled in on the lively escapades of life in Gobabis. Ou Nik tells us that the place can get 'blerry rough' on Wednesday nights, when all the locals gather here for a *skop* (bash), and we learn about the latest love scandal that has ended up in a *helse* divorce (one of 64 last year in 'Little Texas', with its wild social scene!). The biggest danger, however, seems to be driving home from the pub at night after a 'few *dops*'. 'The damn kudu,' says a battle-scarred local, 'are all over the roads; they get blinded by the headlights and the next moment it's heads and horns through the windscreen!' He goes to his *bakkie* and brings back a photograph of a smashed vehicle.

BOTSWANA BORDER FENCE! — 23°27

NAMIBIA WE'RE FORCED TO USE THE OFFICIAL BORDER POST

CAPRICORN LINE — Ross & Co BACK TO THE LINE

A NIGHT OF R&R AT LITTLE TEXAS — GOBABIS

CATTLE FARMS

LEONARDVILLE

BLUMENFELDE

KOUS

REHOBOTH BASTERS

GAMSBERG

PARTIAL ECLIPSE

GRAMADOELAS BOOK SHELTERING DESERT

KUISEB

NAMIB — NAUKLUFT BY BICYCLE

TOPNAARS

KUISEB

GIANT DUNES OF THE ANCIENT NAMIB — ATLANTIC OCEAN —

'I'm lucky to be alive,' he says, fingering a thick blue scar down the side of his face before ordering another double Klippies and Coke. 'Africa's not for sissies, you know.'

The barman makes several attempts at 'Last round, gentlemen,' but it's after midnight by the time we stumble into our soft, comfortable beds. It's a far cry from the Kalahari Desert floor, and I miss the sound of jackals, hyaenas, the occasional lion and the fire at night. I toss and turn, worrying; we still haven't received the written permit from Namibia's Department of Wildlife and Conservation to follow the Tropic of Capricorn across the officially closed-off area of the Namib Desert. Without it our Capricorn Expedition is doomed to failure! It's a sickening feeling.

Days 44–45: The sand will just cover your bodies...

The call to Windhoek about the permit goes reasonably well. Fortunately, they too have seen our recent TV programme, with the calabash and Capricorn Scroll of Peace and Goodwill. We must report immediately to a Mr Ben Beytell, Deputy Director in the Minister of Environment and Tourism, in order to discuss our somewhat unusual request. We make a decision: Ross, Mike and Troy will continue along Capricorn, whilst Mashozi and I race to Windhoek in the other Land Rover. If we're successful, we will meet up again further along the Tropic with permit in hand.

Leaving Gobabis, Mashozi and I wave to a group of brightly dressed Herero women, walking proudly in their traditional costumes based on the Victorian dress of the old German colonial period. They look like colourful animated dolls, with enormous dresses worn over several petticoats and brightly coloured, rolled, horn-shaped, cloth hats that are said to represent the horns of a cow. They wave and smile, but, whilst these ladies might still admire the old colonial style of dress, the Herero people's association with the German colonists was an extremely painful one. Following the German occupation of Namibia in the late 19th century, much of the Herero land passed into the hands of the colonisers. Finally, they rose up against the Germans. The fighting was bitter and thousands of Herero were slaughtered by the Germans under General Lothar von Trotha. Thousands more died of thirst and starvation as they were chased into the Kalahari. It is believed that 75 percent of the entire Herero population was exterminated. But now there's a resurgence of Herero culture – they have a colourful annual cultural ceremony – and, to this day, a holy fire (to keep alive their link to their ancestral spirits) is kept permanently burning at the homes of the Herero headmen.

An oncoming vehicle flashes its lights at us, as a kudu ram with long twisted horns escorts his harem across the Windhoek highway. Most of the wide open thornveld we pass through is taken up with cattle ranching. Close to Windhoek the road snakes through rocky outcrops. Still anxious about the permit situation, we finally arrive in Namibia's relaxed capital city. Originally the area was known by the Khoi-Khoi as Ai-gams ('steam-' or 'fire-water'), due to the hot springs found here, which were used for centuries by the nomadic Bushmen.

With our hearts in our mouths, we're shown into Ben Beytell's office and tea is poured. A map of Namibia hangs from the wall and a large framed photograph of Sam Nujoma, the President, looks down at us benignly. Mr Beytell, in his khaki uniform with its Parks Board insignia, talks on the phone in Afrikaans and we wait for the moment of truth. 'You blokes must be bloody crazy,' he says, putting the phone down and introducing himself. 'I saw you on TV walking across the Kruger National Park. Have you any idea how difficult it is to cross the Namib from east to west? Believe me, it's almost impossible,' he says, pointing on the map to where Capricorn crosses the most ancient desert in the world. 'Kingsley, if you die out there the wind will just blow the sand over your bodies and you will be lost forever. We don't have the resources to look for you, so please don't expect it. Why don't you cheat? There's a good road to the north that would take you to Walvis Bay and the Atlantic.' I patiently explain that our specific object is to follow 23° 27' as closely as possible and that we would really appreciate his help. He hesitates for a while, then smiles and picks up the phone to speak to a ranger by the name of Kobus Alberts. 'Kingsley, he is the only man I know that can do it, and if there's anyone who can get you across the Namib it's him. He will meet you on the edge of the desert. Good luck and here's your permit.' Mashozi and I jump for joy and shake his hand warmly.

Day 46: Kaptein John McNab and the Rehoboth Basters

Along Namibia's Tropic of Capricorn live a fiercely proud and independent people, a community with German, Khoikhoi and Dutch blood in their veins. They are known as the Basters (meaning 'bastards' or 'half-castes'), whose tough, pioneering ancestors trekked from the Cape in 1872 to create a homeland around the place called Rehoboth. The Rehoboth Basters elected a *kaptein* (captain) and lived much as their Voortrekker cousins had done in the old Boer Republics. They preserved their independence and even fought alongside the German colonists in battles against the Nama and the Herero, until the First World War. They had an existing deal with the Germans that they would remain neutral in any 'white on white conflict.' However, come the First World War, when the Germans expected them to fight against the Allied Forces, they returned their uniforms – infuriating the Germans.

The Rehoboth Basters armed themselves and took shelter in a circle of koppies at

Ons die Rehoboth Baster Gemeenskap, as een van die jongste Inheemse Bevolkingsgroepe van die wêreld voel hui by gerard en bevoorreg om op hierdie Rol van Vrede ons hantekening in die te voeg om ook ons bydrae en stem te voeg tot diegene wat aan alle inwoners en nasies van ons planeet vrede en voorspoed toe te wens.

J McNab:
Capt. (Rehoboth Community.
20/06/2001

20/6/2001 – CAPT JOHN McNAB
OF THE REHOBOTH COMMUNITY.
SIGNED AT REHOBOTH

Samkubis, where they bravely fought off their German attackers until the Basters ran out of ammunition. Thinking they were defeated they turned to prayer. Then, as if by a miracle, a South African column appeared and charged through the desert towards the Germans, saving the Basters from certain defeat. That day, May 8th, has since become a day of covenant for the Baster people, and every year the community treks out to Samkubis in the Namib Desert for a commemorative prayer meetings, braaivleis, brandy and the shooting off of ancient weapons.

Waving our permit from the Land Rover window, Mashozi and I meet our fellow Capricornians outside Rehoboth. Everybody is overjoyed and we go in to town to meet Kaptein John McNab (with a name like NcNab, he obviously has a Scottish ancestor who took a local wife). We sit over-

Kobus Alberts, with his dog Roxie.

looking the settlement at sunset. Kaptein McNab is a serious man who is concerned for the future, independence and welfare of his community. We sit and talk and he endorses our Capricorn Scroll.

Kaptein McNab suggests we overnight at the hot springs close to town. Two mischievous little barefoot children guide us to the rather spartan tourist camp, built apart from Windhoek's other amenities – a legacy of the old separate development apartheid days. It's as cold as hell and we are the only guests. We light a fire and throw some Windhoek steaks on the coals. We are entertained by Ross, Troy and Mike's stories of their journey following Capricorn to Rehoboth: they built a small cairn of stones outside Leonardville, as a Capricorn marker.

Day 47: Tales of the Gramadoelas

Chuma and *Susi* are together again now, with written permission to cross the Namib, and so we head off, leaving a dust trail behind us. It's a great feeling as we twist and turn across the spectacular beauty of the stark, windswept highlands, dominated by the thousand-million-year-old flat-topped granite mountain of Gamsberg. We stop to admire the incredible view before snaking down to the desert floor below, where we are to meet our Namib guide and desert expert Kobus Alberts. The Land Rovers simply love this sort of terrain, their constant four-wheel-drive allowing us to keep control on the tight, corrugated bends. Just before noon we stop both Landies in a wide open plain of yellow grass. To the east lie the giant Gamsberg Mountains, to the west the tortured Gramadoelas and the Namib's red sea of sand. Mike takes out the big camera lens and inserts a sheet of plastic. The rest of us, looking like creatures from outer space, put on our planetarium glasses and gaze directly into the sun. A breeze whispers through the yellow grass, the sky is a cloudless blue; we wait. And then it happens: the moon slowly moves across the sun in an 80 percent eclipse that dims the sun and lowers the temperature. Nature goes quiet. It's an eerie feeling, being part of this little band of travellers with their wrap-around cardboard and plastic glasses, in the middle of nowhere. It's a special moment.

By this time Kobus Alberts has arrived in his big, white government V8 Chevrolet truck, with massive sand tyres, ropes, sand ladders and his canvas bedroll. He's also brought his fox terrier Roxy along. He wears khaki shorts and velskoene, and has a pipe in his mouth. I take an instant liking to him. He's about 28 years old, with an open, honest, smiling face. He speaks English with a guttural Namibian-style Afrikaans accent and, best of all, he seems not to take himself too seriously. It turns out that Kobus is the great-grandson of the celebrated Boer voortrekker leader Oom Gert Alberts, who led the Dorsland Trek by ox-wagon into Angola. Kobus's great-grandmother's grave lies in the Etosha Pan, where she succumbed to the hardships of the Thirstland Trek.

'Ag, Kingsley, it's good to meet you at last,' says Kobus. 'I've only seen pictures of you in the *Getaway* magazine and I must say you really looked like a grumpy old f...er!' Well, Ross and Gill just fall about laughing. It makes their day, and for the rest of the journey across the Namib I am referred to as GOF.

Until arriving here I never knew that there was an actual place called the Gramadoelas and always thought the saying, 'He lives out in the Gramadoelas' simply meant 'in the middle of nowhere'. But here we stand, with Kobus, overlooking one of the most inhospitable places on earth I have ever seen: thousands of little gnarled, dry hillocks and mounds, koppies, canyons and gorges. It is as if a greater being has been kneading the landscape like dough.

In an amazing story of survival and endurance, two young German geologists, Henno Martin and his friend Hermann Korn, who were threatened with internment for the duration of the Second World War, escaped with their dog Otto. They lived a Robinson Crusoe-like existence out here in this hostile wilderness for two-and-a half years, before Korn became ill and they were discovered. Fortunately, their story of bravery was viewed leniently by the higher authorities, and they were taken into government service as geologists, where their intimate knowledge of the desert helped them survey well-drilling sites in the Namib. Henno Martin gave his own account of the experience in his book *The Sheltering Desert*. It's now out of print, but was made into a film of the same name in 1992. I find myself often thinking about these two brave, peace-loving men as we make our way across this moonscape of gruelling terrain.

Once through the Gramadoelas and across the dramatic Kuiseb Canyon, we make our way onto the huge open plains of the Namib-Naukluft beyond. Kobus might never have been to Johannesburg, but he knows this area like the back of his hand. The Namib-Naukluft is the largest nature reserve in Africa, covering an area more than twice the size of Wales. From a high, rocky outcrop Kobus points out the various landmarks we will need to follow along 23°

In the wilds of Namibia we stop to view the partial eclipse of the sun - all around us is wilderness and as the sun darkens, there is a hush!

The day of the dark moon. From L to R: Me, Mashozi, Ross and Troy.

27' to get to the Atlantic. The view is endless: thousands of square kilometres of rock desert and, in the distance, a smudge of red sand dunes – the eight-million-year-old Namib Desert. We shake hands; Kobus will meet us again in two days' time at the village of Klein Klipneus, just north of where the Tropic of Capricorn crosses the gravel track that runs to a Namib desert research station at Gobabeb. We set off on our own, after giving Kobus our word that the Land Rovers will travel only along the dry washes (water courses), as tracks made in the desert can remain for well over a hundred years, because it's so arid. The Land Rovers will zig-zag across the plains, but to stay true to the Tropic of Capricorn Ross and I get special permission to cross the Namib-Naukluft Vlaktes (Namib-Naukluft Plains) by mountain bike. We make camp within sight of Mirabib, a giant granite inselberg that shines red and pink in the desert sunset. Springbok, mountain zebras, gemsbok and ostriches are the only other occupants of the vast plain. Ross declares it to be the most beautiful place he has ever pitched camp. We sit around the fire and discuss the challenge ahead. Will we make it across the *vlaktes* by bike and be able to cross the Namib by vehicle? Time will tell.

Days 48–49: **Desert moonscape on two wheels**

After another day of travelling across the *vlaktes*, we're up at sparrow's fart preparing the bikes and checking the kit: full waterbottles, first aid kit, *Rehydrat*, blockout, pump, spare tubes, puncture kit and food supplies. Ross and I say goodbye to Mashozi, Troy and Mike. The emergency plan is simple: if we don't make it to the rendezvous point then Kobus will come back along 23° 27' to look for us. Mike films us leaving the Landies, two little specks of man and bicycle crawling across the great landscape of the Namib-Naukluft.

It's fine while the sand has a hard crust to it, but after a few hours it becomes softer and the wind swings around to blow directly against us. Soon father and son are doing more pushing than riding and by midday the situation has become really tough. We creep into some shade, wedging ourselves into a windblown hole in the rocks. We ration our water and battle through some bully beef and biscuits – it's really too hot to eat – then crawl on, forever west. I wish I were Ross's age and as fit as he is. I hate this body that I live in; at this bloody rate I won't make my allocated three score years and ten. All that keeps me going is the sight of a thin line of green trees that marks the Kuiseb River, bordering the sand dunes of the Namib. Crunch, crunch, crunch, the sound of boots on desert crust. On the bike, off the bike; finally the crust hardens again, the wind drops and we pedal on through the desert moonscape. Ross's GPS tells us that we are almost there and, dead on target, we meet the Gobabeb dirt track and turn right. What did we do before the days of GPS?

Kobus, Mashozi, Mike, Troy and the *Carte Blanche* TV crew are waiting to meet us at the village of Klein Klipneus, a Topnaar village on the dry Kuiseb River. Kobus is rather proud of the GOF and his son, exclaiming that a bicycle ride across the Namib-Naukluft is a world first. Ross and I, too tired and thirsty to care, are more interested in the contents of the expedition coolbox! We load our bicycles on the roof carriers of *Chuma* and *Susi* and go forward to meet Chief Reuben of the Topnaars, who have been described by anthropologists as the modern descendants of the oldest population group in Namibia. They belong to the Khoikhoi people, and it is said that the Strandlopers (groups of beachcombers who lived a nomadic existence along the seashore centuries ago) are amongst the Topnaars' ancestors.

The village is a rag-tag affair of old sheets of corrugated iron, donkey carts, goats, little children and chickens. Chief Reuben cannot sign his name and, like the Bushmen in the Kalahari, he endorses our Capricorn Scroll with a shaky cross. The ballpoint pen is a strange object in the gnarled, weather-beaten hand of a leading member of the ancient Topnaar people, who are probably the last group of humans we will see along Africa's Tropic of Capricorn. Ahead of us lie the shifting sand dunes of the world's oldest desert.

Days 50–54: **Straight down the slipface**

Last night, camped in the desert dunes, I entertained Kobus with anecdotes from our Capricorn journey. No sooner had I mentioned our visit to the Pedi rain queen than the heavens opened and the pelting rain soon had us scuttling for tents and tarpaulins. Kobus couldn't believe it – rain in the middle of the Namib. He giggled with delight as he dragged his bedroll and Roxy the fox terrier off to find a dry place under his Chevy. Late yesterday afternoon, having bid farewell to the Topnaar Chief, we made our way across the dry Kuiseb and into the high dunes of the Namib. It was an immediate baptism of fire, despite the fact that we let our tyres down to one bar of pressure.

We get severely stuck several times today in the steep, soft sand dunes. I can tell that it will be absolute hell for the vehicles. It's only our momentum that keeps us upright as we follow Kobus, racing along the razor-back ridges and clawing our way to the tops of sand dunes, engines screaming in low gear. Having driven our Land Rovers across the Kalahari we are used to sandy, desert-like conditions, but, let me tell you, nothing prepares us for some of the highest sand dunes on earth. It's like being out at sea on a small boat with massive swells, and it's scary.

Kobus has the advantage of very wide sand tyres and a powerful petrol V8 engine, but even he struggles at times. His task is to race ahead and search for a way through the dunes. He flits from one sand dune to another, travelling at breakneck speed, sand flying high and engine roaring. He drives with one hand on the steering wheel, the other resting on the door, Roxy parked in the crook of his elbow and his pipe always in his mouth. To succeed you need nerves of steel. It takes a few hours of digging and winching to make me realise that we will just have to throw caution to the wind. The only way is to drive as fast as possible – break the forward motion and down you go, both diffs stuck in the sand. It's all about speed, even if we risk rolling the Landies; we will just have to go like hell. We strap everything down – seatbelts on, shoes off for better grip on accelerator, clutch and brake – and point *Chuma* and *Susi* west, towards the Atlantic, for the ride of our lives. Forty-five degrees may not sound like much, but that's the pitch the Namib sand dunes rise to, and it's quite something when you're heading down them in a Land Rover.

The trick is to roar up the hard, windblown side of the massive dunes, reach the summit, fly the front half of the Land Rover over the edge to avoid see-sawing, drop a gear without stopping, and then slide the vehicle down the soft sand slipface, some of which are well over 100 metres high. It's an unbelievable feeling. The vehicles cause a sand avalanche that roars in your ears like a jumbo jet. The important thing is to keep your front wheels straight; slide sideways and you will roll to the bottom – and the end of the expedition. It's important to move faster than the avalanche and hit the bottom of the dune ready to give full taps for the ascent ahead. We put the Land Rovers through some precipitous angles that make adrenaline pump through our bodies.

We get stuck in giant conical holes, many the size of a tennis court – Kobus jokingly calls them mouse holes. They're like giant antlion sand traps, except that in this case, the insects are our *Chuma* and *Susi*. The trick is to keep moving and drive the vehicle out in a spiral to the top. Most of the time, though, this fails, and we have to dig, pull and winch the vehicles free. It's taxing on the Landies. Sometimes they slide sideways and the soft tyres get pulled from the rims. At times we lie back in the hot sand, too exhausted to move. I wonder if we will make it.

Kobus's support is unfailing. On day two we make only 12 kilometres in 10 hours, but still a sense of humour and optimism stays with us. It's too dangerous to drive at night, but the isolation and beauty of the desert is mind blowing. One night, too tired to cook a proper meal, I use Captain Morgan rum to flambé some thick steaks on the Land Rover spade. Using a sharp knife, we cut the succulent flesh into thin strips and dunk it in coarse salt, Zulu style. It's delicious. We raise our enamel mugs and toast the Namib, although the thought of the journey ahead is terrifying. The tension is getting to us and we drink too much, too quickly. Mike is full of nonsense tonight. Using the camera light, a sharp knife and a roll of boerewors, he performs a shadow operation on me from behind a sleeping bag sheet, appearing to cut me open and remove metres of sausage-like intestine, whilst giving a comical commentary.

It takes five days to complete the 60-odd-kilometre crossing of the Namib. Five of the longest days of my life: pushing, shoving and digging. To make matters worse, Kobus's Chevy's starter motor packs up, so whenever he stalls in the soft sand he needs a pull start from one of the Land Rovers. I just wish we'd offloaded more of our kit before attempting the crossing. Can you believe it, Mashozi's tin bath is still riding on the roofrack! It's frighteningly punishing work for *Chuma* and *Susi,* but they are proving to be tough enough to justify the names of the two remarkable African heroes that they've been given. This is the toughest Land Rover ride of my life.

We stop at the summit of a high dune, where Mike sets up the camera and waves us forward. The Landies slide down the dune slipface to the blue-green south Atlantic Ocean. On 23° 27' there's a cold Benguela current mist. We've made it.

We're exhausted, mentally and physically spent, but our spirits soar as we are welcomed by hundreds upon hundreds of seals, flapping, flopping and sliding into the cold Atlantic. We empty the Capricorn calabash of Indian Ocean seawater, taken from the coast of Mozambique, into the Atlantic. I gaze across the foam-flecked ocean towards the setting sun. Ahead of us lies South America. I just hope that Chile's Atacama Desert will be easier. Roxy barks and Kobus sucks quietly on his pipe; he's the true hero of our Namib journey. Without him to lead us through the maze of dunes, I doubt we'd ever have made it.

Yes, we've survived Mozambique's unexploded landmines and the Jompa Jozz trail, the man-eaters of the Kruger National Park, the never-ending Kalahari, the Gramadoelas and the *vlaktes,* and now the roller-coaster ride across the dunes of the Namib Desert. Mama Africa, you are now behind us. I look across at Mashozi and Ross, the strain of the desert is etched on their sunburnt faces. We hug and kiss – Capricorn South America, here we come!

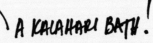

A KALAHARI BATH!

Protea Hotel
Walvis Bay, Namibia
14 September 2001

Hi Taryn

Well, here we are, cocooned in hotel luxury. The Protea Hotel guys in Walvis Bay took one look at us and obviously felt we needed a bit of pampering. Mashozi is still hidden in the depths of a bubble bath. Geraldine and little Tristan are flying in to meet Ross and we've said goodbye to Mike Yelseth, who caught the Joburg plane with seconds to spare (he was desperate and would have chartered a Boeing to get back to Vanessa!).

We've survived the Namib, and Capricorn Africa is finally put to bed. The journey across the dunes and the solitude of the ancient Namib will live with me forever. I thought we knew something about 4x4 sand driving, but never before have I been so utterly terrified as when we slid the Landies down the 45° slopes of some of the highest dunes in the world. One wrong move and it would have meant the end of the Capricorn Expedition. Without Kobus Alberts, chief game warden of Namib-Naukluft, to coax and guide us through the dunes I doubt we would ever have made it.

Taryn, you can imagine the feeling of relief as we slide down the final dune slipface - not a human being in sight, just thousands of grunting seals to welcome us to the end of 23° 27' on the Atlantic Coast.

The Capricorn Scroll of Peace and Goodwill is now dog-eared and sweat-stained. Mayors, chiefs, governors and ordinary people have endorsed it. The journey has taught us that it's humankind that makes the world go round and, although we might come from all walks of life and have different creeds and colours, it's that basic sense of humanity, something we Africans call ubuntu - it binds us all together along this imaginary line called Capricorn.

Got your message. Glad the dogs and house are all okay. Thanks as always for holding the fort.
All our love,
The Crazy Capricornians
P.S. Great news! There was an email waiting for us here in Walvis confirming that Chuma and Susi have a berth on the Alpha Bravery bound for South America. Please thank Duncan Davies from Phoenix Shipping for us.

The out-stretched arms of the massive Jesus Statue welcome us to Rio and the fantasy world of Brazil. Our family Odyssey will take us from Ubatuba on the Atlantic coast, across the Serra do Mar mountains and to the concrete jungle of São Paulo, the largest city along Capricorn. Then it's west to the Rio Parana, the Mato Grosso and Paraguay. They say that 'God favours the Brave'!

Brazil

Days 55–57: **Montevideo, Uruguay**

It is close to midnight when flight PUO229 on Pluna Lineas Uruguays makes a bumpy landing on the Montevideo runway. We're extremely relieved to see our expedition baggage and mountain bikes being off-loaded safely. Our South American adventure is about to begin! Armed with our Zulu calabash, to be filled at the beginning and emptied at the end of each continent's Capricorn journey, and our expedition Scroll of Peace and Goodwill, we'll now cross South America along the Capricorn line, from just south of Rio to Antofagasta on Chile's Pacific coast.

At the old Hotel Lancaster on Plaza Cagancha in downtown Montevideo we meet our lovely goddaughter and latest Capricorn member. She flew to Buenos Aires from London and took the ferry down the Rio Plate to meet us in Montevideo. With her blond hair bouncing and a big grin on her face, Nicola-Jane ('NJ') Balcomb races out to greet us; it's wonderful to see her again.

Just prior to our departure for South America NJ phoned us – she was tearful over a love affair gone wrong. 'Stop complaining. You're only 23 and have got a whole life ahead of you,' I said. 'Leave London for a while and come and cross South America with us! All you'll need is a few bob for the grub kitty and drinks. It's an opportunity of a lifetime.'

The children of our two families, the Holgates and the Balcombs, grew up together in Zululand and had many shared adventures in Africa. I shudder as I remember an occasion when the baby Nicola, wrapped in a blanket, was put down on the ground next to the Land Rover whilst we were unpacking on a camping trip. Not knowing she was there I jumped off the truck. Fortunately, some instinct made me look down as I sailed through the air and I just managed to move my legs in time, landing with a size 13 boot on either side of little NJ's head. Now here she is in Montevideo, and ahead of her lies who knows what! We all hit the town and, this being South America, the pubs stay open for most of the night.

Day 58: **A reunion with Chuma and Susi**

It is with some relief that we hear from Duncan that our vehicles have arrived safely in Montevideo. Just a few weeks ago we said farewell to *Chuma* and *Susi*, with our friends the Zulu dancers from Shakaland, who had come to the docks in Durban for the occasion. I must say that, as the vehicles were hauled up by cranes onto the deck of the *Alpha Bravery*, I found it hard to believe that it was all really happening. South Africans love a great adventure, and Duncan Davies, legendary Durban shipping character and owner of Phoenix Shipping, is no exception. He sponsored the vehicles' passage to South America and Land Rover chased up all the paperwork. And, whilst the Landies went by sea, we expedition members flew to South America, courtesy of Flight Centre.

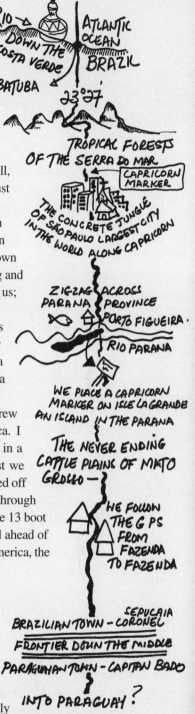

RIO
DOWN THE COSTA VERDE
ATLANTIC OCEAN
BRAZIL
UBATUBA
23°27'
TROPICAL FORESTS OF THE SERRA DO MAR
CAPRICORN MARKER
THE CONCRETE JUNGLE OF SÃO PAULO LARGEST CITY IN THE WORLD ALONG CAPRICORN
ZIGZAG ACROSS PARANA PROVINCE
PORTO FIGUEIRA
RIO PARANA
WE PLACE A CAPRICORN MARKER ON ISLE LA GRANDE AN ISLAND IN THE PARANA
THE NEVER ENDING CATTLE PLAINS OF MATO GROSSO —
WE FOLLOW THE GPS FROM FAZENDA TO FAZENDA
BRAZILIAN TOWN - CORONEL SEPUCAIA
FRONTIER DOWN THE MIDDLE
PARAGUAYAN TOWN - CAPITAN BADO
INTO PARAGUAY?

It was only after the Landies were safely aboard the *Alpha Bravery*, and the Zulus had stopped the chanting and the beating of drums, that Duncan informed me over lunch that all the crew were on danger pay. 'Bloody explosive cargo. I hope your Land Rovers aren't leaking any diesel – the whole lot could blow up!'

Now we are at the docks in Montevideo, and there stand our two lonely Land Rovers. They are covered in salt and grime and some of the tyres are half flat, but in true Capricorn Expedition style, they kick into life at the first turn of the key. Customs and Immigration are, however, not that easy to manage, and our negotiations call for a degree of African patience, much hand-shaking, smiling and the use of a Spanish phrase book.

Montevideo is a picturesque city, with blocks of modern flats competing with beautiful old Spanish colonial buildings. Everybody is warm and friendly, admiring our Capricorn Land Rovers with the South African flag decals on the bonnets and the flags of the ten Capricorn countries running along the length of the vehicles. This, however, does not stop Ross from getting a heavy speeding fine for going just a few kilometres over the limit (he didn't even notice the sign). It's South America and the traffic cops, including a pretty girl, are squeezed into figure-hugging uniforms with plenty of leather, sunglasses, boots, badges, caps and big guns. Ross smiles sweetly at the lady cop. It doesn't help a damn. Our ten words of Spanish, mixed with Zulu and the Expedition Scroll (complete with Spanish letters of introduction), gets us a small discount, but it still takes US$200 from our expedition budget. It wouldn't be too bad for most *gringos*, but for us poor South Africans.... Mashozi mumbles furiously: she's the expedition bursar. She's very annoyed, as it's her task to juggle the tiny Expedition budget.

And so we head north, our right-hand drive landies on the wrong side of the road. Uruguay has wonderful old cars: Chevies, Fords, Pontiacs and Oldsmobiles – all blowing smoke and still in use. It takes us hours to get into Brazil. The big, blond customs official doesn't seem to understand our South African vehicle-registration documents (which are in English), despite the fact that they're attached to the 4x4s' *carnets de passage*. It seems no SA-registered vehicles have ever passed this way before and he wants to know why they are registered in the name of Land Rover SA and not Señor Holgate. 'They could be stolen,' he tells us. The situation calls for big smiles and lots of patience. He speaks only limited English and our Portuguese is virtually non-existent. Finally, we work it all out in broken German with NJ, whose mum is German, saving the day, more with her blond hair and good looks than her linguistic skills. Welcome to Brazil!

Day 59–62: Nightmare journey to Rio de Janeiro

The entry into Brazil brings with it relentless pouring rain and a nightmare journey of over 2 000 kilometres to get to Rio and the Capricorn line. The World Champion Formula One motor racing driver Ayrton Senna is Brazilian and most lorry drivers share his love for speed. We have giant lorry wheels in front of us, on both sides and behind, but the mist, rain and road signs that instruct motorists to '*reduza a velocidade*' ('reduce speed') just exhort them to greater feats of daring. Smashed and crumpled vehicles are lined up at roadside police stations. Believe me, South African drivers aren't too bad! We are eternally grateful for *Chuma* and *Susi*'s constant four-wheel drive in these hellish conditions, with lorries that squeeze us in and push us forward at breakneck speed. The old-fashioned Land Rover windscreen wipers work at full speed, struggling to remove the tropical torrents from the windscreen. The rain pours down in buckets.

Picture pockets of mist, road-building detours, overturned lorries, mountain passes and the joys of driving right-hand drive vehicles on the 'wrong' side of the road at night, against the blinding lights of racing lorries, and you will have some idea of what our journey to Rio is like! It has rained solidly over the four days it's taken us to get here, and it is a tired and weary Capricorn Expedition team that finally pulls into the crowded backstreets of Copacabana.

Day 63: The bronzed bodies of the cariocas

How different this is from the Capricorn line on the desolate coast of the Namib Desert. Rio certainly lives up to its reputation as one of the most beautiful cities in the world.

We try a few hotels on the famous Copacabana strip, but they are far too expensive for our weak South African Rand and so we go back a block or two from the sea. Rio, although beautiful, is known as a rough, tough city and we'll have to watch our backs. Our major concern is for our Land Rovers; we don't want them to get stolen and end up in Paraguay without us. Finally, after much negotiation with a garage owner, we arrange secure parking (we hope) on the second floor of a parking garage. After that we meet Alexandré Miranda, an oddball character who speaks good English and wears a Greek cap, a ponytail, and a bandanna around his neck. He's come to us as a guide and translator, recommended by our 'el cheepo' hotel on Rua 5 de Julho, in the backstreets of Copacabana. He looks fine to guide us around Rio, but with his suave Brazilian looks, he hardly seems the type who would become an expedition member for the difficult journey across Brazil. We ask him to show us around the city, get us survey maps and find a hardy youngster who can speak English, pitch a tent, help cook and interpret for us as we travel across Brazil – perhaps a student.

From L to R: Mashozi, me, Walter Fleita and NJ – at Walter's second-hand auto lot, outside Montevideo, where he sells old Model T Fords and uses an old aircraft as an office.

NJ — NICOLA JANE IS THE ONLY DAUGHTER OF OLD FRIENDS LLOYD AND HELLA BALCOMB FROM MBELEZI FARM, ESHOWE ZULULAND — SHE'S ALSO OUR GOD-DAUGHTER, AFFECTIONATELY KNOWN TO US AS N.J. — NOW SHE'S OUR NEW CAPRICORN EXPEDITION MEMBER FOR OUR JOURNEY ACROSS SOUTH AMERICA!

Tim Chevallier flies in to Rio to join us. As luck would have it he is a Capricornian, born under the sign of the goat. He is also a great old friend and one of the world's best adventure cameramen. We have had many an African adventure together and now he has taken up the challenge of filming our trip across South America for National Geographic. He'd also like to cross Madagascar with us – that's if and when we get there. We couldn't have wished for a better travelling companion, and he's always good for a laugh. During the evening we wander down to Copacabana's beachfront to celebrate Tim's arrival. The beachfront is lit up, and full of locals chatting, playing cards and volleyball, and people strolling and flirting. It's a balmy evening and we blow a week's budget on a seafood extravaganza and *caipirinhas* (local Cachaça rum, lime juice, sugar and ice). My giant piece of calamari is the size and shape of an oven glove. Samba music plays, hawkers sell souvenirs and the *cariocas* (people of Rio) stroll and kiss under the palm trees. Even at this hour there is no let up in the traffic.

TIM CHEVALLIER — WHAT A PRIVILEGE TO HAVE "OLD FRIEND" TIM ALONG — GREAT HUMOUR AND HE'S KNOWN "TO TAKE A SHANDY ON A HOT AFTERNOON" — NOT TO MENTION A "CAPTAIN ON A COLD NIGHT" — BORN IN MALAWI TIM'S AN EXPERIENCED ADVENTURER AND A GREAT CAMERAMAN, WITH A NEVER SAY DIE ATTITUDE — TIM'S OPTED TO DO THE S'AMERICAN LEG OF CAPRICORN WITH US & MADAGASCAR SIYABONGA! TIM —

Day 64: Caipirinhas, the sounds of Samba and a disco called Help!

On the summit of Corcovado ('the peak of the hunchback') we stand in awe at the feet of Christ the Redeemer. Alex explains that the statue was completed in 1931 and that its outstretched arms face the entrance to Guanabara Bay, welcoming visitors to Rio. Gonçalo Coelho, an early Portuguese mariner, was sent to explore the 'new land' by King Manuel I of Portugal. His fleet sailed down the coast, naming prominent geographical features after Biblical saints as they went along. By the time they got to Guanabara Bay on 1 January 1502 they'd run out of saints' names, and, thinking that the mouth of the bay was a river, they named it Rio de Janeiro ('The River of January').

Sandwiched between the Atlantic and the peaks and mountains of the Serra do Mar ('Mountains of the Sea') lies one of the most dramatic cities in the world. Our bird's-eye view shows us that every inch of ground is occupied; the rich in their villas and skyscrapers living cheek-by-jowl with the poor. The *favela*, or shantytown, with nowhere else to go, creeps forever higher up the mountains, giving the shacks some of the finest views of any real estate in Rio.

Down in the city, the streets are joined by 16 tunnels, cut through the mountain ridges that crisscross the city; street children juggle tennis balls for tips and call out the names of the ten Capricorn countries painted on the sides of the Land Rovers. Beautiful beaches with famous names like Copacabana, Ipanema and Flamengo are crowded with sun-bronzed bodies beautiful. Alex explains that no self-respecting *carioca* would be seen swimming in the sea. 'That's for foreigners. If you want to swim, you go to a swimming pool,' he says, with no further explanation, pulling on a Marlboro. 'The beach is our living room, where we socialise, play cards, football and volleyball, chat up the chicks, plan our nightlife (much more important than work) and drink countless *caipirinhas*.' They taste wonderful, but drink it under the hot sun and it's got a kick like a mule. No lines divide the beaches, but the *cariocas* know what 'tribes' hang out where.

ALEXANDRÉ MIRANDA - ALEX 47 WAS BORN A 'CARIOCA' (MAN FROM RIO). HIS FAMILY HISTORY GOES BACK TO THE 1500s WHEN HIS PORTUGUESE FOREBEARS SETTLED IN BRAZIL'S BAHIA PROVINCE AND RAISED CATTLE. THE OLDEST SON OF NEWTON AND STELLA, ALEX FOLLOWED IN HIS FATHER'S FOOTSTEPS TO BECOME A WELL-KNOWN RIO DE JANIERO LAWYER — DISILLUSIONED BY 25 YEARS OF BABY ADOPTIONS AND THE MESSY BUSINESS OF RIO'S DIVORCE COURTS, HE LEFT TO FOLLOW HIS PASSION FOR BRAZILIAN HISTORY, GUIDING AND INTRODUCING VISITORS TO THE FASCINATING CULTURAL KALEIDOSCOPE OF RIO — WE ASK HIM TO SHOW US AROUND HIS CITY, GET US SURVEY MAPS AND FIND A HARDY YOUNGSTER, WHO CAN SPEAK ENGLISH, PITCH A TENT, AND CAN HELP COOK AND TRANSLATE AS WE FOLLOW CAPRICORN ACROSS BRAZIL! ALEX WHO'S NEVER CAMPED OR BEEN ON EXPEDITION BEFORE TAKES THE CAPRICORN CHALLENGE. IT WILL BE INTERESTING!

Everything and anything goes in this city of relaxed sexual and social barriers. There are gay beaches, near-naked nymphet beaches, marijuana smokers, elderly citizens walking their dogs, prancing fitness fanatics with tattoos and oiled muscles, and a sprinkling of foreigners sunbathing outside their hotels. We can only imagine what it must be like at carnival time! What a pity the Tropic of Capricorn doesn't cross Rio and that this is only a staging point for our journey to the start of 23° 27'. At night the sounds of samba music fill the streets, and those looking for professional female company go to a disco called 'Help!'. There are clubs for every taste, but in true Capricorn fashion Tim, NJ, Ross, Mashozi, Alex and I end up at a dingy corner bar in Raimundo Correa Street in downtown Copacabana. We spend a wonderful evening chatting to locals and drinking countless Cachaças – straight. Beer crates are put out on the pavement for people to sit on. We dance to MPB Radio and eat bowls of fatty beef stew, delicious brown beans and *farofa* (cassava fried in pork fat). Passing prostitutes and out-of-town traders join us for drinks.

Alex makes several calls but can't find us any English-speaking students young or crazy enough to accompany us on our ridiculous journey. 'I've never been on an expedition or camped before,' says Alex with a grin and a pull on his Marlboro, 'but remember, you guys, you're not in Africa and you will never make it without an interpreter. So, if you'll take along a not-too-sober ex-lawyer, well then, I'm your man!' We laugh and shake hands; after all, there is no better way to get to know someone than getting drunk with him. And so Alex becomes one of the team. But will he survive the rough Capricorn life across Brazil? I wonder if he fully understands the effort it takes to follow an imaginary line.

On a gut feeling I decide to take a chance on him – a middle-aged academic who's about to become an adventurer. He's enthusiastic and has an in-depth knowledge of Brazil. I think back to our African journey with Troy: he started out a city slicker and ended up a suntanned Capricornian. Thinking of the team, I notice that NJ is still a little heart-sore. She and Mashozi are having a good old heart-to-heart talk; knowing NJ as I do I'm sure that the Capricorn adventure will soon push the 'affairs of London' out of her mind. To Mashozi and me she's like the daughter we never had. She and Ross scrap a bit; they always have. But deep-down they're like brother and sister. Tim has a daughter NJ's age and he understands what she's going through.

Days 65–66: Off to Ubatuba

After a few days of clear weather in Rio we head south out of the city and down the Costa Verde – the beautiful green coast. I've nicknamed Alexandré 'Judge Alex' because of his legal background. So that I can get to know him better, he moves into *Chuma* with me (*Chuma* is the 'bread van' type of Land Rover Defender, with only two front seats and the Capricorn Expedition kit behind and on top). Mashozi joins Tim, Ross and NJ in the stationwagon *Susi*. After our harrowing trip to Rio we've become 'old hands' at driving in South America: when in doubt put your right foot down, blow the hooter and go for it! It's absolutely hair-raising.

Our two 4x4s, battered and abused from this gruelling adventure, creak and growl towards the town of Ubatuba and the start of 23° 27'. Between the Atlantic and the high, forested range of the Serra do Mar is the exquisite Costa Verde region. The rain clears to reveal literally hundreds of picturesque tropical islands, white sandy beaches and forested coves.

We hoped to make Ubatuba by evening, but the rains delay us. We find a small *pousada*, or inn, and Mashozi goes in with Judge Alex to bargain over the price. Alex quips that although the writing above *Chuma* and *Susi*'s rear doors reads, '*Alrededo Pourtierra del Mundu*' ('Around the World by Land'), it would be more accurate if it read 'by Rand'. On this expedition, we are already dipping into the old pension fund, but fortunately Brazil is good value, even for South Africans.

WE FILL THE CALABASH IN THE RAIN

Day 67: Forever in the rain

Surely Parati must be one of the loveliest towns in Brazil – certainly along the Costa Verde. It's about 300 kilometres south of Rio and its full name is Vila de Nossa Señora dos Remédios de Paraty – but these days it's just called Parati. UNESCO rates it as one of the best examples of Portuguese architecture in the country and the ancient city has been declared a national monument. The churches and homes are beautifully restored, with the doors and window frames painted in a variety of pastel shades. People wave and smile, and even the dogs seem friendly. While our real objective is to get to the Capricorn line, we can't resist the temptation to wander along the town's cobbled streets, which are out of bounds to motorised transport. The cobbles are arranged in channels, to drain off storm water and allow the sea to enter and wash the streets at high tide. The town has been inhabited since 1650 and was once a prosperous trading port, rivalling Rio de Janeiro. Over time its fortunes declined and, apart from a short-lived coffee-shipping boom in the 19th century, Parati has remained off the beaten track, keeping its historical character quietly intact.

It is late afternoon by the time we arrive in rain-drenched Ubatuba, on the Tropic of Capricorn. Alex, who by this time is eyeing the beachfront bars, says that the town's name should be changed to Ubachuva, which means 'forever in the rain'.

Day 68: South America's first Zulu calabash?

In the early morning of 27 September we dip our Zulu calabash into the Atlantic for the start of the South American leg of the Expedition. Local fishermen dragging their *pirogues* (dugout canoes) up onto the beach are astonished to see two Landies and a bunch of *gringos* dipping a calabash into the sea. They sign the Capricorn Scroll of Peace and Goodwill; one old fella simply makes his mark. He is illiterate and has been fishing here on 23° 27' for over 30 years.

Judge Alex asks one of the fishermen if he knows where the Tropic of Capricorn lies. He answers, 'Well, we know that it runs out of this bay here and across the Serra do Mar. But every single mayor we've had puts up his own sign to impress the tourists. Nowadays there's even a Capricorn sign out at the airport.'

23°27'

The forebears of many Brazilians came over the sea from Africa as slaves to work on the Portuguese sugar and coffee plantations. Trussed up, the early slaves on this coast were called 'Angolan chickens'. It was a despicable business that continued for some 30 years after the abolition of the slave trade.

So much of Brazil is like South Africa, and we feel a link to our Mother Africa. We see it in people's faces and taste it in their food: mealies, cassava, brown beans and bananas. Brazilian cities have their shacklands too, and in some areas there's a great deal of unemployment. There's also crime, drugs and poverty, but we can learn a lesson from Brazil. They're united as a nation, they all speak Portuguese and love football, as well as enjoy the same music and eat the same food. In Brazil we are experiencing a level of racial tolerance we have never seen before. It certainly is an example of Third World 'survival with a smile', despite all its problems.

Day 69: Chief Aua, cachimbo tea and the peace pipe

The Capricorn line runs over our first great obstacle, the tropical jungles and high peaks of the Serra do Mar. The uncomplaining 4x4s grind their way through thick mud and tropical forest, and the wipers click across the windscreen. Mashozi and I follow Ross, NJ and Alex in the vehicles. We stop at little rain-soaked forest villages to ask directions. Children peep at us from under the dripping eaves, and villagers walk by, feet in the mud, under colourful umbrellas.

We're about 12 kilometres south of the Capricorn line, and need to move north, through the thick forest, to the base of a peak known as Corcovado, 'The Peak of the Hunchback'. We're told there's an Indian village at the base of the mountains. The mist lifts for a moment and we gasp in disbelief; it's the first time we see ahead of us what seems to be an impenetrable mountain forest – a mass of thick, green tropical vegetation. The curtain of mist soon closes again, and we splash the Landies across a shallow stream. The rainforest drips and sweats. Ross stops under a canopy of trees, and we consult the GPS, while water from our raingear drips onto the maps. Judge Alex does plenty of interpreting, as we continually have to ask directions. Very few of the village people we come across have ever heard of this imaginary line. But they can point out the village we're heading for. Finally, we slip and slide into a Guaranese Indian village at the base of the mountains.

It was local Indians who first led the Jesuit priests, the founders of São Paulo, across these mountains and we are determined to follow in their footsteps, west, along Capricorn. We are well received by Chief Aua and he invites us to sit around the fire and sip *cachimbo* herbal tea through a silver straw. Through Alex we painstakingly explain the reason for our journey and request that he and some of the men from the village guide us through the wet tropical jungles of the Serra do Mar. There is no road or vehicle track that follows Capricorn and we will have to proceed on foot. Chief Aua is an extremely good-looking man, with long black hair, warm kind eyes and a ready smile. We talk and talk, and smoke the communal pipe. Yes, he will endorse our Capricorn Scroll of Peace and Goodwill and we are welcome to sleep in his village, but, as for guiding us across the Serro do Mar in the rain, that's difficult. The paths are steep and slippery; it is best to take ropes and very little luggage he tells us. 'Can the chief guide us across?' I ask. Alex doesn't think there's much chance.

The rain continues to fall in sheets. Mashozi cooks us a simple meal on the smoky wood fire in a high, thatched A-frame hut. Geese and chickens wander in and out and we throw our

bedrolls onto the mud floor. Later on, Chief Aua joins us to discuss our journey. Wearing beaded necklaces and a feathered headdress, he offers us fresh forest palm hearts cooked over the coals. He is joined by his wife, and a forest hunter by the name of Albino. His oldest sons are called Diago and Donezetti.

We share our simple meal with the chief and his sons, and Ross, NJ, Mashozi and I sing a few Zulu songs. In turn Chief Aua calls for the rest of his family. Out comes a guitar and the beautiful little kids screech along merrily. The roof leaks and we keep having to move around to dodge the drops. I show Chief Aua photographs of our African crossing, explaining how other great chiefs have also signed the Capricorn Scroll of Peace and Goodwill. Chief Aua tells us that the god of the forest is known as Nhandaru. He will ask him for guidance and then tell us if it's possible to assist us. I am quickly realising that such a negotiation needs patience, just as with an African chief from whom one needs a favour. Alex, himself fascinated by life in the village, proves his worth as an interpreter, allowing us to talk into the night. NJ is adopted by the girls in the homestead, and they present her with a feathered headdress and some Indian beads.

After several hours have passed, Chief Aua raises his hand for silence: he, his sons and Albino the hunter will guide us through the forests and mountains of the Serra do Mar, but only because we have become friends. In the morning, before we leave, there must first be a blessing to Nhandaru. We shake hands on the deal and they move off to the large family hut that they all share. 'Boa noite!' I look across the smoke-filled hut and give Ross, Mashozi and NJ the thumbs up.

Day 70: A red ochre blessing to Nhandaru

Judge Alex only realises the mistake of rolling out his sleeping bag under a small leak in the vast roof when he wakes up wet. I wake early to find him sitting upright in a camp chair, drinking a cup of coffee and smoking the first Marlboro of the day. He gives me a lopsided grin: 'You really are a bunch of crazy gringos.'

It is still raining when, at about 7 am, Chief Aua arrives to escort us solemnly across to the family *oca* – a hut that is somewhat larger than the one we slept in. Here simple sleeping cots are draped with mosquito nets, and there is a cooking area with some stools around the central fire. Hanging from the roof are bows and arrows, blowpipes and feathered headdresses. As I enter the hut I can sense a serious atmosphere. The young children are all sitting on the floor with their mothers; Albino the hunter, Donezetti and little Diago are standing, and the air is filled with smoke. In hushed tones, Chief Aua explains that he is about to perform a blessing to the forest god Nhandaru. Only Tim, Ross and I are brought forward into the centre of the hut. NJ, Mashozi and Judge Alex sit with the family. Chief Aua chants a request to Nhandaru to bless our journey across the rainforests of the Serra do Mar. There's a strange and eerie feeling; the look in Mashozi's eyes tells me that she feels it too. She's sensitive to the spirit world.

Albino is already in a deep trance and shudders as if possessed. Chief Aua shuffles around the hut's interior, shaking hand rattles and exhaling smoke from a large-bowled pipe. The incantations continue in a deep, monotonous drone for some minutes, and one of the children brings forward a container of red ochre. The atmosphere becomes increasingly eerie. Ross is told to take off his shirt so that they can rub red ochre onto his torso, arm and legs. I looked up at Tim; he's wide eyed. Alex begins to ask questions, but the Chief tells him to be quiet. Albino rubs red ochre onto Ross's face while Chief Aua blows smoke over the two of them. Then it is my turn. I look into Chief Aua's eyes – they are bloodshot and very serious, and his lips twitch as he mumbles the blessing. When it's Tim's turn, he stretches his arms out to make the 'ochre treatment' easier. Mashozi, NJ and Alex look on. They will be taking the 4x4s around by a different route; obviously the blessing applies only to those mad enough to journey through the forest world of Nhandaru.

WE MEET CHIEF AUA – HE SIGNS THE CAPRICORN SCROLL AND AGREES TO LEAD US OVER THE SERRA DO MAR

Then, suddenly, it's all over. The chanting stops and everybody is smiling and jolly as they prepare for the climb over the mountains. I whisper to Mashozi, and she goes out to *Chuma* and comes back with some Zulu beads and shells from Inhambane on the coast of Mozambique, which we present to Chief Aua and his family.

Ross sits with Mashozi, NJ and Alex. He scribbles a map, working out a route that will bring *Chuma* and *Susi* around to meet us at a forester's hut on the other side of the Sierra do Mar, which Chief Aua says he can get us to. If they are unable to make it in the Landies they will send a note with a runner. If we don't arrive by tomorrow evening, then they will alert the foresters and the police to send out a search party. Judge Alex has never driven a 4x4 before and so, quite rightly, Ross hands NJ the keys to *Susi*. It continues to rain.

We're told to bring only the minimum of supplies, as the dogs will hunt for armadillos to provide food for the journey. The Indians arm themselves with bows and arrows. Tim, Ross and I, carrying only the bare essentials and some rope, leave with the Indians, and soon we are drenched to the skin. It's really heavy going as we pull ourselves up the mountain using roots and tree trunks as hand- and footholds. The mud and sweat is endless, and the rain continues. The rainforest is astoundingly beautiful. The Indians recce ahead in search of the way and shout back to us from the hilltops. The hunting dogs race off into the forest in search of armadillos. I twist my right knee, and an old expedition injury returns, so that I am forced to limp forwards, helped by painkillers. Tim's camera breaks down; the humidity and rain is too much for modern technology.

It's almost nightfall by the time we find a small clearing. Ross checks the GPS – that damn machine that rules our lives – to find we're only a few metres off the Capricorn line. The Indians make cups from wild banana leaves to gather drinking water from forest trickles. There's no armadillo for supper, so we share our bully beef, tinned beans and Captain Morgan with the Indians (it was supposed to be emergency rations only). The hunting dogs shiver in disgrace and curl up wet and cold outside the tents. It's too wet for a fire, we're miserable, the tents leak and our sleeping bags are damp. There are seven of us in two small tents, in the endless rain; Ross, Tim and I are in the one tent, the Indians are in the other, and for miles around us is this incredible forest. Tim's concerned about his camera, but then Ross cracks a joke and we all chuckle. The dogs scratch outside the tent, and the Indians, shivering with cold in their tent, ask for more rum. I wish we had some! We're in for a long night.

Days 71–73: The only human beings on earth

The morning sun allows us a brief view of the peak of the Hunchback just above us, and we feel like the only human beings on earth. We manage to get the camera working, which improves everyone's mood (we're all miserable after a terrible night). We start climbing through the mist, and my knee feels as if it's the size of a football. I've had a couple of patch-up jobs on this knee, but the last time I saw my doctor he suggested a replacement. It will just have to wait till after

ATLANTIC OCEAN
UBATUBA 23°27'
COASTAL PLAIN.
CHIEF AUA'S VILLAGE
TOUGH CLIMB OVER THE SERRA DO MAR MTS – THICK WET TROPICAL RAIN FOREST
FORESTER'S COTTAGE –
MEET LAND ROVER TEAM
DIRECTION SÃO PAULO 23°27'

23°27' WE'RE IN THE FOREST WORLD OF NHANDARU.

Capricorn. Sometimes I hate having to live in this ageing body of mine. A friend once said, 'Kingsley, you should consider slowing down – they're starting to fell in our plantation now!'

Chief Aua is first to reach the summit of the Hunchback. He stands on the edge of the sheer cliff, raises both arms and shouts his praises to Nhandaru. As if on cue, the mist rises and we get a brief glance of the magical forest world beneath us – an endless canopy of bright green that drops steeply to the coast below. Then, as quickly as it lifted, the mist closes in again.

My mind goes back to our crossing of Africa. Nowhere, along that whole section of the Tropic of Capricorn, did we encounter such forests and mountains. I think of the high Andes ahead of us, but that's a long way away and, first of all, we have to get out of these mountains. We slip and slide. Diago helps Tim with the camera equipment. The river crossings are hell for my knee; one slip off the wet stepping stones and it could dislocate. Chief Aua cuts me a long walking stick, which helps me balance. I'm woozy from the painkillers I'm taking, but I'm still able to appreciate the beauty of our surroundings. Tim is in good spirits now that his camera is working again.

Our communication with the Guaranese is through a wet Portuguese phrase book and sign language. They talk to each other in Guaranese, and we learn a few words. A narrow path leads us through a thick bamboo forest – the stems thin and straight. Chief Aua cuts one and demonstrates how they make great blowpipes from them. By midday we're all starving. Still no armadillo (I'm secretly pleased that we don't have to kill one of the little blighters). Albino, with his hand-carved tobacco pipe and bows and arrows on his back, is fit and tough. Donezetti just smiles all the time and recces ahead. Diago sticks close to Tim, watching his every move with the camera – he's even learnt to put up and level the tripod. Chief Aua is kind and helpful – he's very concerned about my knee – and I connect with him. A few strokes of his razor-sharp machete bring down a young palm tree, and soon we're all munching hungrily on fresh palm hearts, steamed over an open fire and washed down with river water. Tim's got a tube of Super-C sweets and we each get a half.

At times we get a bit lost, and there's much discussion amongst the Indians. Ahead of us is another steep, forested ridge. Prickly vines tear at our skins and clothes. Using the rope we haul ourselves upwards through the mud and the wet. At the top of the ridge we all flop down utterly exhausted, except for Albino, who lights up his pipe and sets his hunting dogs off into the bush. They all start yapping and he grabs his bows and arrows and darts off after them, shouting dog instructions in Guaranese. In sign language, Chief Aua excitedly, and with much smacking of his lips, indicates how tasty armadillo is. But after a short while the dogs go quiet, and Albino the great hunter returns sheepishly. The thought of a hungry night in the forest galvanises us all into action. We move down into a valley, following a mountain stream. The path broadens and we're able to quicken our pace. Chief Aua indicates that we must speed up. He makes a triangle with his hands and points down the path. I presume he means we're on course for the forester's hut. I take two Myprodol and clench my teeth – it's *vasbyt* time.

It's dark by the time we reach the forester's little wooden hut at the edge of the mountains, but there's no sign of Mashozi and the rest of the Land Rover party and there's no note. We boil up some sweet tea on the forester's wood stove – we're all starving. Finally, lights appear in the distance; it's the mud-covered 4x4s. NJ is wide-eyed. They've had a hell of a journey. She can't believe the mud they have driven through, nor the punishing places where you can drive a Land

Rover! The adrenaline is pumping through her. I smile; I knew she would soon forget London. I don't think Alex enjoyed the trip too much, though. This bundu-bashing is not what's he's used to. Normally spotless, he's now covered in red mud.

Day 74: São Paulo - the largest Capricorn city

To the west of us lies another great jungle through which the Capricorn Line passes. It is the massive, sprawling São Paulo: a jungle of great wealth and poverty, of cathedrals, warlords and drugs, where, instead of crawling ants, there are streams of motor vehicles and the giant trees are a seemingly endless line of skyscrapers. The Land Rovers are covered in mud and the expedition members in forest bites and welts, where vines and creepers have torn at our skin, our limbs stiff and sore, as we limp into the largest city in South America. Our objective is to reach the old church and Jesuit mission in the centre of the city, where São Paulo was founded.

We decide to treat ourselves to a meal in a typical *chuascaria* (a sort of barbeque restaurant). In many restaurants in Brazil they weigh your food and you pay only for what you eat. Here, though, it's all-you-can-eat, and the meat just keeps coming: chops, steak, pork, chicken, beef and sausages. Waiters bring a never-ending supply of skewers to our table, from which pieces of meat are sliced straight onto our plates. Glance over your right shoulder and there's always someone waiting, a razor-sharp knife in hand. One wrong move and there goes your ear! There are mountains of salads, tiny quail's eggs, local Cachaça rum and, of course, Brazilian music. Judge Alex is in seventh heaven. He's clean again and

THE CONCRETE JUNGLE OF SÃO PAULO AND THE LARGEST CITY ALONG 23°27'

there's a Cachaça in his hand. If we allow him to, he'll drink us all under the table. 'Beats camping!' he says, raising his glass.

Judge Alex has got an amazing constitution. He starts each morning with black coffee, so thick you can stand a teaspoon in it. His other early-morning fix is a handful of guarana pills (full of yet more caffeine), not to mention all the Malboros. By midday he's generally managed a beer or two, and the late afternoon and evening Cachaças help to calm his nerves and enable him to cope with expedition life. I don't know how he does it – he just keeps floating along.

Day 75: 'Rio is a beauty, but São Paulo is a city,' Marlene Dietrich

We wake refreshed after a good night spent in a cheap hotel in the northern suburbs of Gaurulhos, as close as possible to the Tropic of Capricorn, which runs through the northern part of São Paulo. This morning the sun comes out and we dry our clothes. What a difference after all the rain and mist; it's like a new world. As someone who has spent most of his life

全人類の熱望するもの
それは平和

平和は愛によってのみ
得られる

2001年10月2日

ブラジル日本文化協会
会長　岩崎秀雄

CAPRICORN'S SÃO PAULO HAS THE LARGEST JAPANESE POPULATION OUTSIDE JAPAN –

in the African bush, how do I begin to describe the sheer size and concentration of humans and traffic that make up a city like São Paulo?

We park *Chuma* and *Susi* and take public transport to São Paulo's traditional centre, the Praça da Sé. There's a heaving throng of people, endless feet pounding pavements, exhaust fumes, and everywhere you look something is for sale. The Paulistano women are able to squeeze themselves into the tightest jeans imaginable. I wonder if the breadwinner, on payday, says to his wife, 'There you are darling – take a hundred bucks, and go get something tighter than the neighbour!'

We stop to buy an ice cream from a street vendor. Nearby, an exuberant fellow is selling cosmetics from a barrow. He plays a product video and delivers his cheerful sales-pitch through a scratchy microphone powered by a car battery – but there're no takers. I catch his eye and he smiles a greeting. I step in, taking the mike to give a ridiculous sales-pitch in English, Zulu and Afrikaans. A crowd soon gathers and, can you believe it, he gets a sale and the crowd roars with laughter. Then the little Capricorn team moves off down the street; Ross shadowing Tim, making sure no-one grabs the camera.

Along Rua Boa Vista is the place where this city originated. We stand outside the whitewashed Portuguese Baroque Pátio do Colégio, a replica of the building that formed the centre of the mission station founded here in 1554 by Jesuit priests José de Anchieta and Manuel da Nóbrega. We photograph the relief carving that pays tribute to the early Jesuits, who like ourselves were guided across the mountains and forests of the Serra do Mar, and to the role of the Indians, who led the first Jesuit priests here to start the mission that became this city.

São Paulo has the largest Japanese community outside Japan (they came as immigrants, working largely in market gardening), and there are entire streets lit with Japanese lanterns. We meet with the head of the Japanese cultural centre, who endorses our Capricorn Scroll of Peace and Goodwill in Japanese script, and we all bow several times from the waist.

Days 76–80: West to the great Rio Parana

Our journey along Capricorn takes us west out of bustling São Paulo. As it's late afternoon I suggest to Judge Alex that we pull into one of the numerous out-of-town motels for an early night. 'Oh, no!' he says in his slight American accent, 'They're only for f...ing.' The well-lit motels have names like L'Amouré, The Fanny Motel, The Hanky Panky and Le Savage. Later, even deep in a rural Catholic farming area, we find an establishment proudly called Angels of the Night, just a short distance from a large Tropic of Capricorn sign. We go in to ask the 'girls' to sign the Scroll of Peace and Goodwill, and one of the 'angels' signs her name Angelique. After all, our story is about the people of Capricorn. Alex gets really uptight. 'Be careful, be very careful, the bouncers will spank you!' he shouts. We roar with laughter. We spend the night at a relatively sedate *pousada* called The Colonial.

WE FILL THE SYMBOLIC ZULU
CALABASH WITH INDIAN OCEAN
SEA WATER — TAKEN FROM THE COAST OF MOZAMBIQUE

BULLET HOLES AND BUSHMEAT.

LEGLESS LANDMINE VICTI[M] ENDORSE THE SCROLL OF PEACE & GOODWILL

MOZAMBIQUE HAS BEEN RAVAGED BY FLOODS!

MAPUTO'S FREEDOM WALL

THE BLOODY TUBE DEVELOPED A HERNIA IN THE HOT SUN & IT BURST AND HAD US DIVING FOR COVER!

MASHOZI TAKES HER
EARLY MORNING BUSH BATH
WATER RATION - ½ LITRE

BARRY LEITCH
AND DAWN
A FAREWELL FR
SHAKALAND

OUR SANDBANK CAMP ON THE RIO LIMPOPO

THE SANGOMAS BLESS THE EXPEDITION!
AND THE BRAND NEW LAND ROVERS

THANKS TO
DUNCAN DAVIES
CHOMA AND SUSI
ARE LOADED FOR
SOUTH AMERICA.

COPACABANA
Rio de Janeiro

BRAZIL IS STILL
VW-BEETLE COUNTRY

RIO'S SUGARLOAF

COPACABANA &
IPANEMA! SUN BRONZED
BODIES & THE SOUNDS OF SAMBA—
THIS IS THE FANTASY WORLD OF BRAZIL!

EARLY DAYS IN MONTEVIDEO —

IN RIO - COMPLETE WITH BRAZILIAN FLAG.

CAPRICORN EXPEDITION

EXPEDIÇÃO CAPRICÓRNIO LAND ROVER SOUTH AFRICA

GUARANESE INDIAN CHILDREN

BRAZIL'S FAVELAS

THEY COULDN'T WEAR THEM ANY TIGHTER IF THEY TRIED!

WELCOME TO PARAGUAY
PLEASE CAN I JOIN THE
EXPEDITION SHE ASKS?

BRAZIL'S BEAUTIFUL
COSTA VERDE.

ALBINO THE HUNTER

CHIEF AUA AND HIS CHILDREN

THE AWESOME CATARACT OF THE IGUASO FALLS.

WE MEET CHIEF AUA

FAR RIGHT: Our crossing through the forests of the Serra do Mar.
BOTTOM RIGHT: Writing up the leather-bound expedition journal.

Our bodies are smeared with Red ochre as a blessing to the forest god 'NHANDARU'

THE VILLAGE KIDS LOVE N.J.

IT WAS THE EARLY GUARANESE INDIANS THAT LED THE JESUIT PRIESTS ACROSS THE SERRA DO MAR MOUNTAINS TO SÃO PAULO — WE FOLLOW IN THEIR FOOTSTERS.

THE ENTRANCE TO SÃO PAULO

Ayrton Senna

AQUI PASSA O TRÓPICO DE CAPRICÓRNIO

THE WET, WHITE CLAY IS LIKE SNOT ON A MIRROR – IT'S EITHER FOOT-FLAT OR WINCH – WE END UP DOING BOTH!

CROSSING THE RIO PARANA AT LAST!

THE FISHING FESTIVAL NEARLY KILLED US! – BUT FINALLY WE CROSS THE RIO PARANA.

THE KIDS JUST LOVE OLD TIM

WET TENT.

THE BEARD.

N.J.

MASINDZI

A FRIENDLY DOG FROM WHERE

GUAY →

TIM USES A BIKE TO GET OUT OF THE MUD! AND GO AHEAD AND FILM —

JUST A SIMPLE BEACON FOR A BORDER AND WE'RE INTO PARAGUAY —

RIGHT: A rose and a decorated pillow – it's our 33rd wedding anniversary – on the Tropic of Capricorn.

HAPPY 33 RED ANNIVERSARY xx

SHOZI

ROSS

SWAMP ROAD:

IG

ITS TOUGH GOING THRU
THE TROPICAL JUNGLES
OF PARAGUAY.

No time off for the Capricorn team: we just keep on heading west, following the GPS and survey maps, constantly asking for directions and always searching for tracks and roads that will keep us as close as possible to 23° 27'. We are all looking forward to reaching the Rio Parana, where we'll enter a more remote section of our journey. Once across this area, known as the Mato Grosso (meaning thick bushes or trees), we will reach Paraguay. As we travel further west, the Brazilians we met seem quite paranoid about us entering Paraguay, warning us about its dangers – the lawlessness and hijacking of vehicles. Alex says that there's no way he'll continue with us into Paraguay.

The Tropic of Capricorn takes us directly from the city of São Paulo, across São Paulo Province, and then across the northern part of the Province of Parana to the Rio Parana. It's mostly agricultural land, with pigs and cattle, farmed by the descendants of immigrants who came out to Brazil as a result of the labour shortage after the end of the slave trade. The old Ford F250 trucks, horse-drawn carriages and villages with the bottom part of their tree trunks painted white (to stop the ants and help the drunks get home safely) remind me of the old Portuguese colonial time in Mozambique. Brazilian cowboys, or *gauchos*, on horseback wave as we pass and old men playing cards in the shade of the town square look up at these strange *gringos* in their colourful right-hand drive vehicles. The faces of Europe are mixed with those of African and Indian slaves. Some of the towns have Indian names like Ipatetininga, Itai and Taquai. Others we travel though have distinctly European names like Cariopus, Jundia do Sul, Nava Fatima, São Jorge do Ivai and Rondon.

Our destination on the Rio Parana is the river town of Porto Figueira. Ross, Judge Alex and I spread out the survey maps on a Land Rover bonnet and, with a series of dots, mark out the roads and tracks that will keep us travelling as close as possible to the Tropic of Capricorn. Following an imaginary line is extremely time-consuming and difficult. Close to the Tropic of Capricorn there's a ferry (or so our survey maps tell us) that crosses the Parana to the wide open spaces of the Mato Grosso. The rain stops and the Landies don't miss a beat. We stop at a small stick mill owned by a lovely old man who uses a VW Beetle to tow the mill to the side of the road every day. On request, he starts up the mill with the pull of a rope: in goes a single stick of sugar cane and a lime for extra flavour, and out pours the thick, sweet juice. It's wonderfully refreshing, although sickly sweet. The old man is fascinated by us and the Land Rovers. Alex explains our Capricorn journey to him. He laughs out loud, refuses to accept payment and offers us more juice, '*Munto Obrigado Señor*! *Tchau*!' ('Many thanks! Cheers!').

The rural areas of Brazil's Parana Province strike us as very relaxed – girls ride bicycles and jog on their own, and rapes and muggings are unusual out here. The wide-open farming areas have the feeling of the American Midwest mixed with Mexico, but there's really only one Brazil, where the *gauchos*, in their wide-brimmed hats and jeans, dance with their girls in the street to their own brand of country-and-western music. American pick-up trucks of all vintages are the norm here, so our Land Rovers are a rarity, and people gather around to ask questions. The Brazilian flag, amongst the nine other Capricorn flags, invites comment and helps the 'Judge' with his endless explanations. He's a wonderful diplomat and loves taking centre stage, but, oh, how he hates camping! I think it's a South American thing: people who have made it a bit in life don't camp. Alex tells us that camping is only for the poorer classes.

We're fast learning how much Judge Alex hates roughing it. He's slightly effeminate and is extremely fussy about his personal hygiene. He wears his hair in a ponytail and constantly washes his hands. He puts us all to shame, taking great care over his dress and somehow managing to wear a spotlessly clean T-shirt every day. He mistakenly calls his underrods 'panties', about which we tease him. He flirts a bit with NJ – it's a Brazilian thing. She just raises her eyebrows and cuts him off with a toss of her hair.

Day 81: Porto Figueira - Rio Parana at last

We reach the Rio Parana at sunset. It's a huge, brown snake of a river, bordered by some of Brazil's last remaining tropical forests along the Capricorn line. The good news is that there is an old ferry that crosses from here to the Mato Grosso on the other side. There's great excitement in Porto Figueira, as the river port spruces itself up for its annual Fishing Festival. In fact, some of the revellers have already arrived. A big, motorised dugout weaves up the river, and there's much shouting and laughter from the occupants of the boat. A nearby fisherman tells us that they've been out all day looking for wild honey on the islands, but, from the laugher and the erratic route taken by the boat, it seems they've found more than just honey. Noticing Nicola, they shout: 'Welcome to Porto Figueira!' – hoping that NJ has arrived for the Fishing Fiesta.

We find digs in the village and discuss the next leg of our Capricorn journey. Of course we're thrilled to have reached the Rio Parana, but the great river runs south to an even more incredible place, and one that is way off the Tropic of Capricorn. If we go there, it will mean a detour of some 800 kilometres there and back, and, to remain true to our mission, we'll have to come back here to Porto Figueira to carry on the journey along Capricorn. Should we do it? Do we have the time and money? No, we don't. We gaze out over the river. 'C'mon, let's feed the cat another goldfish!' Mashozi gives me that, 'What about the bucks?' look. I say, 'Come on, let's just do it!' Our minds are made up, and everybody leaps with joy. Tomorrow we're off to experience one of the greatest natural wonders of the world: the Iguaçu Falls.

Day 82: Mosi Oa Tunya or Iguaçu?

One of my favourite places is Africa's Victoria Falls on the mighty Zambezi, and as we travel south we wonder which will be more beautiful – Vic Falls or the Iguaçu. Because we're on a tight budget, we pitch our tents in a forest camp near the main entrance to the falls, in the town of Foz do Iguaçu, so that we don't have to pay for formal accommodation. We introduce ourselves to the park rangers and show them our Capricorn letters. Judge Alex does a great PR job and they say they'll let us in first thing in the morning before the tourist gates open. We're honoured – for a few hours we will have the entire place to ourselves. When night falls the debate continues: could Iguaçu possibly be more spectacular than Mosi Oa Tunya, 'the smoke that thunders', Dr David Livingstone's great Victoria Falls? Tomorrow we'll know. In the meantime, knowing that the falls are bordered by Paraguay and Argentina, we ask Alex to put out the word for an English-, Guarani- and Spanish-speaking guide from Paraguay, who can interpret for us across that country. Alex still fears the worst, declaring that we'll never survive the Capricorn crossing of Paraguay.

Day 83: The splendour of Iguaçu

Our first response to the falls is disappointment, but we soon realise that we are looking at only one tiny section. The falls go on forever: 275 in total, cascading over a precipice three kilometres wide. The surrounding tropical rainforests are pristine, and full of beautiful birds. I sit looking over the cascades, writing up the expedition journal. The blue sky, the green forests, the cataracts and falls – like layers of white lace curtain – the roar of the water and the fine, cold spray: it's all unimaginably beautiful. And then the floodgates open and the busloads of tourists arrive, spoiling the unbelievable beauty and magic that is Iguaçu. More beautiful than the Victoria Falls? Well, let's just say they're different. Somehow, experiencing the beauty and splendour of Iguaçu gives the expedition a huge lift. However, when we camp for a second night, this time in the rain, Alex gets completely washed out. He hasn't attached his flysheet properly, and the wind blows it off, turning his tent into a swimming pool. I hear him shouting in the night and go to his rescue, but everything is already soaked and he swears never to camp again.

Day 84: Will she charm the banditos?

The news of our expedition spreads like wild fire, and when we wake up we find a Guaranese Indian girl by the name of Salia (I guess it would be Celia in English) waiting outside our camp. 'Just what you need,' says Judge Alex, 'a pretty girl who can speak Spanish and Guarani (Paraguay's two official languages). She'll charm the officials and, hopefully, the *banditos*.' We all laugh nervously. Salia seems both tough and sexy. Her English isn't all that good, but what choice do we have? She agrees to take the bus up to Porto Figueira in three days' time. We agree on the 'bucks' and shake hands on it. Ross is not all that happy; believing that Paraguay will be physically tough and possibly dangerous, he'd rather we had a bloke. Mashozi thinks she's great – she likes her no-nonsense, confident manner. The journey will tell. We pack up our wet tents and head back towards Porto Figueira and the Capricorn line.

Days 85–88: Porto Figueira Fishing Fiesta

We've arranged to meet with the Department of Wildlife's chief of the Isle la Grande, Brazil's youngest national park, consisting of an island in the Rio Parana near Porto Figueira. The Tropic of Capricorn runs across the park and we want to explore the island on our way back up the Rio Parana. The Department of Wildlife's Chief is called Maude Motto (her grandmother came from England). What a card! She's about 45 years old, plumpish, with smiling eyes and a cheerful grin, has two boys (but there's no sign of the father), is full of bounce and seems to have a lot of clout with the officials. She and Judge Alex hit it off immediately, and, before we know what's hit us, she's in her camouflage shorts, bush jacket and hat, we're all bundled into lifejackets, and the lot of us are flying up the Rio Parana in an aluminium boat to view the south of the Island. Maude smokes incessantly, drinks like a fish and talks non-stop about her plans for the future of the park. We see plenty of birdlife and some shy capybaras; the world's largest rodents, they're like giant guinea pigs, the size of a normal domestic pig, and are quite cuddly, with sweet faces. Maude is now firmly ensconced as one of the Capricorn team, and travels with us up to Porto Figueria to show us the northern Capricorn part of the island.

Back in Porto Figueira all hell has broken loose. The Fishing Fiesta is on, with street stalls, music, Cachaça rum and mountains of food. Maude puts us up at the Department of Wildlife's headquarters, which is right in the centre of town. No international tourists come to Porto Figueira, so we are something of a novelty. She instructs the local police to look after the Capricorn *gringos* and, in a flash, Mashozi, Ross, Tim, NJ, Judge Alex and I are all prisoners of Brazilian hospitality at the Porto Figueira Fishing Festival!

The party never stops, all night and all day, for three days. Everyone promenades and struts or shows off their latest V8 trucks, some with sound systems that take up half the back of the pick-up. If we're lucky we might manage to catch a few hours' sleep from 4am till 8am, and then Brazil's fantasy world fires up again.

We erect a rough Capricorn sign on 'Maude's Island' (Isle la Grande), and she tells us that a proper cement and stone Capricorn beacon will follow. Back in Porto Figueira banjos and guitars belt out the sounds of Parana and Mato Grosso as we all dance barefoot on the sandy banks of the Rio Pirana.

We are treated like gods. The local TV station does a story on us and 15 mayors, who have gathered from nearby villages for the celebrations, invite me to give an after-lunch talk about our Capricorn journey. They sit smoking their cigars, some of them dozing off; the air-conditioning has packed up and it's as hot as hell. Judge Alex does his usual great job of interpreting. I have a few drinks at lunch, and then I relate how we were mock charged by elephants in Africa, and how we dodged landmines and faced man-eating lions (I ham it up a bit here – Alex even more so as he translates). 'But,' I say, 'never before have we been as close to death as here in Porto Figueira, Brazil.' They all sit bolt upright in their chairs – eyes wide. 'Yes,' I continue dramatically, 'we're being killed by Brazilian hospitality. Please, sirs, we want to leave! Ahead of us lie five more Capricorn countries.' There are roars of laughter. We can leave tomorrow, they say, but first let's celebrate!

They sign the Capricorn Scroll of Peace and Goodwill, and next day the *gendarmerie* escort us onto the ferry. One fellow gives Ross his police shirt, another presents me with his cap; they salute and wave. Dear Maude travels with us to the next ferry and the border between Parana and the Mato Grosso.

We come across a lovely, wrinkled old man who lives alone in a wooden hut on

A MESSAGE TO ALL BANDITOS.
WE'RE HOPING THAT SALIA
WILL CHARM THE EXPEDITION
CROSS PARAGUAY —

Our expedition is brought to a halt by the continuous merry-making of the accordion-driven forro (pronounced fawhaw) – the word originates from the English 'for all' and refers to the dances financed by the early English engineering and plantation companies for their manual labour. The locals simply won't let us leave. It appears we are prisoners to Brazilian hospitality.

the Rio Parana. He is nearly blind and almost burnt his hut down recently by knocking over a candle. Mashozi digs in her bag and gives him her spare pair of spectacles. His face lights up; he can see again! He signs the Capricorn Scroll shakily, sitting on the step of his wooden shack alongside the banks of the Rio Parana, here on the Tropic of Capricorn.

Day 89: Farewell to Judge Alex and the Parana Province

We are sad to say goodbye to Judge Alex. Despite our misgivings about how he'd cope, what a useful addition to the expedition the *Carioca* has turned out to be. We hug and shake hands, as is the Brazilian way. 'You crazy *gringos* – I'll see you one day in Africa!' he shouts as the ferry leaves. Alex and Maude keep on waving until we are out of sight. I think they fancy each other. Only this morning I found her sitting on his bed as he combed her long hair. I look across at Salia who joined us yesterday at Porto Figueira. She looks confident, dressed in her expeditionary kit. 'Welcome to Capricorn,' I say. 'Let's hope we make it across Paraguay.'

Now almost all the tropical forests that were once here in the Mato Grosso have gone, and thousands of square miles have been turned over to cattle. The area is so vast that in some cases cattle are counted by aircraft. Many of the wealthy cattle owners live in the city. When night falls we camp at an isolated *fazenda* (cattle station). Maria, the farmer's wife, welcomes us. She's alone here, with just the workers – her husband is away 'fishing'. We camp next to the homestead, and she offers us cold *yerba maté* tea, sipped from a gourd through a silver straw. It's passed around and we all have a little. Salia explains that bacteria don't stick to the silver and it's easy to clean. Tim helps Salia with her tent and she arranges for us to use a tap and a toilet. Tonight we hit the hay early, with no grog – we're still recovering from the unforgettable fiesta at Porto Figueira; a fishing festival at which I never saw a single fish caught!

23°27'

Days 90–92: A journey across the Mato Grosso

Travelling from one *fazenda* to another, we make slow progress across the Mato Grosso, and a lot of our time is spent thinking about the crossing into Paraguay. 'Will we be safe?' I wonder. Judge Alex really filled our heads with scare stories, and the Brazilians continue to try to scare us off with wild stories of *banditos*.

As we enter one *fazenda* close to the frontier, the lady owner races off on horseback to warn the neighbours and soon a fully armed posse arrives to intercept the '*banditos* from Paraguay'. Salia quickly explains our journey. She's terrific, but, like Judge Alex, is beginning to struggle a bit with the rough living involved in following an invisible line and camping where you end up each night. But she seems tougher than Alex, and understands our need to adhere to this imaginary line. She's patient, as we ask hundreds of questions, and she continually has to ask people for directions.

A family allows us to camp in front of their plain wooden house. They nickname Ross '*Perigoza*' ('the dangerous one'), saying that he looks like a gangster from the movies. What friendly, simple folk they all are. Salia, NJ and Mashozi soon get invited in to use the bath – our turn comes later – and they offer us firewood, drinking water, home-made cheese and fresh milk. We sit around the fire and, through Salia, ask them questions about their lives here on Capricorn. They, in turn, want to know more about our adventure, especially Africa.

We notice NJ is covered in welts and insect bites, and warn her not to scratch them. Some are already going septic, so Mashozi gives her antihistamines and cream for them. Tim, Ross and I break open some of our precious Captain Morgan. It's so much better than the local 'blow the top of your head off' rum – even NJ's developed a taste for Ye Olde Captain's! Salia sticks to the *yerba maté* tea known as *tereré* (that's what it's called when served cold) and sits and chats to the farmers.

We're all starting to miss home a bit, but it's especially tough for *Perigoza* Ross to be away from little Tristan for so long. Tim is a happy camper; he's an old 'bush man' and puts his tent up meticulously. Then there's the puffing and blowing as he pumps up his mattress (generally with ribald shouts of encouragement from the other Capricornians). He lays out his sleeping gear carefully, knowing the importance of a good night's sleep, and puts his Walkman and small bag of tapes next to his sleeping bag. He's a great music lover and has learnt to break the tension of long expeditions by listening to music, both morning and evening. Sometimes he and I ride together in *Chuma* playing tapes and talking about the old days. We often amuse ourselves by taking the piss out of the old colonial British, especially when there's a tense situation. Tim pipes up with, 'I say, old chap, anyone seen Carruthers? He hasn't claimed his war pension and is said to have taken off with a local girl somewhere along Mato Grosso's Capricorn line. Damned unfortunate! You haven't seen him have you? Red nose, bloodshot eyes, takes a shandy on a hot afternoon...'

In the morning there's a commotion well before sunrise: cattle amongst the tents, loud music and dogs everywhere. A *gaucho* gallops into camp, with eyes only for NJ and a sick calf dangling across his saddle. The *fazenda* owners let us use their small wooden shower room, and before we leave we all share a massive bowl of home-made ice cream. The *fazenda* mama takes the signing of the Capricorn Scroll as a great honour. They will always remember *Perigoza* Ross, the dangerous bandit, and we will always remember their wonderful hospitality.

PERIODO
TÍQUETE DE ESTAC
Válido das 07:00 h até as 06:59 h c
nas áreas identificadas de Estacion
Obrigatório o preenchimento à
AO ESTACIONAR, ACION
PR
Mês
JA N   F E V   M A R
U   AG

When we reach the Paraguayan frontier I once again feel the familiar anticipation and anxiety that come with not knowing what lies ahead. The closest border town to the Tropic of Capricorn is called, rather grandly, Coronel Sepucaia on the Brazilian side and Capitán Bado on the Paraguayan. The frontier is a street down the middle of the town. There are tarred roads and modern buildings on the Brazilian side, dirt tracks and humble wooden buildings on the other. People mass around our two Land Rovers, and we are offered *maté* tea, sipped cold from a cow horn. A tall blonde girl in a tight black dress escorts me over to Paraguay, but Paraguayan Customs and Immigration is closed. Friendly off-duty officials tell us that we won't be able to drive the Landies across the road into Paraguay. Not because they don't want us, but because the Brazilian federal police allow foreigners to check out of Brazil only at Ponto Porã, approximately 100 kilometres to the north. We get the impression that it's the 'Brazilian Giant' that's trying to control things here and not little Paraguay.

And so we travel north of the Capricorn line to check out with the Brazilian federal police. Then we cross into Paraguay at Pedro Juan Caballero. We show our Capricorn letter from the Paraguayan Embassy in South Africa and it works wonders. A letter of safe passage is typed out for us by the Head of Immigration on an old typewriter. There is much hand-shaking and more *tereré*. Everybody is just so friendly. Sure, things are a bit buggered, but can these be the Paraguayans the Brazilians so fear? Is it just typical cross-border paranoia or is there still some tension left over from the horrific war between Paraguay and Brazil? This conflict was known as The War of the Triple Alliance. It raged from 1864 to1870, during which time the adult male population of Paraguay is said to have been reduced by the war and famine from over a million, in 1864, to under 20 000. Today the country's total population is approximately 5.5 million, with barely half living in urban areas. More than 75 percent of Paraguayans are Mestizos Indians, whose mother tongue is Guarani. Most indigenous Paraguayans, about three per cent of the population, inhabit the Chaco (great plains of white clay, palm forests and bush-veld) in the west of the country, through which the Tropic of Capricorn passes. Thanks to the war, Paraguay lost 150 000 square kilometres to Brazil. Although Paraguay is tiny by South American standards (looking on maps like a small umbrella in the middle of the continent), at 407 000 square kilometres, it is larger than Germany and almost exactly the size of California.

SILVER STRAW

MOUTHPIECE (SILVER TO STOP BACTERIA)

FILTER

'YERBE MATE'

THE TEA IS MULCHED INTO THIS CONTAINER, WHICH CAN BE A GOURD, A COW HORN OR EVEN A HOOF

WE SOON GET USED TO THE HABIT OF DRINKING MATE — SOUTH AMERICAN HERBAL TEA — DRUNK HOT IN THE MORNING & EVENING ,, IT'S CALLED "CALIENTE" MY FAVOURITE IS WHEN IT'S SERVED COLD DURING THE DAY — A BREW WHICH IS CALLED 'TE RERÉ'.

Paraguay

It's a small umbrella of a country, in the centre of the great S. American Continent. The Tropic of Capricorn runs through the old Spanish colonial city of Conception on the Rio Paraguay. The Brazilians say we won't make it and that the Landies are sure to get hijacked! But coming from South Africa... well! We'll just take our chances. Printed in Spanish on the side of the Land Rover are the words `EXPEDICION DE CAPRICÓRNIO ALREDEDO PÖR TIERRA DEL MUNDO' (CAPRICORN AROUND THE WORLD BY LAND) I hope it helps!

Days 93–94: *República del Paraguay!*

It is not 10 minutes after we arrive in Paraguay that we come to our first police roadblock. I suppose we should remember that Paraguay was once a notorious police state. Salia flicks her hair and looks the guys up and down: they are dressed in camouflage, with big guns, sunglasses, badges and cigarettes. We were just starting to feel at home in Portuguese and now it's Spanish – Salia explains our journey and we show them our letters. The Paraguayan flag displayed on the side of the 4x4s helps a lot too.

Back on the Tropic of Capricorn the humidity thickens and the rainclouds gather, as we make our way down the forested mountains of Cordiliera del Amambay. We are soon heading into tropical rainforest and the road becomes a track. A tropical downpour breaks the humidity and turns the road into something worthy of the Camel Trophy Challenge. We slip and slide for hour after hour; everything is covered in red mud and the Land Rovers are pushed to their limit. We push, dig and winch, soaked to the skin. Every one of us is covered in painful insect bites. The rain continues. Ross, driving through thick mud, slides into a log. There's a loud bang and we all leap out, fearing that the front suspension has been ripped apart. Ross slides underneath *Susi* in the mud and rain to find that the protection bar is bent against the steering mechanism. Off comes the protection bar, which we throw in the back, and we continue through mud, endless mud. Somehow *Chuma* and *Susi*, wheels spinning, just keep growling forward.

We spend the night on the verandah of an *estancia* (an estate or cattle farm carved from tropical jungle). The owner, Senõr Ramon, is a swarthy character, who slaughters a pig for us.

In the morning we have a feast of pork, rice, beans and cassava. Salia is doing a great job of interpreting, and the Paraguayan cowboys love her to bits. After the sumptuous meal Senõr Ramon wipes his face on the table cloth and we all follow suit. We pack up the Landies and, as we leave, he waves cheerfully from his hammock strung between two trees. In Paraguay an afternoon siesta is part of life. We stop a little way on from the *estancia* to wash the red mud from our filthy bodies and clothes in a waterfall. The sun comes out and bathes the tropical forest in light. Beautiful, but I get bitten to hell by red ants.

As we go west, into the setting sun, we are dismayed by what we see: lorries carting giant hardwood logs out of the magnificent forests. The practice of slash and burn clearing is turning tens of thousands of hectares of tropical forest into cattle ranches. We ask who is doing it and why, and are told that this massive destruction is the work of large Brazilian companies. The local Indians claim

BRAZIL
CAPITAN BADO
PARAGUAY

FORESTED MOUNTAINS – DIFFICULT!

ESTANCIA OF SENÕR RAMON –

TERRIBLE DESTRUCTION OF THE TROPICAL RAIN FORESTS!

MUD! ENDLESS MUD. TOUGH! GOING.

VILLAGES

ESTANCIA KLAUS WE NEARLY GET SHOT...

RIO PARAGUAY 23°33'

CONCEPTION

1000's OF PALM TREES

PANS

MUD & MORE MUD

BUSH COUNTRY MOZZIES GALORE!

NIVACLÉ INDIAN TRIBE

ARGENTINA – FRONTIER

23°27'

that they don't have a say in the matter: 'The Brazilians do deals with our government officials in Ascunción (the capital) and there's nothing we can do.' It's an ecological disaster.

Our destination is Conception. A muddy track heads west, close to Capricorn – it's a bonus after sliding through the tropical rainforests, and we decide to push on into the night. A stuck truck full of odd-looking characters blocks the road. They wave us down and we winch them out of the mud. I don't like the look of them, especially the one fellow, who's balancing a TV set on his lap. Contraband is a fully-fledged way of life in Paraguay, and I warn NJ, Mashozi and Salia to stay in the 4x4s.

It's pitch black, with no stars, and looking for a safe place to sleep we drive on to an *estancia*. The next moment we are blinded by bright searchlights, and we hear dogs barking furiously. A tall white man leaps up from behind a hedge and sticks a gun in my face. I shout out a nervous greeting to him in English and he answers in German: 'It's very dangerous in Paraguay to arrive unannounced in the dark.' I believe him. His name is Klaus and he is a descendant of one of the many German settlers who came out to Paraguay. He offers us a place to camp, and some water and firewood. NJ practises her German and Salia chaffs him into letting us use the bathroom. Then it's time for the tiring routine of pitching camp. Mashozi and NJ knock up a meal of spaghetti and Tim moves off into the shadows to pitch his tent – he likes his privacy. We have been pushing hard across Paraguay and everybody is dog tired, especially Salia, who is now afraid of the insects and has taken to sleeping inside one of the Land Rovers. Ross has been very quiet these last few days. It's a difficult job navigating along an invisible line, and the conditions over the mountains and forests of the Cordiliera del Amambay were extremely tough. Never before have we taken our Land Rovers across such difficult terrain, but *Chuma* and *Susi*, bless their hearts, haven't missed a beat.

Days 95–96: Conception, on the Rio Paraguay

Over the last few days, Ross has taken to waking up very early in the morning and going for a run. It's a way of relieving the tension of the journey and, more importantly, of breaking the incredibly long hours spent in the vehicles. Tim has also started doing some exercises in the morning. For me this is one of the few moments of the day that I get to write in the Capricorn Expedition journal.

Today we really hope to reach the city of Conception. We keep the revs up, travelling as fast as we possibly can through the open farmland and scattered palm trees, and finally we make it to the bustling market town of Conception on the Rio Paraguay, in the sticky heat of midday. It's a small, colourful city and Paraguay's largest along the Tropic of Capricorn. We are told you can buy anything on the streets – from nuclear weapons to cocaine – but all we are interested in is fresh fruit and vegetables. Standing in the market, we guzzle down slice after slice of sweet, red, juicy watermelon. As a special treat, after the hardships of the rainforests, we spoil ourselves with a night at the gracious Hotel Victoria, a decayed colonial structure with the great delights of noisy air-conditioning and squeaking fans – a welcome night away from the forest insects. We celebrate Mashozi's birthday across the road at a local bar. The heavens open and the tarpaulin roof leaks like a sieve – but that doesn't stop us dancing the night away. Salia is a great hit with the locals.

23°27' – FOLLOWING A COCAINE TRAIL ACROSS A SWOLLEN RIVER BLOODY CRAZY! – THE CAPTAIN ALSO GOOD FOR CHASING INSECTS!

There are lots of guns and some seedy-looking characters, but so far we've found the Paraguayans to be the some of the most casual and laid-back people we have met in South America. Many Paraguayans have a mixture of Guaranese Indian and Spanish colonial blood. The Mestizos Indians welcomed the Spanish into their social system and allowed them access to their women. In Paraguay today the official languages are Guarani and Spanish.

In the morning, just outside Conception, we find a Guaranese Indian community, sadly living in squalor. They are beautiful people, and the kids immediately befriend Mashozi and NJ. An old Guaranese elder endorses our Capricorn Scroll. He struggles to hold the pen, and it reminds us of the Capricorn line in the Kalahari, when the two old Bushmen also signed this document with a shaky cross.

Day 97: **Across the Rio Paraguay**

Bushman signature

From Conception we cross the Rio Paraguay, a huge ribbon of water that links Conception to Asunción. We travel due west through a immense palm tree belt, interspersed with vast swamplands. The intense heat and humidity numbs the mind. It's no wonder the locals spend much of the day at siesta! South America is determined to throw everything at us – once again the skies open and soon an almighty tropical downpour blots out the sun. Ahead of us lies the huge area of the Chaco (white clay plains, palm forests and bushveld).

Still some 270 kilometres from the border with Argentina, we have our passports stamped out of Paraguay at a lonely petrol station that also serves as the customs post. It's obviously placed at this junction because there's a road here that comes down from Bolivia in the north, and there are virtually no roads between here and the border. The friendly, red-eyed immigration officer warns us that the tracks through to the border will be impassable. He says that is it unlikely we will be able to follow the Tropic of Capricorn and, 'If you do succeed,' he says, 'it will be the f...ing Argentinians that will give you a hassle. Those bastards!' He rummages in a leather bag and pulls out a huge, long-barrelled, silver revolver. 'This is what they need,' he says, pulling back the hammer and thrusting the weapon into his open mouth. Oh my God! Does he really hate the Argentinians so much that he is going to blow his brains out in front of me? Seeing the horrified look on my face, he roars with laughter and returns the shining revolver to the leather bag. He stamps our passports with a flourish and shakes hands all round.

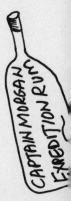

From here we slip-slide, winch, push and dig for kilometre after kilometre, through a massive belt of palm trees. With groaning winch cables, spinning wheels and drenched bodies covered from head to toe in mud, it seems hopeless. It takes us seven hours to do 36 kilometres, and finally our progress is halted by three stuck lorries that have slid across the road. We decide to camp here and grind through the thick clay, forcing the Land Rovers between the palm trees at the side of the track. In a vain attempt to keep out of the rain, we string a tarpaulin between the two vehicles and pour out some Captain Morgan to revive the wet spirits, and then a bit more for no reason at all!

The rain continues to pelt down, and a dog pitches up at our camp, wet and shivering. It takes cover behind our tent, which makes Mashozi homesick for our animals back in South Africa, and she befriends it. Salia is desperately unhappy; the romance of becoming an expedition member has now become a nightmare and she sits in the Land Rover covered in insect repellent. Even little NJ is despondent, but I soon coax her into being the bar lady.

23°27'

Despite the rain, or perhaps because of it, we have an incredibly merry evening, as we play the harmonica and do the odd jig. Every so often we have to push the tarpaulin up with a spade as it fills like a swimming pool in the rain. The result is a miniature Iguaçu and an unwanted shower for the inmates who sit huddled in a tight circle beneath the covering. Our night in the rain ends up being one of the most memorable evenings of our journey across Paraguay – it shows that life is what you make it.

NJ is now so full of bites she is convinced she is going to die. She's made the mistake of reading the insect-borne diseases section of the South American guidebook. In the dengue fever section she reads that aspirin should be avoided, as it increases the risk of haemorrhaging. There is no vaccine against dengue and the best precaution is to avoid mosquito bites at all times. Then, of course, there's malaria, Chagas's disease, filariasis, leishmaniasis and typhus! Under the cuts, bites and stings section there are bedbugs, lice and *bichos de pê* which burrow into the thick skin of the foot at the heel, toes and under the toenails and appear as dark boils. We pull her leg mercilessly and, being the Zululand farm girl that she is, she takes it in her stride.

Day 98: West to the Pilco Mayo

The sun lights up the muddy track and in our camp alongside it we sink up to our knees in water. Everybody is scratching away at insect bites, and the flags that mark the Capricorn countries on the side of the Land Rovers are covered in grey mud. Shotgun blasts and music break the morning silence. The lorry drivers are awake and shooting breakfast, which turns out to be a European stork.

The Nivaclé chief signs the scroll

We drive around the lorries and, travelling in low gear, with the difflock on to help the wheels find traction, we grind west, and by late afternoon we reach the village of Escalante and the mission of San Leonardo. In a clearing under a giant tree, elderly Nivaclé Indian women dance in a circle, each carrying a stick topped with goat-horn rattles. The lead dancer wears an orange-feathered headdress. Indian men with stern faces keep up the rhythm with drumbeats and calabash rattles. Their deep-voiced chants take them back to the time nearly a hundred years ago, when this community (which now numbers 260) first settled here. The Chief signs the Capricorn Scroll. He's got a very dignified face and his people have a great sense of pride – these citizens of Capricorn have stood the test of time. From Escalante it's just 12 kilometres to the Rio Pilco Mayo and the border with Argentina, so we press on, two small 4x4s dwarfed by the orange ball of the setting sun. We camp just before the border (so we can get an early start tomorrow) in dry Kalahari-type scrubland that reminds us of home.

FOREVER WEST

FORESTS INTO CHARCOAL — A SHAME!

A BRAAI GRID, LAND ROVER AND A HAT! WHAT MORE DO YOU NEED?

IN PARAGUAY ITS MUD — ENDLESS MUD!!

Argentina

I half expected Argentina to be relatively first world and easy, but the Capricorn belt in the far north of the country is rough, tough and somewhat wild! — There are military police to contend with, no bridge across the Rio Bermejo and then it's into the foothills of the Andes — South America's Capricorn line seems to be throwing everything at us!

Days 99–100: Don't cry for me Argentina

We awake to sunny blue skies and the sound of thousands of bird calls, which make us homesick for Africa. After all the rain, it's so good to feel the sun again and to be dry. The dried-up Rio Pilco Mayo forms the frontier line, with a simple iron beacon that reads 'Paraguay' on one side and 'Argentina' on the other. Unfortunately, things are not that easy. The Argentinian military checkpoint in the border village of Lamadrid will not let us through. They make numerous radio calls and search the Land Rovers. 'Yes, you can proceed on foot,' they say, 'but no vehicles!' The commanding officer is adamant. We try every diplomatic line in the book: the Capricorn Scroll, the Spanish letter from the Paraguayan Embassy, newspaper clippings and the flags on the Land Rovers. Salia flirts and charms but the answer remains a firm, military, 'No.' They won't even let us speak to their superior on the radio.

Foreign, South African 4x4s filled with expedition kit and strange, travel-worn Capricornians are obviously a rare species here. For the first time on our entire journey we seem to be inviting suspicion. I remember the words of the drunk Paraguayan immigration official who thrust the silver revolver into his own mouth. The people of Lamadrid feel so sorry for us that we are given a huge chunk of beef, cut from a freshly slaughtered carcass hanging in a tree. Three wandering Nivaclé minstrels play the accordion and guitar, the red wine flows and we drown our sorrows a little, as the locals prepare for a feast.

We are hugely disappointed: all the mud and all the discomfort – all in vain; now we have to turn back into Paraguay. For the first time the sun sets behind us, as we turn away from the Capricorn line we have so diligently followed. Thwarted by Argentinian bureaucracy, we are forced to detour down to Asunción where we hope to cross into Argentina at the regular border post. It means a 700-kilometre round trip that will dig deeply into our depleted cash and time budgets. Fortunately, the roads are now dry and we race though the night. At Asunción we get an introductory letter from the Argentinian consulate addressed to Argentinian customs. It helps us cross the border just outside Asunción, and soon we have the military *gendarmerie* posing for pictures next to the Capricorn Expedition Land Rovers. They welcome us to their headquarters in a beautiful old *hacienda* on the outskirts of the border town of Clorinda, and the Commandant signs the Capricorn Scroll and gives us a

PARAGUAY

RIO PILCO MAYO – DRY

ARGENTINA

A SIMPLE SIGN MARKS THE BOUNDARY BETWEEN PARAGUAY & ARGENTINA

MUD!

LAMADRID
THE GENDARMERIE ARE TWITCHY AFTER SEPT 11 AND WERE FORCED TO DETOUR TO ASUNCIÓN

FORCED DETOUR BACK THRU THE MUD!

23°27'
BACK ON CAPRICORN

DRY CACTUS
DUST-HOT

FORMOSA PROVINCE

SALTA PROVINCE

CASA SALVANTO-NIO

GAUCHO MANUEL

RIO BERMEJO
ROSS CROSSES ON HORSEBACK – FOLLOWING ILLEGAL COCAINE ROUTE DANGEROUS!

SUGARCANE FIELDS AND CLOUD FORESTS

PURMAMARCA

CERRO DE LOS SIETE COLORES

SALT PANS

SUSQES

ACROSS THE HIGH ANDES SNOW-CAPPED VOLCANOES! BITTERLY COLD

CHILE

stunning coffee-table book on Argentina, as well as a letter of safe passage that will get us through all the checkpoints back to, and along, the Capricorn line. They apologise, asking that we please understand that the border with Paraguay is a sensitive one. There is a strong military presence in Argentina, as they have to be on guard against contraband and drug trafficking from Paraguay. We wonder, however, if it's not the current hysteria about international terrorism that is hampering our journey – the 11 September 2001 twin towers disaster has shaken the whole world.

Sometimes you have to get into trouble to get help, and now the military can't do enough for us. Major Nikolini, in his smart military fatigues, gives us one of his men to escort us into the town in search of an English-speaking translator who can help us along Argentina's Tropic of Capricorn. We are told that the conditions are tough and dry in the northern provinces of Salta and Chaco. They also say we should be wary of drug smugglers and bandits from Paraguay (poor little Paraguay; I know it exists off contraband, but it's a beautiful country. It's no wonder that some South Africans have settled here, many on huge cattle ranches, and now even some Zimbabweans are looking to escape Mugabe).

Day 101: **Goodbye to Salia**
Argentina is the world's eighth-largest country. At 2.8 million square kilometres, it is only slightly smaller than India.

We've finally made it to the halfway mark of our Capricorn Expedition across South America. Who knows what lies ahead? *Chuma* and *Susi*, despite having been punished so terribly, are still strong and willing, as is our little Capricorn team. Last night at Clorinda we stayed in a rundown hotel, most of which had been burnt out in a fire. Still, it was hugely expensive, since everything here is linked to the American dollar and is at least three times as expensive as in Brazil and Paraguay. The locals tell us that the economy is in trouble.

We need to get back into the bush and back onto the Capricorn line as soon as possible. Mashozi, who is getting really nervous about the budget, keeps saying that we don't have the bucks to reach Chile's Atlantic coast. That's my cue to change the subject! We say goodbye to Salia and put her in a taxi to the nearby Paraguayan border, from where she'll take a bus back to Foz Iguaçu, clean clothes, a hot bath, boyfriends and her insect-free apartment. We couldn't have got across Paraguay without her. She really did do her best to keep us going along Capricorn; it was just tougher than she expected, but I'm sure she'll remember this journey forever. I certainly will.

Day 102: **Martin Escudero joins the Capricorn circus**
A young man, Martin Escudero, is introduced to us in Clorinda. He's not yet 20, speaks basic English and for a change we find someone who likes the outdoors, camping and canoeing. Martin is filled with enthusiasm and can't wait to join the expedition; he's even got his own tent. But, before we take him on, we go to meet his parents at their home. We agree with them on a fee of US$25 per day and write down their telephone numbers in case there's an emergency. They are obviously a bit concerned about letting their son go off into the wilds with a gang of *gringos*, but our letter from the local commandant and a friendly introduction from the *gendarmerie* smooth the way.

ITS AS HOT AS HELL!

Day 103: **Back on 23° 27'**

And so, with Martin aboard to interpret, we head north, back up to 23° 27' and the province of Salta. We camp close to the Baralari line separating the Salta Province from Formosa. Here it is hot, dusty and incredibly dry; there's no water, just thorns, so we call our stopping place for the night 'Cactus Camp'. Martin enthusiastically pitches his own tent and shows us how to mush and prepare our own *maté* tea (we've even bought our own apparatus, complete with silver straw). This herbal tea's said to have a calming effect, something we all badly need, in what is becoming a race against time across South America. We have to complete this leg in time for the vehicles' shipment and our booked flights – in just over two weeks. We sit round the fire and update Martin on our adventure – he's fascinated by it all. He's too young and boyish to spark any interest from NJ. *Buenas noches*!

Martin Escudero – our young spanish interpreter – signing the Capricorn Scroll.

Day 104: **Luna Muerta and our camp in hell**

As usual the day starts with maps and the GPS. We set a course for a dot on the map called Luna Muerta ('place of the dead moon'). We force our way down narrow tracks and paths – the scrub tears at the Landies' sides. The terrible sound of thorns and branches screeching on aluminium reminds me of our journey through Mozambique. We get clear of the scrub only to have sticky-bottomed pans halt our journey. The water is not very deep, but the wet, white clay underneath is as slippery as snot on a mirror. The 4x4s' wheels can't get any grip on the surface and they just spin. There are a number of pans in our path, with solid patches in between, and there are only two ways forward: either we winch the vehicles across each pan or we hit them at high speed – foot flat on the accelerator – and hope to slide across. We end up using both methods and continue inching west, but we never find Luna Muerta – maybe the place itself is dead and gone.

The Rio Bermejo is the only large river along this part of the Tropic of Capricorn, and the map shows it to be wide, with numerous sandbanks. We hope it isn't too wide or fast-flowing for us to cross it with the Landies. While searching for the river, we get lost in thick bush. It's sheer hell: the vehicles churn through fine choking dust and it must be at least 50° C. Finally, at the end of the day, the human members of the party run out of steam and we decide to camp where we are. I take a narrow cattle path through the bush, down to where the river should be, but it's obviously changed its course. In an effort to keep cool, we wet our shirts and hats, only to find that the moisture attracts swarms of bees and insects. At least there's good firewood here, but the bugs are horrific and our groundsheets trap the heat from the baked earth we're camped on. It's like sleeping in a sauna; I've never been so uncomfortable. Mashozi and I wet our sleeping bags and lie naked on them in our tent. Eventually I creep outside in an attempt to catch the faint breeze that's come up. It's a little cooler, but I get eaten alive by bugs. There's much complaining from the other tents. It's obviously hell for everybody.

Day 105: Stricken cattle

An hour on from our camp, we reach a mission station called Chakenya. I hope we'll be able to get directions from here to the Rio Bermejo. Amazingly in this overwhelmingly Catholic country, the little mud-walled church here is an Anglican one, built

HIS CATTLE LIE DYING IN THE SWAMP

in 1926. Inside the church, to the strumming of guitars, three beautiful Indian girls, Graciela, Lucrecia and Roxanna, sing 'What a friend we have in Jesus' in their local Witche language. The men of the village sit outside the church chewing coca leaves. Their teeth are stained brown from years of doing this and some of them look really mean; I wouldn't want to cross them. This is not the Argentina that I expected – here in the north-east of the country, it is every bit as wild as Paraguay.

Julio, the mission doctor at Chakenya, is a friendly little fellow. He speaks reasonable English and is originally from Buenos Aires. He warns us strongly against attempting to cross the Rio Bermejo. 'It's a cocaine smuggling route,' he says. 'If the *gendarmerie* don't get you the drug smugglers will. It's also too deep to get your 4x4s across and there are, like a fish...' he battles to explain to us in English, but I think he means a type of eel or stingray, which, if you step on it, will give you septic ulcers that remain with you for the rest of your life. As I listen to him my mind goes back to the crossing of the flooded Limpopo, when everything was against us. After coming through all that, we're certainly not going to give up easily now.

The doctor explains that most people here chew coca leaves, a centuries-old practice that came from the Incas. It alleviates hunger, keeps one awake and dulls the effect of the heat. It's legal to chew coca leaves – even the kids do it – but illegal to trade in them. However, some workers still get paid in coca leaves, and I notice that the little trading store at Chakenya sells them quite openly – even giving you your change in leaves!

How are we going to cross the Rio Bermejo on the Tropic of Capricorn? We hire a short, thick-set Witche Indian by the name of Raoul, who claims he knows the way down to the river. Young Martin is caught up in the adventure and loves the excitement. His English is not too good, but he tries his best to interpret as we take the narrow, twisting, turning track down to the Rio Bermejo. It turns out that the doctor is right: it is too deep and wide to cross the river by 4x4. It's still as hot as hell and everybody's tired out and a bit disappointed. Raoul, green coca-leaf slime oozing from the corners of this mouth, says that the only way is to attempt it on horseback.

So, leaving Ross, Tim and NJ on the riverbank, Martin, Raoul, Mashozi and I take off in search of horses. Raoul takes us to a small shack – it's here that we meet the delightful Manuel Morena, a tough *gaucho*, who welcomes us to his humble abode, Casa San Antonio, which is built from planks, thatch and corrugated iron. We are invited to sit round the table in the open-sided, mud-floored living room. Horse tack hangs from the wall; there's an outside cooking area with a clay oven, a long drop and a well with a hand pump. Manuel brews up some *maté*, and we sip it from a cow's horn. Only once we have relaxed, in true polite rural style, does Manuel ask Martin what the purpose of our visit is: who are these *gringos* in the strange Land Rover?

Manuel offers us some coca leaves and begins to chew contemplatively as he listens. Yes, he'll help us across the Rio Bermejo, but not today, maybe not even tomorrow. He's got a serious problem: his cattle are caught in the mud of the *pantanal* (swamplands) and he needs to use his horse to pull them out. Manuel is on his own, so I suggest we help him to free the animals. Mashozi, Martin and Raoul go back to call the others at the river, leaving Manuel the *gaucho* and me to try to communicate in sign language. He's a thick-set, stocky man, with a large, wide nose and a smiling, round face – made even rounder by his constant chewing of coca leaves (he looks as if he's nursing a gum boil). He offers me some leaves; they taste bitter, but I chew politely, hoping he'll help us get across the Bermejo.

Slowly, he gets dressed in his leather chaps and apron, and his *gaucho* hat with the wide brim turned up in the front. His horse has already been saddled up and kitted out with a lasso, long bush knife and animal skin-covered water bottle. To protect himself and the horse, two large sections of sundried cowhide are tied in front of the saddle; they act as armour plating against the sharp thorns of the arid Chaco. We fill our waterbottles from the hand pump. The heat is oppressive – it's worse than summer in the Zambezi Valley. Surely it has to rain soon.

Manuel takes off on horseback and we all follow in *Chuma* and *Susi*. He cuts through the bush and we meet him at the swamp. The sickly odour of death hangs in the air, as hundreds of black vultures feed on the bloated carcasses of the cattle that got caught in the swamp and eventually drowned. They died a painful, agonising death. Smelling the water, the thirst-crazed animals braved the sucking mud to quench their thirst. They drank until their bellies were full, but for many it was their last drink. As the swamp claimed them, their struggling only made them sink deeper and deeper into the clinging grey mud. Giant storks pecked their eyes out while they were still alive. Then came the vultures, and even the gluttonous half-wild pigs fed on the carcasses. It is a dismal killing field and we leap in to help the surviving animals.

Ross takes command. Using the Land Rover winch cable, and a canvas rope around the animals' horns, we slowly pull the cattle out of the ooze, obviously being careful not to break their necks as we do so. We save three this way, but there's still a big brown steer lying deep in the mud. He's been fighting for his life for two days. The oozing grey mud is now up to his nostrils and he's taking what would have been his last few breaths. Slowly, we drag him to safety.

I'M TAKEN INTO THE VILLAGE TO MEET MANUEL'S FAMILY THEY ENDORSE THE SCROLL AND FEED ME HUGE CHUNKS OF BEEF & BOOZE INCREDIBLE HOSPITALITY!

MISSION CHIKENYA

CASA SAN ANTONIO - MANUEL'S HUMBLE HOME

(HOT)

'PANTANAL SWAMPS – DROWNING CATTLE'

RIO BERMEJO

MANUEL LEADS ROSS ACROSS THE WEST BERMEJO ON HORSE BACK — ILLEGAL COCAINE CONTRABAND ROUTE! DANGEROUS!

Mashozi pours our valuable drinking water into his nose and mouth and clears the mud from his nostrils. Raoul cuts down green branches with his machete and soon the beast is munching away; happy, no doubt, to be alive. I ask Manuel to give it the name 'Capricornio'. Poor Manuel has lost nearly ten percent of his herd.

By the time we get back to Casa San Antonio, the rainclouds are gathering. Manuel invites us to stay overnight with him and we all cluster around the hand pump to wash the grey slime from our arms and legs. Water is carried into the hut for a shower and the horse is unsaddled. Manuel and I go back to the mission to drop off Raoul, who presents me with a beautiful, delicately hand-carved humming bird for Mashozi.

After we say goodbye to Raoul we go on to visit Manuel's parents, who live near to the mission. They are delightful old people who, like their son, live in humble simplicity – although they do have a giant gas deepfreeze. We're offered cooldrinks and big chunks of beef with home-baked bread. It's a Saturday and a number of friends and relatives have gathered. I take photographs and shake hands all round.

Manuel's parents give us a number of plastic two-litre cooldrink bottles filled with water and frozen. They are like gold bars in this place, as the heat is intolerable and it is getting worse now in the late afternoon. The Capricornians can't believe their luck when we return with the ice blocks and soon everybody is merry. Mashozi cooks up a stew with the last of the meat and we drink strong *maté* tea with Manuel. The old-fashioned 'grandma's' feather bed is dragged out of Manuel's bedroom into the roofed dining area. 'It's for the old timers,' he says in Spanish, pointing at Mashozi and me. The others roll out their sleeping bags on the mud floor; only Tim puts up his tent in the courtyard.

Sometime after midnight it hits us – massive cracks of lightning and thunder such as I have never experienced before, not even in equatorial Africa. Bolts of lightning light up the room and Mashozi and I cuddle onto one side of the feather bed, trying to keep out of the rain blowing in from the open side of the room. The others have moved under the table. Manuel, the tough *gaucho*, appears, trembling, at the foot of our bed, terrified by the fury of the storm. Finally the heat has broken.

Day 106: Down the cocaine trail

We wake to find pools of mud and water on the floor. Before breakfast, we do the rounds with Manuel, feeding the pigs, chickens, turkeys, goats, dogs and numerous cats that live with him in his compound. He explains that he has approximately 200 head of cattle (about 20 died in the swamp), which graze over a massive area of dry thornscrub in the Chaco (an old Indian word meaning 'the hunting place'). It was to this region that the Incan hunters came for puma and wild animal skins, and for colourful feathers, horns and claws for ornaments. In Manuel's bedroom there is a picture of his grandparents, early pioneers and settlers on the Chaco. But Manuel Morena's lifestyle is not the romantic storybook one of the *gauchos* in the Pampas, to the south. Here, in this harsh country, he has to fight to keep his cattle alive.

Manuel seems in no hurry to get going. Few people come this way and I think he is enjoying having Sunday guests. There are only two horses, so it'll be just Ross and Manuel who risk the Rio Bermejo crossing. The rest of us will take a longer way round in the Landies. I notice he loads up a .32 revolver, spins the chamber and puts it in his bag. Manuel seems a bit nervous about the whole thing, which makes me concerned for Ross's safety.

Just before we leave Casa San Antonio, Manuel reverently opens two wooden doors to reveal a wonderfully detailed shrine to the Virgin Mary, decorated with plastic flowers. He takes off his hat, lights a candle and mumbles a silent prayer. Then the hardy *gaucho* leaps onto his horse, and he and Ross gallop off to the Rio Bermejo, with Manuel's dogs in hot pursuit. This is the only way we can stick to Capricorn, and Ross is loving every minute of it – the opportunity to get out of the Land Rovers and have some action. We follow in *Chuma* and *Susi* to see them off. There are some very unsavoury-looking characters knocking about the riverbank, and they eye us up and down mistrustfully. I look at Ross and he says, 'Let's get the hell out of here!'

He and Manuel swim their horses across the Bermejo, followed by the dogs. It's deep and there's a fast current, thanks to last night's storm. They jump off their horses and try to swim while still holding onto the reins, but the brown water washes them and the dogs downstream. We shout encouragement and Tim keeps the camera rolling. Finally they all reach the opposite bank – they've made it across the Rio Bermejo! We watch them – two specks on horseback, followed by the even tinier specks of the dogs – disappear over the horizon and into the rain. Then we get back into *Chuma* and *Susi*, and take a long detour over a bridge and around to the other side of the river. We find Ross nursing his saddlesore backside. It's dark by the time we say farewell to Manuel: an honest, humble, friendly man who has taken us into his heart and home. I think he's sad to see us go and, as I shake hands with him, I remember his words from yesterday evening, when I asked him what his greatest wish was. His answer: 'To share this lonely life with a señorita.' The rains come and we drive, wheels spinning, through the mud and into the night.

Day 107: **A race against time**

We leave the dry Chaco region behind us and enter sugarcane plantations and a beautiful zone of tropical cloud forests known as Serrania de Calilegua. We're racing against time, desperately trying to make up for the

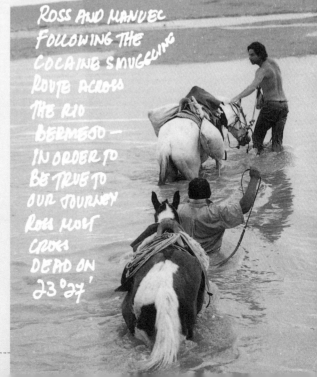

ROSS AND MANUEL FOLLOWING THE COCAINE SMUGGLING ROUTE ACROSS THE RIO BERMEJO – IN ORDER TO BE TRUE TO OUR JOURNEY ROSS MUST CROSS DEAD ON 23°27'

delays in Brazil (the Fishing Fiesta, the detour to the Iguaçu falls, the mud and the rain, and then the hassles of getting into Argentina). We have to complete South America within the next 12 days, to stick to the scheduled dates for *Chuma* and *Susi* to be shipped to Brisbane, Australia, for the next leg of the Capricorn Expedition. South America's finishing date is cast in stone, as Tim's due on another shoot, NJ has to get back to London and our flights out of Santiago have already been booked by our sponsor, Flight Centre.

The pace of the journey is starting to tell and we're all suffering from fatigue, but our spirits are still high and, as long as the Landies keep firing on all cylinders, we can carry on going. We spend the night in a cheap *pousada*: just little cubicles with beds and mozzie nets. Mashozi organises for the kitchen to cook us up South African-style steak, egg and chips – bloody luxury! Ross and NJ scrap a bit; they're as bad as brother and sister, but I know that if push came to shove they'd support each other. Old Tim is just fine and still looking for 'Carruthers'! Young Martin has been interpreting as best as he can, and Mashozi and I are feeling quite exhausted.

Day 108: The Hills of the Seven Colours
By evening we reach the foothills of the Andes; it's like a dream come true. It's a different world, with the feel of Bolivia and Peru, and the people too are different. Their Incan heritage shows in their dark, tanned skins, like roasted chestnuts, and in their colourful hats and shawls, woven from alpaca and llama wool. We hear melancholy flutes and the strumming of banjos coming from nearby as we arrive in the village of Purmamarka. It's freezing cold: no bugs, mosquitoes or dengue fever here. Smoke pours from the chimneys of the thick-walled adobe houses, in a village filled with courtyards, alleyways and narrow cobbled streets. The hills around us resemble the many-coloured layers of sand sold in bottles. It's breathtaking: the blues, mud-ochre reds, mauve, charcoal, browns and greys, and the green cultivated valleys of maize, wheat and grapevines – these are the Cerro de los Siete Colores, the Hills of the Seven Colours.

Shepherds bring in their flocks and, as the sun goes down behind the high Andes, it turns even more bitterly cold. We meet two Danish adventurers who have just come over the mountains. Their sunburnt skin is dry and chapped. We enjoy a few too many drinks with them and they tell us about their journey. They complain bitterly about the cold and wind, saying that at times they have had to build up piles of rock as a windbreak for their camp at night. We eat savoury maize cakes cooked in their leaves at a mud-walled, reed-ceilinged local restaurant, and find warm rooms with a fireplace in a local boarding house. Our budget says that we really should be camping out, but, 'C'mon Mashozi, let's get used to the cold first,' we cajole. Our plan is to take the old trade route over the Andes and into Chile. Already I can feel the effects of altitude – slight nausea and a dull headache – and drink lots of water to help counteract them.

Days 109–110: Cordillera Los Andes
Martin is as sick as a dog this morning. He's got a temperature, is vomiting and has a runny stomach. We dose him up with Imodium, but he still looks absolutely miserable. I think it is a mixture of a hangover and altitude sickness. We should know by now that booze and altitude simply don't go together! We all ate the same food last night, so it can't be the grub.

THE SHEPHERDS' FLUTES WELCOME US
TO THE LAND OF THE INCAS —

Martin thinks it's the water. Once we're in the Andes it will be difficult for him to get home from there if he's not well enough to carry on, so I suggest he take public transport back from here, but he will have none of it. He's determined, he says, to make it all the way to the Pacific and to the end of the South American leg of the Capricorn Expedition.

In the village we buy some thick, Andean woollen hats and gloves. Before we leave Mashozi kneels inside the whitewashed, thick-walled 17th-century church to pray and light a candle; she knows that we've got a tough journey ahead of us. At the nearby cemetery, a miniature of the same church stands as a gravestone and bunches of plastic flowers brighten up the sombre scene. It's such a far cry from the noisy world of Brazil. I suppose the joy of following Capricorn around the world lies in these contrasts. Gone are the days of steamy, wet, tropical jungles, swamps and the mind-numbing, prickly heat of the dry Chaco. Now we must prepare to climb our Land Rovers over the Cordillera Los Andes, following one of the ancient mountain passes originally used by mule trains to link the Andean north-west to the Pacific Ocean, in present-day Chile.

We set off, with young Martin lying curled up in the foetal position on the back seat. He's still got a temperature, but at least he's feeling less queasy now. I feel sorry for him, and guilty that I didn't force him to go back from Purmamarka, but he still insists that he wants to continue. I hope we are doing the right thing; it's too late for him to turn back now and there are no hospitals or clinics out here.

Jeez, it's cold! We get out often to have a look at our surroundings, dressed like Michelin men. We all look double our normal size, padded with jackets and tracksuits, and our cheeks and noses are red from the cold. It's also difficult for *Chuma* and *Susi*; we're having to work hard to keep our revs up at this high altitude – the engines scream in protest and stones from the dry river beds fly out from behind the wheels as we tackle the steep gradients of the high Andes. In my ignorance – I suppose it's because I'm used to our Drakensberg mountains – I expect us simply to climb up and over. But the great Andean chain is over 200 kilometres wide, with range after range of jagged mountains that run like dragons' backs from north to south down the continent. As we climb to over 4 000 metres, we all start feeling the effects. There's a glorious feeling of height and isolation, but, oh, the altitude sickness!

We leave the track and, using the GPS, make our way across a massive plain between two ranges of mountains. We're at the edge of a giant salt pan. It's arid up here and the only vegetation consists of tough little Karoo-type bushes, the stems, roots and branches of which are dry enough to use as firewood. We use the Landies to block off the howling wind and stack our grub boxes in a line between the wheels as a further windbreak for our camp. We all have to help with each other's tents – the flysheets billow out like spinnakers on a yacht. Tim and I get the giggles: 'I say old chap, has anyone seen Carruthers? Last spotted out in the Andes, desperately trying to reach the Pacific...' Ross struggles to light the fire and we have to lay one of the old East African camp chairs on its side to provide enough shelter. Finally, the bushes leap into bright orange flames, blowing sideways with the wind. Little NJ, shaking like an epileptic from the cold, is first to warm her outstretched hands. 'I-I've n-never b-been sooo c-c-cold in my my l-l-life,' she stammers. 'But you're the one from London!' we tease her.

Young Martin's a little better. We make sure he drinks lots of water, has only a piece of toast and soup for supper and is off to bed early. He's still miserable and in his youthful inexperience thinks he's letting the side down by being sick. I tell him that it could happen to any of us and to keep his chin up. As we're still acclimatising ourselves to the altitude, there's no Captain's rum for us tonight, just plenty of sweet tea... well, go on then, just one renoster coffee for the cold! The wind buffets our tent all night. Mashozi and I put on every stitch of clothing we have – I even wear my padded cycling shorts. I struggle to sleep with a headache and nausea from the altitude. Mashozi tosses and turns throughout the night. In the morning I learn that we have all had very vivid technicoloured dreams.

I am first up. I put the old, dented kettle on the fire to boil and watch frozen human forms struggle from their tents: first Tim, then NJ (still shaking), Mashozi and Ross, but no Martin. Mashozi takes him some sweet tea. He's burning up with fever and has a runny stomach again – he looks bloody terrible. Ross and I go into a huddle: if he's not right by midday we will treat him for serious dysentery. In the meantime we give NJ the task of making sure he drinks frequently from a waterbottle filled with *Rehydrat* solution. I think the altitude is aggravating Martin's condition; even NJ, who is normally full of bounce, is struggling with altitude sickness and has gone quiet. Tim, who is dressed in his woolly hat, is doing a slow camera pan of the snow-topped, blue mountains ahead of us, the white salt pan and the yellow-green bushes – it's incredible, and there's not another human being in sight.

Today's destination is the hamlet of Susques, close to the border with Chile. Following the shoreline of the salt pan Ross, with NJ and Martin in *Susi*, breaks through the crust and the 4x4 sinks down to the axles in the wet, grey, salt-laden goo. He stops immediately, knowing it's futile to try to drive out; that only spins the wheels, causing the vehicle to sink even deeper. He shouts and points to the right and, with the engine screeching, I drop a gear and immediately take evasive action, stopping on a hard piece of crust several hundred metres away. There's absolutely no way I am taking *Chuma* closer. If we both go down out here – I don't even want to think about it. We head over to *Susi* and push and dig. Out come all the mud ladders; at this altitude just unpacking them makes us pant and wheeze. Martin's too weak to help and lies in *Chuma*'s shade, as it's starting to get hot. There's nothing to winch from and, with the mud ladders under the wheels, we make only a few metres at a time. It's back-breaking work, shovelling up the goo from under the wheels, pushing in the ladders, riding over them, digging them out again from where the weight of the vehicle has pushed them deep into the mud, and then starting the whole process all over again. Sometimes we use the high-lift jack to raise the Land Rover before packing in the ladders again. We also try using the rubber sandmats, but they are for sand and desert use and soon clog up with mud. The salt crystals cut our hands and fingers.

The sun burns down, and we strip off our fleeces and jackets in the dry, high-altitude heat. Tim and I are up to our elbows in goo. Ross is tough and fit and works tirelessly. Mashozi has been through all of this before in her life and sets about preparing some food. When it's ready we stop working to have brunch. Martin looks ashen and NJ is also feeling ill. She's sitting on the ground with her head between her knees. We seem to be getting nowhere.

Then, mumbling something about a 'spare wheel', Ross starts digging a deep hole some 30 metres in front of *Susi*, away from the edge of the salt pan. We all get stuck in and bury

ALTITUDE SICKNESS STILL A HASSLE!

the spare wheel with the winch cable attached. 'We've got one go at this or we'll have to sleep here, so let's do it properly,' says Ross. 'Have you got that Carruthers?' I say to Tim. We all laugh as we lay out the mud ladders. It takes nearly an hour before we're ready. I drive, Ross directs and operates the winch control, and the others push. '*Hamba*!' shouts Ross and I slowly inch forward in low gear, with the difflock on. The winch cable creaks and groans; I just pray the buried spare wheel doesn't come hurtling through the windscreen. Then, finally, after a total of six hours, we're out.

As if to test fate – but there's no other way to do it – we race the Landies across a drier section of the pan, white salt dust flying, at over 80 kilometres per hour. I feel the odd shudder as a wheel half falls through the crust. The adrenaline pumps. If both vehicles go down out here they will end up as Capricorn markers for future travellers, and it'll mean the end for us. But, with true Capricorn luck, we make it! We spend another bitterly cold night in this mountain paradise – now we're really running late.

Day 111: Susques and sunsets

It's late afternoon, and a day late, by the time we reach Susques, just four kilometres off the Tropic of Capricorn. It's bitterly cold and the dust blows in spurts down the narrow streets. Fortunately there's diesel and water here, so we're able to fill our containers. Susques is a sombre place, made even more so by a funeral procession that slowly wends its way to the terracotta-coloured, adobe-walled cemetery. The bell tolls mournfully from the mud-brick church tower. The mourners are dressed all in black; the only bright colours are the plastic flowers on the graves. Even the thin village dogs look sad as they walk past.

In the centre of the hamlet, adobe houses and courtyards line the cobbled streets and the serious, coffee-coloured inhabitants look like the Incas. Nobody is smiling in Susques today and the death bell continues to toll the passing of another Andean resident. Further into the town we come across a magnificent 17th-century church with thick mud-plastered walls, a bell tower and a roof of yellow thatch. The interior rafters, cut from the strong, fibrous stems of the cardon cactus, are bound with rawhide thongs and the old murals take us back to the time of the Spanish conquistadors and the introduction of Catholicism to the Andean Incas.

Ross is in a hurry to get going again in this race against time and budget restrictions. I urge him to be patient – we'll only travel this road once in our lives. I sit down on the ground resting my 'Land Rover back', sore from driving all day, against the inside of the arched gateway to the church and, as I scribble these notes in the Expedition journal, I think of all the feet that have worn away the flagstones here at the church entrance. I imagine the intrigue, happiness and sorrow that the people who come here must feel, and what a respite this church must be for the worshippers who gather under the centuries-old beams of the thatched roof – an escape from the harsh task of daily survival in the Cordillera Los Andes.

Off-road again, amongst the dry, barren mountains, we follow the GPS and struggle through soft sand. It's like a desert here between the mountain ranges. As we continue, the sand becomes even softer; it's like churning through brown sugar. We reduce tyre pressure and finally force the 4x4s up into a high, dry gully beneath a barren peak, and out of the roaring wind. We leap out of the vehicles, eager to stretch and set up camp. But Mashozi won't move. She refuses point blank to sleep here or even to get out of the vehicle. 'This place is bad.

23°27

There're evil spirits. There's absolutely no way we're camping here,' she says with a scowl. The wind howls, Ross looks at me and raises his eyebrows. I try to reason with Mashozi, but she's not budging. Finally, I give up, flash my lights at Ross and we drive all the way back down the gully. Mashozi and I have a few minutes of 'no speak'. She's got a thing about 'spirits' and we've learnt to go along with it (the Zulus at home believe she has some *sangoma*-like traits). Maybe this time it's the altitude. We drive past our first wild llamas, known as *vicuñas*. They're impala-coloured, with long necks, and are very skittish.

We carry on driving and at last arrive at a small pan, no bigger than a tennis court. 'Are the spirits okay here, Mashozi?' I ask. She nods and smiles. The small depression is surrounded by snow-capped peaks, and the wind still howls around us. We all help Martin put up his tent. We've treated him with antibiotics, but his eyes are sunken and his lips chapped from fever blisters. Mashozi toasts some bread on the fire and gives it to him with Bovril and sweet tea. He mumbles '*gracias*' and goes straight to his tent – this is not the expedition he imagined. Mashozi tries her best to mother him, but I still think we should find transport home for him from the next bit of civilisation, which will be in Chile. Martin has helped us enormously with his interpreting, especially during our time with Manuel the *gaucho* and the Rio Bermejo crossing, but now it seems as if his illness has broken the poor lad's spirit. Talking about spirits, maybe Mashozi was right.

The view from here is outstanding and the struggle against the freezing, demonic wind is made worthwhile by the most incredible sunset we've ever seen in our lives: a kaleidoscope of light and colour that continues for nearly an hour. Even Tim, who has filmed countless sunsets in Africa, has never seen anything to compare with it and doesn't know which way to point his camera – at the sunset itself or the snow-capped mountains opposite, which keep changing colour in the reflected light. Afterwards we all feel drained, in the same way as when you've just come out of a really good movie. I'm enjoying the great solitude and the feeling of space here. Tim and I sit up till late around the warming fire, talking of adventures past, present and future. Hopefully we'll reach Chile tomorrow. Who knows, we might even find Carruthers!

CAPTAIN MORGAN EXPEDITION RUM

Day 112: Time is running out

The Zulus call it *thamala elanga*: to sit like a baboon facing the early morning sun, warming up the bones. The only difference is that we're each clutching an enamel mug of strong coffee and condensed milk. Martin is still extremely weak and listless, and has got bad stomach cramps. He hates the *Rehydrat*, but Mashozi forces him to drink it. We also feed him vitamins and continue the course of antibiotics to stop his dysentery – poor bloke! Ross is missing home terribly. He talks about little Tristan Kingsley constantly: 'Will he even recognise me? Will he be crawling by now?'

Up here in the Andes, you can turn around the full 360° and still see no buildings, no corrugated iron shining in the sun – just mountains, sand, distant salt pans shimmering yellow-green, brown scrub and wispy threads of white cottonwool clouds stretching out across the huge blue sky. It makes the soul and the spirit fly. On the down side, fatigue is now constant. We're very high up, over 4 000 metres above sea level, and are all suffering from the dull headaches and nausea of altitude sickness. We're feeling the strain of forever moving forward, pitching and breaking camp, and sorting out fuel, water and supplies. The GPS and survey maps are our only guides in the challenge to stay on, or as close as possible to, 23° 27'. This bloody imaginary line! Why can't we just go wherever we want to? We wind our way over the Andes – two little Landies, dwarfed by God's mighty creation of beauty. We climb higher, and nearer to the border between Argentina and Chile. In a wide, windswept valley, we come across the small, lonely Argentinian border post, built from rock; smoke billows from the chimney. It is operated by the *gendarmarie* and they are expecting us, as Major Nikolini has obviously radioed to them from Clorinda. Like naughty children waiting to see the headmaster, we sit outside the small Argentinian border post under the country's flag. For the last time we produce our military papers (this time they make sure they hang on to them). They won't let us film anything here, but it's all handshakes and smiles as they endorse the Capricorn Scroll. Goodbye,

Argentina – *bienvenidos* to Chile. There's no official Chilean border post up here, just a sign welcoming us to the country. We sit and look back over Argentina. Mashozi rustles up a celebratory lunch of bully beef, tinned sweet corn, peas, beans, asparagus, tuna and processed cheese triangles. We even risk a wee drop of Captain Morgan at high altitude! Martin has improved a bit and is able to nibble on some lunch; we're greatly relieved.

MANUEL MORENA OF CASA SAN ANTONIO

MASHOZI IN GAUCHO OUTFIT →

SALT PANS IN THE HIGH ANDES

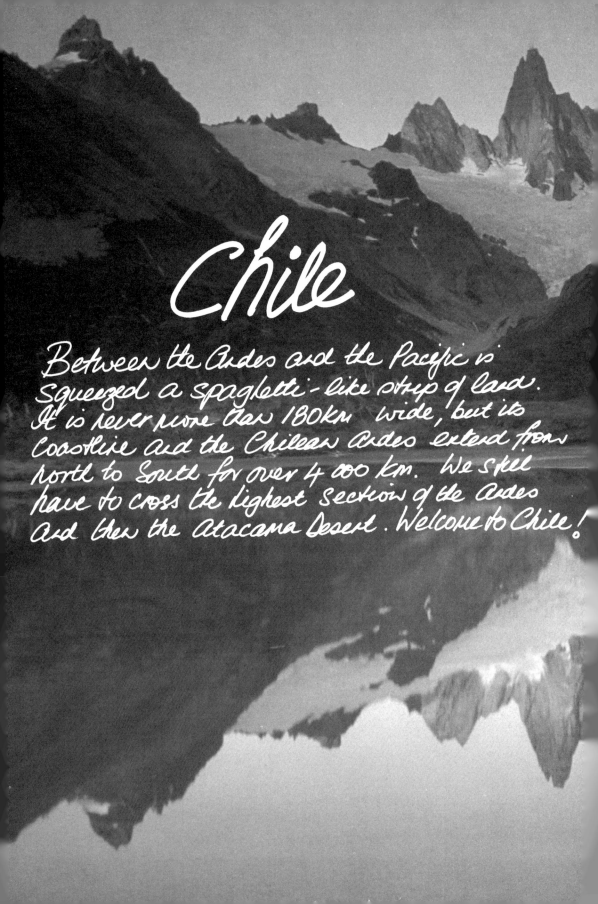

Chile

Between the Andes and the Pacific is
squeezed a spaghetti-like strip of land.
It is never more than 180km wide, but its
coastline and the Chilean Andes extend from
north to south for over 4 000 km. We still
have to cross the highest section of the Andes
and then the Atacama Desert. Welcome to Chile!

Days 113–114: Land of fire and ice

We are at an even higher altitude now, close to 5 000 metres above sea level. Tall stone obelisks protrude from the sand like an Andean Stonehenge and all around us are magnificent snow-tipped peaks and volcanoes

As we continue west it becomes even more beautiful, and even drier. Clearly visible to the north is snow-covered Lincancabur. At 5 900 metres it is one of the highest extinct volcanoes in the Andean chain. Determined as always to stick to the Capricorn line, we make an expedition base camp in a deserted Atacama Indian village. It's strange and eerie, and we wonder why this place is empty. Several hundred people must have lived here. There's no sign of an earthquake or past volcanic eruption and everything is undisturbed. I hope there's no strange disease lurking here.

We camp here, in order to get out of the terrible cold and wind, at the base of the 5 154-metre-high Volcano Lascar, which blows smoke vigorously into the air. Ironically, the biggest danger is not an eruption but the landmines planted by Chile during the recent period of territorial disputes with Argentina and Bolivia. And we thought that our journey through Mozambique was the last time we would have to worry about these horrific devices.

Our expedition camp in the deserted village has a spiritual feel to it. The thatched roofs have long since caved in, but the thick stone walls shelter us from the icy wind and there is a stream for water. We wander through the living rooms and kitchens, and the nearby terraced fields fed by stone irrigation canals. The altar in the collapsed church has moon, cactus, sun, stars and llama symbols carved into its stone. Is it the altitude that fuels the imagination or, in the night, do I really hear the clip-clop of hooves and the shouts of a passing mule train making its way along the tortuous contour path cut into the side of the mountain above us (an old Andean trade route to the Pacific seaport of Antofagasta)?

Early in the morning Ross heads out to follow the contour path on foot – in order to stick as close as possible to the line – while we descend from the Andes in the 4x4s, and head down into the Atacama Desert, the driest place in the entire world. In this desert is the Salar de Atacama, a massive dry salt pan through which our Capricorn line passes. But, before we get there, we must first cross legally into Chile. We don't want a repeat of our first attempt to get into Argentina, so we travel a short distance to the north to report to Customs and Immigration in the

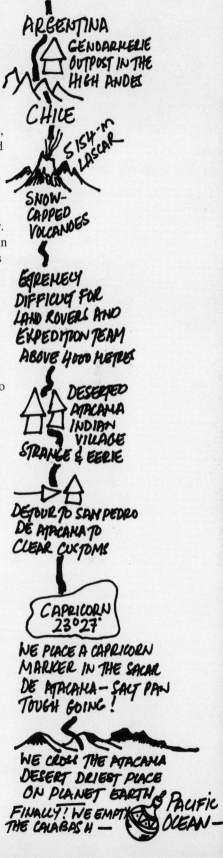

ARGENTINA

GENDARMERIE OUTPOST IN THE HIGH ANDES

CHILE

5 154 m LASCAR

SNOW-CAPPED VOLCANOES

EXTREMELY DIFFICULT FOR LAND ROVERS AND EXPEDITION TEAM ABOVE 4000 METRES

DESERTED ATACAMA INDIAN VILLAGE STRANGE & EERIE

DETOUR TO SAN PEDRO DE ATACAMA TO CLEAR CUSTOMS

CAPRICORN 23°27'

WE PLACE A CAPRICORN MARKER IN THE SALAR DE ATACAMA – SALT PAN TOUGH GOING!

WE CROSS THE ATACAMA DESERT DRIEST PLACE ON PLANET EARTH

FINALLY! WE EMPTY THE CALABASH — PACIFIC OCEAN —

I SENT THIS PIC TO PAUL
MELHUISH THE M.D. OF LAND
ROVER SOUTH AFRICA —

Hi PAUL—THEY'RE RUSTING A BIT
BUT I'M SURE THEY'LL GET US HOME!
GREETINGS FROM ANTOFAGASTA—CHILE

oasis town of San Pedro de Atacama. The customs people are wonderfully friendly and efficient, and most of them speak English. But, as we've arrive from Argentina, all uncooked foodstuffs, grains, beans (what about Mashozi's tasty bean stew?!) rice and meat are confiscated. Our personal bags are also searched by Foot-and-Mouth and Disease Control. As any form of plant material invites suspicion, we wonder how they'll react to our Zulu calabash. We decide that silence is golden, and keep our fingers crossed. Somehow, to our relief, it escapes the notice of the searchers. Once they're done with our bags, they empty the vehicles and spray them with high pressure hoses. Only then are our passports stamped.

Parked alongside the border post is a blood-splattered, crushed Land Rover Defender, with expedition logos still on the doors. We don't know what happened here, but they clearly didn't made it, and I think of how fortunate we've been as we've followed the dangerous mountain trails across the Andes. One wrong move and this could've been us.

After the solitude of the Andes, the crowded tourist town of San Pedro de Atacama – with its restaurants, dollar prices, internet cafés and tourist buses – comes as a shock to all of us. Now that we've entered Chile legally, all we want to do is get back onto the Capricorn line.

Days 115–116: The straw that breaks the Capricornians' backs?

Back on 23° 27' the sharp, fragmented rocks of the Salar de Atacama are proving an absolute nightmare to drive over. Sharp, fragmented salt crystals protrudes into the desert sky like sharks' teeth. If the Landies break through the crust, then we will sink into grey slippery mud. Worse still, there are giant sinkholes of crystal-clear saltwater, deep enough to swallow an entire 4x4. We station someone up on the roofrack at all times to look out for them. We camp for the night on the pan, which is so inhospitable, that we gaze back longingly at the Andes. It's a bitterly cold night and we huddle around our small fire, built from the roots and stems of dry, Karoo-type bushes, to try to get warm before we go to sleep.

After breakfast we drop coins into a sinkhole in the salt; each making a wish to the ancient gods of the Atacama. We crunch west through the rough salt craters, and thank God for the Land Rovers' excellent suspension. High up in the Andes I carved the word 'Capricorn' into a piece of soft sandstone I found there. This we place in the middle of the giant salt pan on 23° 27' – a monument to our little expedition. In time maybe some exploring archaeologist will stumble across it and wonder at its strange Andean origin. The placing of this Capricorn sign in the Atacama is something of a milestone for us: if we survive this obstacle, surely we can make it to the Pacific.

Martin chooses this moment to drop a bombshell. He comes up to me sheepishly, saying that he simply can't go on. I'm furious. Why didn't he tell us when we were still in San Pedro? I want to make him walk from here, but Ross and Tim quieten me down. 'Let him go,' they say, 'his heart's not in it.' It takes us several hours to take him all the way back to the road that leads to San Pedro de Atacama. He'll have to hitchhike from this point.

He still hasn't fully recovered from the effects of his illness, and last night he was very quiet and uncommunicative. He didn't say as much, but I think he took one look at what lay ahead of him across the dry Atacama and decided that, since the tourist town of San Pedro de Atacama was still in reach, this was the time to quit the expedition. Now we're on our own, with barely 10 words of Spanish amongst us.

It's punishing terrain for *Chuma* and *Susi*, but they carry on tirelessly. We have to be extremely careful to allow enough space between the two vehicles as we go. Should the front Land Rover break through the crust into the mud or go down a sinkhole, we need to be able to winch it out quickly before it sinks. We progress painfully slowly, bouncing over mounds of jagged salt crystals. My fear is that if we have to walk out of here our boots will soon be sliced to pieces by the sharp salt crystals. As it is we've inflated our tyres for fear of the sidewalls being cut open – it's a terrible journey. The Capricorn Expedition team is looking a little ragged around the edges: the salt, fierce sun and wind have dried our skins to parchment, strained our eyes and chapped our lips, so that we almost blend in with the ground! But luck is on our side – we find a route across the pan, and, what's more, it roughly follows the Tropic of Capricorn. We can't believe our good fortune and soon we're belting along the narrow, hardened track, heading due west – it's perfect.

Then comes a major obstacle: a sentry tower, a very official-looking boom gate and an even more official-looking armed security guard. It's the entry to a salt mine. We really need our Spanish interpreter. Right now Martin is probably sipping an ice-cold beer and chatting to his girlfriend on the phone. We paid him what we owed him and more, and here we are stuck with no Spanish! Out comes my phrase book and Spanish documents.

There's much hand-shaking and pointing at the vehicles, and I introduce all the Expedition members (whispering to NJ that she should smile sweetly), but the security guard will have none of it and demands that we retrace our steps and take a road to the south. I shake my head and point to all the flags on the side of the Land Rover, reading out the Spanish words 'Expedicion de Capricórnio – alrededor põr tierra del mundo' ('Capricorn Expedition – around the world by land'). He nods in a confused way, clearly not understanding why a bunch of *gringos* want to follow the Tropic of Capricorn across this forlorn salt pan. He radios Mr Big from his control tower, but the answer remains a firm 'no'. Still I persist; making a big show of the words 'National Geographic'. He makes another radio call and this time I gather our man is saying, 'These crazy *gringos* must follow Capricórnio – they're from National Geographic.' I do my normal nodding and smiling bit

We leave the smoking volcanoes of the Andes behind us and head for the Atacama – Antofagasta and the Pacific!

23°27'

and finally we get waved through to where huge pyramids of salt are being loaded onto waiting trucks by conveyor belt. We don't stop to ask questions, and continue west.

The jagged white salt finally changes to red-brown rock and sand. At last we've made it across the salt pans and to celebrate we pour valuable drinking water over our heads, wet our caps and even do a jig. Now we roar over the copper-red dunes of the Atacama; the surface is harder than the Namib and we are able to follow old mining tracks. There seem to be no living things here: no grass, no animals, nothing. No precipitation has been measured in this desert since the Spanish colonists first came here in the 16th century, earning it the reputation of the driest place on earth. We camp in the dunes. It's a beautifully clear night and the Capricornians are visibly excited; everybody has perked up at the thought of home – finally we can all taste victory. I couldn't have wished for a better team.

With the Land Rover engines roaring and stones flying from behind the wheels we alternately bounce and grind to the top of the coastal mountains. It is with an incredible feeling of jubilation and relief that we get our first sighting of the Pacific Ocean on the rugged Atacama coast of Chile. I wonder just how much more punishment *Chuma* and *Susi* can take. Below us lies the small, deserted, rocky island of Santa Maria. Ross consults the GPS – we are dead on track. Mashozi waves the calabash out of the Land Rover's window, as we race across the last stretch of dry, stony, windswept Atacama to a small beach of broken shells. Pelicans fly overhead, seagulls hover and whiskered sea lions eye us curiously. Here, at least, there is life.

With mixed emotions – I always have a feeling of anti-climax after all the effort – we empty our traditional Zulu calabash of Atlantic seawater, taken from the coast of Brazil, into the Pacific. We are all alone; just a little group of travel-weary Capricornians and our two battle-hardened Landies. As the well-travelled seawater glugs from the calabash, I glance up at the team: Ross, sunburnt and serious, with his head wrapped in a Bolivian scarf, has succeeded in navigating us across South America along the invisible line of Capricorn. Mashozi, dressed in a warm Captain Morgan fleece top to protect her from the cold brought by the Humbolt current, has tears in her eyes, and NJ's blonde hair blows wildly in the wind. When she's back in London I'll send her a before and after picture. She looks sunburnt and healthy – a far cry from the pale little 'English' girl who arrived in Montevideo all those weeks ago. Tim Chevallier stands behind us with his camera, documenting the moment for National Geographic. His team spirit, good humour and sense of adventure have never failed. We have all stuck together through thick and thin across this continent, and now it's over – time to celebrate.

We dig in the coolbox and bring out a chunk of beef bought at San Pedro de Atacama. The spade that helped free the Land Rovers from tropical mud and Atacama salt is scrubbed clean with sea sand and used to fry the steaks over glowing driftwood coals. Our 'steaks à la spade', flambéed with Captain Morgan, are cut into strips and eaten with coarse salt, Zulu style. The wind howls and we sing and dance (I even have a vague recollection of dancing with a huge piece of seaweed at one stage, but I may be wrong!).

Too exhausted to put up tents, we sleep under the stars to the sound of crashing waves. We've made it to the Pacific! But, sadly, we still can't find Carruthers: 'By Jove, Tim, there's a rumour that he's heading for Down Under.'

Muchas gracias, South America. You've been a tough but wonderful host.

HEADING UP INTO THE FOOTHILLS
OF THE HIGH ANDES

SCENES FROM THE VILLAGE OF PURMAMARA IN THE ARGENTINIAN FOOTHILLS OF THE ANDES.

LEFT: In the cemetery at Purmamarka there's a grave with exactly the same design as the village church.
BELOW: Surely this is the first time that two South African-registered Land Rovers have come this way?
FAR RIGHT: Quecho Indians knit colourful jerseys and warm hats from llama wool.

COBBLED PAVEMENTS AND THICK ADOBE-WALLED HOUSES IN THE FOOTHILLS OF THE ARGENTINIAN ANDES—

MULTI-COLOURED FOOTHILLS OF THE ANDES—

GHOST TOWN —

GRUBS UP —

WE CAMP IN A DESERTED VILLAGE —
BENEATH A 5000 M HIGH SMOKIN
VOLCANO —

VOLCANOES
AND GRAVES

WELCOME TO CHILE

FOLLOWING CAPRICORN OVER THE ANDES INTO CHILE —

N.J.—
ALTITUDE?
NOT
ATTITUDE!

A DESERTED VILLAGE CF OLD
RAILWAY CARRIAGES - ATACAMA.

A COLOURFUL MURAL IN ANTOFAGASTA - CHILE

ROSS AND MANUEL — FOLLOWING THE COCAINE-
SMUGGLERS' ROUTE ACROSS THE RIO BERMEJO —

WE REACH THE PACIFIC !
ON 23° 27' ——

THE NEVER-ENDING
RED BULLDUST!

CROSSING THE SIMPSON
OUR LIVES ARE RULED
BY THE GPS

SETTING OFF FROM THE
COAST OF QUEENSLAND

NEVER BEFORE
HAVE WE KNOWN SUCH
SOLITUDE ----

BLOODY FLIES

MY BEST ADVICE IS TO GIVE WAY TO THESE — KINGS OF THE ROAD

THE EXPEDITION REFLECTED IN A ROAD TRAIN HUBCAP!

BLOODY RED DUST
COVERS EVERYTHING.

AND THE WORLD BY LAND

BLOODY
SPINIFEX —

LITTLE THORNY DEVIL

Another `Road Kill'
Tens of thousands of
`roos' are killed on the
roads

IN MADAGASCAR — RICE PRODUCTION
IS A MEASURE OF LIFE ITSELF!

FINALLY WE BRING MASHOZI TO
BENINITRA! THE LOCALS CAN'T
BELIEVE IT — A WHITE WOMAN
ON A ZEBU CART —

MADAGASCAR HAS THE WORLD'S LARGEST CHAMELEONS.

THE GREYBEARD AND THE CALABASH — BAY OF ST AUGUSTINE MADAGASCAR —

MADAGASCAR COMPLETE

THE ALL IMPORTANT CAMP SPADE - IT BOLTS ON TO THE ROOFRACK, FREES THE LAND ROVER FROM MUD AND SAND - IS GREAT FOR COOKING STEAK À LA SPADE AND IS USED FOR BUSH ABLUTIONS

VICTORY IN THE MOÇAMBIQUE CHANNEL - KINGSLEY, ROSS AND B.

Valparaiso, Chile

Hi Taryn
Thanks for the email – I got it today. Glad the dogs are fine and all is
okay at home. Well, South America is done now; it's been an unforgettable
adventure. I cast my mind back to Rio, with its big Jesus statue, and
Copacabana, with the food, music and bodies beautiful that introduced
us to the amazing world of Brazil. We'll never forget the journey with
the Guaranese Indians: Ross, Tim and me smeared with red ochre and
we battled through the rain-drenched tropical forests of the Serra do
Mar. Then São Paulo, Capricorn's great concrete jungle and the largest
city on 23° 27', followed by the Parana River and the Mato Grosso.
Alex, our Brazilian translator, claimed we'd never make it across
Paraguay. But, somehow, we did. For poor Chuma and Susi it was mud,
sweat and gears as we forced them through the jungle to the border with
Argentina. The Argentinians... well, they took one look at the battered
Capricornio travellers in their two South African 4x4s and said, "No
entry!" We were searched from bumper to bumper and sent back to
Paraguay, down to Asuncion, and then across the border to report to the
Argentinian military at Clorinda. But it all worked out in the end and
soon we were back on the Tropic of Capricorn; this time with military
papers from the gendarmerie.
   In the dry Chaco of Argentina we winched drowning cattle from the mud
of the pantanal, and in return a gaucho led Ross on horseback down an
illegal cocaine route and across the Bermejo River, on 23° 27'.
   Some days we didn't think we'd make it, when, wheezing and puffing,
with engines screaming and stones flying, we faced the high altitude of
the Andes, before dropping down into the Atacama Desert. Finally, we
emptied our Zulu calabash of Atlantic seawater, taken from Ubatuba on
the coast of Brazil, into the ocean a short distance north of Antofagasta,
on the coast of Chile. There wasn't a human being in sight, just sea birds,
whiskered sea lions and the windswept Pacific.
   After that we rested up for a day and a night in the colourful port of
Antofagasta. It's full of character, with painted fishing boats and
brightly-coloured wooden houses set between the Pacific and the rocky,

brown Atacama coastal range. For the first time in weeks we slept in hotel beds, and ate juicy chickens straight off the spit with mountains of 'slap chips' at a street side pub. Then we pointed Chuma and Susi south, down the Pan-American highway, for a 1 500-km dash to Valparaiso. Small shrines, many decorated with plastic flowers and known as animitas (little spirits) lined the highway – many Chileans believe that the spirits of those who have died violently in accidents continue to roam the areas where they met their deaths and that they can intercede for the living – and we throttled back for the sharp bends and dangerous corners to avoid joining them.

With only hours to spare we reached Valparaiso and met Captain Angus Shaw, who had arranged the shipping of the Landies to Brisbane, Australia. It was a strange feeling leaving Chuma and Susi, as the two 4x4s had been our home for months, and the cowbell we bought outside the village of Kang in Botswana's Kalahari Desert was still tinkling from Chuma's bullbar. We got rid of all our left-over food and cleaned all the kit and both the vehicles; we'd heard that the Aussies were really fussy about not bringing in any alien plants or foot-and-mouth disease. Let's just hope that Chuma and Susi arrive all right in Brisbane – the success of our expedition depends on it.

Having now completed eight out of the ten Capricorn countries, I'm really looking forward to Australia. At least it's English speaking! But what about those vast red deserts and Aboriginal lands? Well, that's the next great Capricorn challenge, isn't it? Tomorrow we fly to Santiago, then on to Jo'burg and Durban via São Paulo. With Flight Centre's assistance it's easier for us to wait in South Africa for the vehicles to reach Brisbane and be cleared, and it gives us the chance to touch base and get our paperwork together for Australia. So, Taryn, the good news is that we will see you in a few days' time – can't wait!

Siyabonga and gracias,
The Capricornians

CAPRICORN
SCROLL OF
PEACE &
GOODWILL

CAPRICORN
CALABASH

THE AUSSIES WON'T BUDGE — I HOPE IT'S NOT BECAUSE OF THE CRICKET! AND SO WE WAIT —

Mud on the undercarriage

...luland adventur-
...velling around the
...along the line of
...corn have arrived
...stralia on the next
...their journey.
...sley Holgate takes
...the story:
...then just as we
...bout to launch the
...lian Capricorn leg
...Captain Morgan
...corn Expedition 'a
...shell', like the
..., hit us for a six.
...ralian customs
...uarantine inspec-
...und some South
...can mud under-
...he two Land Rov-

...ave been given 14
...get them out of
...ia - what a mess!
...we have survived
...dmines in Mo-
...ue, walked across

jungles, the high Andes
and Chile's Atacama
desert, driest place on
planet earth - but now,
can you believe it, the
future of this world first
expedition is being
threatened by mud on
the undercarriage and
dead insects on the radiator!

We sent the Aussies this appeal:
'HELP! We are a South
African family attempt-
ing a world first by land
around the globe along
the Capricorn line. We
have completed Mozam-
bique, South Africa,
Botswana, Namibia,
Brazil, Paraguay, Argen-
tina and Chile and now
there is just Australia
and Madagascar to go.
'We have put our fam-

'If any of the expedi-
tion kit in the vehicles is
a problem you have our
permission to destroy it
- anything in an effort to
save the expedition.'

PS - Australia, Africa
and South America were
once all part of the Su-
per continent of
Gondwanaland. All we
are trying to do is give
them a bit of their mud
back.
Wish us luck! A spe-
cial thanks to our spon-
sors Land Rover, Cap-
tain Morgan, Flight Cen-
tre, Continental Tyres

and African Satellite
Corporation.

CAPRICORN *adventure*

Race day

The   Empangeni
Rotaract Club is hosting
a 'Day at the Races' on

Disc Jockey will host this
inaugural derby and eve-
ryone is assured of an

CAPRICORN
adventure

It has been a while since hearing from our modern day explorers who are on an incredible journey around the globe.

With eight of the ten countries now behind them, Kingsley, Gill and Ross Holgate's next challenge is to cross Australia from east to west along the Capricorn line.

This is a distance of over 4000km through some of the toughest desert and Aboriginal country in the world.

The same two Land Rover Defenders, Chuma and Susi that departed from Shakaland, armed with the Capricorn Scroll of Peace and Goodwill and the Zulu calabash, have arrived in Australia.

Another exciting leg of this Capricorn adventure is about to begin.

We pick up the Capricorn saga in Kingsley's words:

Looking back on this journey of many months I'm really beginning to realize just how difficult it is to follow this imaginary line around the world. Traveling from east to west means long hot tropical afternoons, driving, walking or cycling into the sun. Our lives are ruled by maps and the GPS. It is amazing just how focused one becomes on 23°27' and the will to succeed in this crazy world-first attempt to circle the world.

I assure you that having come this far we are determined to make it. Unfortunately the low Rand against the Aussie Dollar, like the cricket, is giving us a bit of a hiding. We are going to have to tighten the belt, eat only bush tucker, sleep in our 'swags' down by a billabong, play the didgeridoos, boomerang roos and learn to quaff Fosters and Bundies (don't worry, we will still have our Captain Morgan).

Captain Morgan are our funding partners in this world first odyssey and will be carrying some of their expedition brew to sustain us on our journey.

Flight Centre are handling all our flights to Australia.

This is the year of the Australian Outback and we are getting a great response from the Australian Station owners through whose vast lands we must cross.

The route

The Australian leg of our Capricorn Expedition travels through Queensland, the Northern Territory and Western Australia. We will commence with the filling of the Zulu Calabash in the Capricorn section of the Australian Great Barrier Reef. The line then travels through Rockhampton and Longreach, the Simpson Desert (largest parallel sand dune desert in the world) then just north of Alice Springs through the Gibson Desert, the Little Sandy Deserts to end at the Ningaloo Marine Reserve where we empty the Capricorn Calabash.

Conditions across the giant red deserts of Central Australia we know will be tough. The Royal Flying Doctor's service will be keeping an eye on us. Our communications, by courtesy of African Satellite Corporation and Globaltrack, will be tracking our journey by satellite across Australia.

I imagine these two little specks of white Land Rovers racing across endless red dust deserts - on the bonnets are South African flags and around the sides of the vehicles are the flags of the 10 Capricorn Countries (Mozambique, South Africa, Botswana, Namibia, Brazil, Paraguay, Argentina, Chile, Australia and Madagascar). Inside the vehicles are the Holgates, Kingsley, Gill and Ross, Luke Cormack the South African Cameraman (who will be documenting this leg for Carte Blanche and the National Geographic Channel), and old friend, Linda Sparrow and her dog! Linda, an Aussie 'Sheila' was an expedition member on our 1997 Zambezi Source to Mouth Expedition. She's our Aussie link and I just hope her cooking's improved.

Dust and flies

There is always a feeling of nervous anticipation at the commencement of yet another Capricorn Continent. I know there will be endless sand, dust and flies. For the rest we don't quite know that to expect.

With Africa and South America now behind us I've been reading up on Australia as we prepare for our mid April departure.

Bill Bryson's comical book 'Down Under' reads: 'Australia is the world's sixth largest country and its largest island. It is the only island that is also a continent, and the only continent that is also a country. It was the first continent conquered from the sea, and the last. It is the only nation that began as a prison.

'It is the home of the largest living things on earth, the Great Barrier Reef, and of the most famous and

striking monolith, Ayers Rock Uluru to use its now official spectful Aboriginal name). It more things that will kill you t anywhere else. Of the world's most poisonous snakes, all Australian. Five of its creatur the funnel-web spider, box je fish, blue-ringed octopus, par sis tick and stonefish - are the r lethal of their type in the w This is a country where ever fluffiest of caterpillars can lay out with a toxic nip, where shells will not just sting you actually sometimes go for yo

'Pick up an innocuous cone from a Queensland beach, a nocent tourists are all too wo do, and you will discover tha little fellow inside is not jus toundingly swift and testy, b ceedingly venomous. If yo not stung or pronged to dea some unexpected manner, may be fatally chomped by s or crocodiles, or carried help out to sea by irresistible cur or left to stagger to an un death in the baking outback. tough place.'

Wish us the best of luck we'll keep poste

Australia

Days 117–135: Our appeals fall on deaf ears

We stay put at home in SA, waiting for a positive response, but get no reply to our appeal to 'Mr Big' (the Head of Australian Quarantine Inspector Services, or AQIS) and our telephone call to Canberra (AQIS headquarters) goes something like this: 'Sorry, mate, we simply can't take the risk. Your two Land Rovers must leave the country.' 'But...' I begin. 'No "buts", fella. You've got two weeks to get them out of Australia, and there's no guarantee that we'll allow them back into the country once they're cleaned. If you don't move them we're going to take legal action. Sorry, mate, in Australia we've got our rules and there's no way around them.' And so our Australian nightmare begins.

Just a word of advice to any traveller to Australia. Given the recent foot-and-mouth disease outbreak in Africa and Europe, the Aussies are extremely skittish – now made, understandably, even worse by the threat of international terrorism. The sight of our two Landies decked out with the national flags of the ten Capricorn countries – all cattle countries – is the AQIS's worst nightmare. *Chuma* and *Susi* have, for the moment, lost the freedom of the open road and sit locked up in quarantine in Brisbane Harbour. The Expedition seems doomed to failure. They're a bunch of stick in the muds.

Days 135–178: Cousin Fish

To our surprise we find out that a distant cousin living in Perth, Australia, saw our story on the Land Rover website and contacted Lesley Sutton at Land Rover South Africa to track us down. My cousin Ian Fisher, known to his mates as Fish, left Zimbabwe 27 years ago and made his bucks from pearls, property, furniture and a massive cattle ranch above the Capricorn line in Western Australia. Fish is a great adventurer, with a never-say-die African attitude. We share our problem with him and he leaps into the fray. His email to me reads, 'Hi, Kingsley. Don't worry, mate; some of these governmental officials are as useless as tits on a bull! I've got a mate in the shipping business and he'll send your Landies to Singapore for cleaning.' He's a great comic, and signs off with '*Die ou Vis met die groot piesang*' ('The old Fish with the big banana').

Singapore proves difficult. We have no-one there to whom we can consign the vehicles, it

DIE OU VIS! COUSIN FISH. WITHOUT WHOM WE'D NEVER HAVE MADE IT –

will cost a fortune in shipping and we are required to give six weeks' notice to the Australian authorities for a Quarantine Inspector to fly there to ensure that the cleaning is done to Australian specifications – flights and all expenses to our account, of course, plus a mere US$250 per day for his services! The best bet now seems to be Papua New Guinea, but the Head of Quarantine at Port Moresby, Papua New Guinea, doesn't want to hear our troubles. 'Mr Big' in Canberra suggests we send *Chuma* and *Susi* all the way back to Valparaiso in Chile – hoping, I think, that he'll never see them again. Things look bad. Are we going to have to do Australia by camel or just pack it in?

But, finally, Fish and another old Perth friend and great African adventurer Vic Hall (known to the Zulus as Dwala, meaning 'a big stone') hit on a possible solution. We will send the 4x4s to Dili. Well, sure – the whole thing is driving us completely bloody dilly! Dili is the capital of East Timor, a small island between Australia and Indonesia, not far from Papua New Guinea, and until very recently a war zone. In 1999 East Timor voted to break free from Indonesian rule. This triggered a bloody rampage by pro-Indonesian militants in which hundreds died and 250 000 people were forced to flee their homes. Australia sent a UN peacekeeping force to East Timor, so there is an Australian military base there. Because of the movement of their vehicles in and out of Australia, a professional anti-foot-and-mouth disease cleaning service and a Quarantine Inspector are based on the island.

In a few weeks' time up to 200 000 East Timorese, a quarter of the population, are expected to gather at a field near Dili, to celebrate the birth of the world's newest nation. Hopefully Land Rovers *Chuma* and *Susi* will arrive at much the same time, to be stripped down and sprayed. The three-legged cast iron pots, bicycles, toolbox, mud ladders, braai grids, tents and camp chairs – every speck of dirt or dust on this equipment must be scoured off. Every bit of undercarriage mud, every dead insect carcass and grass seed, must be removed from the radiators with high-pressure hoses.

Of course, all this will be possible only if we can find a ship that will take the 4x4s to Dili. We're chatting to the Crocodile shipping line that goes to Dili via Darwin. Our telephone bills are mounting up. I speak to a shipping agent in Dili called Bruce, and the conversation goes along the lines of (I suggest you try reading this out loud with an Australian accent!): 'No worries, Kingsley, we'll sort it out. Only problem is, your Land Rovers might get re-infected over here. Have you heard of Siam weed? You haven't? Well, it's worse than your mud, mate. It grows to the size of a bloody house and you need an army tank to move it. If Siam weed seeds get on your vehicles while they're being cleaned here, you're stuffed, mate. When we fly into Darwin they sometimes even confiscate our boots and socks!'

No-one can give us any promises. We're told by Canberra that, even after the 4x4s have been professionally cleaned in East Timor, there's no guarantee they'll let them back into Australia. 'Come on, that's not cricket!' we protest. 'Sorry, mate, those are the rules,' is the reply.

Thanks to our wonderful sponsors, we're managing to hang in there financially. Struik, the publishers of this book, offers to advance some dough; Captain Morgan steals a bit from next year's budget to give to us; and Land Rover agrees to back us all the way with shipping costs to Dili. To save time and money, we'll ship the Land Rovers from Dili to Darwin, as opposed to Brisbane (the port closest to East Timor, in the north of Australia) and, if we get them cleaned there in Dili, we'll have to drive them down to 23° 27' in the

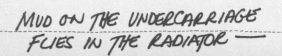

MUD ON THE UNDERCARRIAGE
FLIES IN THE RADIATOR —

south-east. This will be an expedition on its own, before we even start with Capricorn, but we don't have a choice. We've only got two more countries to go (Australia and Madagascar) and we just have to make it!

Oh, by the way, I phoned the South African Foreign Affairs Department yesterday. All hell has broken loose in Madagascar, with fighting between the factions loyal to Madagascar's two rival claimants to the presidency. We'll keep you posted.

Days 179–228: Round one to the Holgates

After all the tension, the money problems, the waiting and waiting – it's finally happened. We're notified that the *Chuma* and *Susi* have left Dili for Darwin. Flight Centre has come to the rescue: all our old tickets have to be reissued for the new dates, after all the delays. Barry Robinson-Butler, their Marketing Director, is a star!

At last we're off – racing to Durban airport to catch our flight for Perth. On the way we stop at the side of the highway to meet our friend Peter Wize. He comes running down the embankment from his crocodile farm and hands us a package. In it is a Nile crocodile skull; a gift to an old friend who owns a crocodile farm on the east coast of Queensland, close to the Tropic of Capricorn. It's hard to believe that with all the hassles we've been having we're now tempting fate with the AQIS boys again: this time with the skull of a Nile crocodile! But it does have the appropriate veterinary certificate.

There are tears at the airport as Ross says goodbye to Geraldine and little Tristan. It's a long flight from Durban to Australia, and it seems strange to be flying east, out over the Indian Ocean; our whole Capricorn journey has taken us in the opposite direction. Through the window of the aircraft I see Madagascar, our last Capricorn challenge, lying over to our left. Unfortunately, the island is now in a state of civil war. I recently spoke on the phone to Mr Bruno, the Madagascan Consul in Johannesburg. 'Steer clear of Toamasina (Tamatave),' he said. That's now the old President's stronghold, protected by his Algerian-trained palace guards. 'Contact us again when you've completed Australia,' Mr Bruno suggested. 'We hope that by that time there will be peace and your Capricorn Expedition, with its Scroll of Peace and Goodwill, will provide much-needed positive publicity for Madagascar.' A Cape Town journalist, an old African hand, phoned me for an article a few days before I spoke to Mr Bruno. His interpretation of the Madagascan situation was somewhat different: 'It's like bloody Afghanistan or Somalia,' he said. 'It will become full of warlords, and ungovernable. You wait and see. And the bloody Aussies!' he said 'You'll have fun and games there. When you do your visa application they'll ask if you've got a criminal record. "Didn't know you still needed one," you should put! I understand you're having all sorts of problems getting your Land Rovers in. I've never known a country so bloody full of rules and regulations. Good luck – you'll need it!'

His comments, and our experiences up to this point, have made me terribly nervous. Imagine if we get there and the Landies are turfed out again; our finances are already stretched to breaking point. Ahead of us lies the moment of truth. If we are turned back, what will we do? We're spending the family pension fund and, in any event, with six South African rands to the Australian dollar, we're really going to have to tighten our belts. All these thoughts and many more race through my mind as we fly through the night.

23°27'

Australia

It seems as if the new world 'Down Under' is not too welcoming. Not only have they evicted Chuma and Susi, they've also forbidden us entry into some of the vast Aboriginal lands, through which the Tropic of Capricorn passes. They tell us it's impossible to cross the Simpson Desert by vehicle along 23°27', but having come this far we'll just have to take it one day at a time.

Day 229: A reunion in Perth

As we stand in a long queue under the 'Foreign Passport Holders' sign, a black sniffer dog on a short leash shows interest in Ross. 'Must smell my dog at home – she's on heat,' says Ross sheepishly. 'No, mate, my dog's only interested in cocaine and heroin,' responds the dog's handler. Luckily the dog moves on to more interesting smells, and the Quarantine inspectors are so interested in the Nile crocodile items and the Zulu Capricorn calabash (both have veterinary certificates) that they overlook the case of Captain Morgan rum, our solace for when we cross Australia's great red deserts.

During the customs search the Expedition's medical kit shows up on the baggage-scanning machine's screen: antibiotics, painkillers, pills to stop diarrhoea, water purification tablets, malaria preventatives and cures, and the like. It turns out that we haven't declared the 'milk thistle, with dandelion' pills for my tired, malarial liver. For the Australian Quarantine inspectors this is just too much, and Mashozi gets hauled over the coals. Heaven forbid that we should shit one of these pills out.

Here to meet us at the airport, after we finally clear customs, is our friend Carmel Hall, whom we haven't seen for years. We're all thrilled at the reunion – we embrace warmly and load our expedition kit into her Jeep. In the 1970s Carmel and her husband Vic came to Zululand for a week and stayed a year. I will always remember their farewell party at Eshowe, and their old orange Australian Land Rover loaded to the hilt as they set off to cross Africa. Now they live in a beautiful home in Perth, furnished with African artefacts. Vic's made a fortune in the oil business and we spend the evening poring over maps and catching up on old times. Vic's got his own winery, so naturally we taste 'the goods'! Jetlagged and full of the noo, we fall into bed at midnight.

Day 230: Darwin at 'The Top End'

We leave Perth for Darwin in the early morning. The affairs of 11 September 2001 have led to much tighter security here at Perth International Airport. I am strip-searched and even have to take off my Zulu bangles, boots and belt

AUSTRALIA! DOWN UNDER.

WE FINALLY DIP THE CAPRICORN CALABASH ON THE FLOOR OF THE GREAT BARRIER REEF (FINALLY!)

BY BICYCLE ACROSS THE COASTAL PLAINS OF QUEENSLAND

FITZROY RIVER

23°27' ROCKHAMPTON BEEF CAPITAL

QUEENSLAND GEMFIELDS SAPPHIRE & RUBYVALE

BARKY AND THE TREE OF KNOWLEDGE

LONGREACH GATEWAY TO THE OUTBACK.

CARLO STN

DIAMANTINA CHANNEL – TOUGH! COUNTRY GOING-

THE DREADED SIMPSON LARGEST PARALLEL SAND RIDGE DESERT IN THE WORLD! RED DUST!

ALICE SPRINGS

EAST MACDONNELLS

WEST MACDONNELLS

HAASTS BLUFF AND OTHER ABORIGINAL LANDS!

GIBSON DESERT (ENDLESS!)

L. MAC DONNELL

L. DISAPPOINTMENT (BLOODY FLIES!)

23°27' JIGGALONG

CAPRICORN ROADHOUSE (NEVER AGAIN!)

NINGALO REEF

before being let through for the Darwin flight. We fly over the Little Sandy Desert and the Bungle Bungles (a sandstone massif that's eroded into hundreds of dome-shaped formations) – thousands upon thousands of square kilometres of sweet bugger all! This is the sort of terrain we will have to cross.

We arrive in Darwin (at Australia's 'top end') to find that, although it's mid-winter, this tropical city is still warm and slightly humid. It's the height of the holiday season and most of the accommodation is booked out. At last we find some digs at the Leprechaun Motel, around the back of which is a campsite full of Aussie youngsters, with old Holden station wagons, camper vans and tents, and 4x4s covered in jerry cans, winches, high-lift jacks, roo bars ('anti-kangaroo' bars, like bullbars) and dusty canvas bedrolls (known here as swags). Somehow it feels a bit like Africa and I can sense the same spirit of adventure. We get settled in and then head down to the docks. Our friendly taxi driver explains that Darwin folk drink more booze than any other Australians do. Sadly, the first Aborigines we see are staggering down the road: 'Useless bunch!' says our driver. 'They get pissed and walk out into the middle of the highway,' he tells us with a grin.

When we reach the docks we learn that *Chuma* and *Susi* have arrived, but are still in their containers. We race up-town to Customs and Immigration. They tell us we have to book our vehicles in at least 24 hours in advance for the quarantine test. We phone AQIS. 'Oh, you're the guys who've been dropping South American mud all over the place! You'll have to get your ship's broker to make an appointment with us.'

'Can't I do that now?' I ask. 'No, mate, there're no short cuts,' I'm told. And so we wait.

Kristin from Customs proves really helpful, but it all hinges on our appointment with AQIS. We go down to the docks and, finally, I find our two lonely Capricorn Land Rovers parked next to their containers. They're shining clean. All the kit has been thrown into the back and the keys are in the ignition. I open the door to inspect them and am firmly but politely chased out of the yard by the foreman. 'You don't want to be seen here mate, not until Customs and AQIS have inspected your vehicles. They're going into that shed over there. No worries, mate.'

Darwin, NT (Northern Territory) – it really stands for 'not today', 'not tomorrow', 'not in three months'! I am feeling tired and tense. What if they kick the 4x4s out of the country again? We simply don't have the financial resources to keep going. Finally, Kristin the Customs lady comes down to check us and the vehicles out. She's very pleasant, and it takes her only a few minutes to sign our vehicles into Australia. No worries, mate! She gives us a bright smile and her big, blue eyes look rather serious as they take us in. What she sees, I guess, is this forlorn little South African family: Kingsley, Gill and Ross. I wonder if she can tell how desperate we are to get going on our journey along Australia's Capricorn line. 'Are we free to go?' we ask anxiously. 'No,' she says. 'There's this AQIS report; your vehicles haven't been passed.'

My blood runs cold as she hands us the report from the Darwin authorities. They've found some dirt above the extra fuel tanks, around the winches and the plastic spotlight covers. 'Well, can't we just clean them ourselves?' I ask. Oh, no – this will have to be done by the professional shipping cleaners at the cleaning bay, then another appointment must be made with AQIS and another inspection will be done, after which they will have to go through all our personal gear. Rick, the cleaning man, is a true-blue Aussie, and he feels sorry for us. With the promise of a bottle of the Captain's best, he takes the vehicles off immediately for

NO MUKIN FURRIES MATE – THIS IS DARWIN!

cleaning. *Chuma*'s engine turns but it won't fire and it has to be taken away by a forklift. When we left them in South America they were running like a dream, but that was months ago. Twenty minutes later both Landies have been cleaned with a high-pressure hose. So easy. I wonder why it couldn't have been done this way right from the beginning in Brisbane. Now, AU$15 000 later, we're doing it all again. The cleaning done, we have to wait for the next AQIS inspection. By this time we're matey with all the guys at the docks and everybody is doing their best to help, but this is Darwin – a very laid-back city – and things take time.

MASHOZI

Day 231: Legal at last?

Back at the docks – today, we hope, is the day of the final inspection, and once again we're on the phone to Greg the shipping agent. By 10 am we still don't have an appointment. Then a fellow comes racing down in his ute with a message from Greg saying that there are a couple of AQIS guys on site. 'Go and chat to them – they might help you now,' he says.

The yard foreman points out a rather serious fellow in a khaki cap and the word 'Quarantine' embroidered onto his shirt. 'He'll sort you out,' he tells us. So off Ross and I go, into the lions' den. Stuart seems friendly enough but there's no doubt he means business. 'Go and lay out all your PEs and we'll come and inspect.' says Stuart. We presume 'PEs' means 'personal effects', and so we spread everything out for inspection.

LINDA

When Stuart comes over to have a look, Ross seizes the moment and asks if he minds speaking a bit for the camera. Ross explains to him that the whole quarantine thing has been a real drama, which is why we'd like to cover it in the documentary. Stuart, who's quite reserved, says he'll have to clear it with Canberra and he goes off to make the call. I try to do a hurried bit to camera, but am so tense that I'm absolutely useless. Stuart returns: 'Permission granted,' he says with a smile, so we mike him up for the moment of truth. From his pocket he takes out a yellow torch, and then he slides under the Land Rovers on a mechanic's dolly. Ross rolls camera as Stuart checks the vehicles, probing every bit by hand. From under the bonnet he removes the air-filter elements. 'These must be confiscated,' he comments, as he checks the thin sleeves of the element looking for dust and seeds. To our immense relief, both the Land Rovers are passed, but we still have to get our Expedition kit approved.

The vehicles are in a bit of a mess now: the carpets and door rubbers were ripped out in East Timor, the radiators were removed and, unfortunately, some of the kit has been stolen – good stuff, like our Captain Morgan fleece jackets for the cold desert nights. The old braai grid, dented camp kettle, three-legged cast-iron pot, old green canvas East African camp chairs and the *ugqoko* (Zulu meat platter) survived the journey – so at least the main African elements of our journey are still there! Now comes the PEs check. Stuart goes over each piece with a fine-tooth comb; even the seams of the tents are inspected. Some of our stuff goes into the bin and another cleaning of the PEs is required by Rick, one of the dockhands, who does it there and then. How much easier it is when things are done face to face.

Then, suddenly, it's all over – we're told that we have finally succeeded in getting our vehicles and Capricorn Expedition kit passed by the AQIS. We are free to go! Ross asks Stuart to do a final piece on camera. 'What should I say?' asks

DURBAN FALKIRK
THE OLD CAST IRON POT

Stuart shyly, to which Ross replies: 'How about a formal apology for having mucked us around so much?' We all laugh and shake hands – no worries, mate. It's been three months since the vehicles arrived in Brisbane; now, at long last, all our equipment is legally in Australia.

We still can't get *Chuma* to start, so we tow it to the Land Rover dealership. It seems *Chuma* needs a new fuel pump, but, this being the Northern Territory, which is relatively isolated, a replacement pump has to come from down south (from Sydney, I presume). 'Nothing till Monday,' they tell us, 'and that's if you're lucky. Have a good weekend, mate.'

Day 231–232: Stuck up north

It's Monday morning and there's bad news waiting for us. Turns out the fuel pump's okay – the real problem is *Chuma*'s electronics: they're wet and corroded. It looks as if they half submerged them in the cleaning process in East Timor. 'Not sure if we can get the necessary parts in Australia,' the mechanic says, adding that he, 'can't ring Sydney now – time difference, mate; they're closed. You should be okay by the end of the week. No worries, mate.' And so the frustration grows.

After a day at the garage, we spend the evening on a pub-crawl, along with hundreds of backpackers from the Old Vic hotel, sunburnt and trendy, and enjoying the Outback. Darwin has a vibrant nightlife – we go to Shannigan's Irish Pub, then on to Kitty O'Shea's, The Blue Heeler Bar and (can you believe it?) the Rorke's Drift Bar, complete with a Zulu shield in a glass case! I take a photograph for Zululand friend Dave Rattray, the famous Anglo-Zulu War historian who lives near the actual Rorke's Drift. Finally, we settle down at the Uno Restaurant for pasta. Some oilmen at the next table have ordered massive rump steaks and the best wines. They're obviously on a different budget from us poor Capricornians!

Day 234: Barramundi, box jellyfish, spiders, snakes and koalas!

There's a big military presence here in Darwin, because of the situation in East Timor, and jets constantly fly overhead. Memories of 1942, when a ferocious Japanese air raid virtually wiped out Darwin, still haunt the city. American naval vessels dock here from time to time, creating so much business that one of the local brothels reportedly closed up shop – the girls simply couldn't cope! Up the road from the Leprechaun is a drive-in bottlestore, the first we've ever seen. The owner recognises us from a recent National Geographic programme and is very chatty. A hullabaloo and wolf whistles are coming from the pub next door. 'What's going on?' we ask. 'Nothing much, mate. There's just a young Sheila taking her kit off.' The sign outside the pub reads: 'Winnerli Hotel – Strip and Prawns'!

Some of the locals come over to the Leprechaun Motel, and we all sit outside in the heat for a beery chat. We bring out a precious bottle of Captain Morgan rum and are soon entertained with rough, raw Aussie humour. Robbo, with singlet and tattoos, is flying back to Queensland tomorrow; he's been in Darwin for three years. 'Spoke to my mum on the blower this morning. She said it's safe to come home now; the coppers have stopped knocking on the door.' Tommo, who's living with a Chinese girl called Jenny, has just moved to Darwin: 'I used to be a concierge in a five-star hotel down south. Now I do nights driving limos – leaves me free to go fishing. Yeah, mate, mostly barramundi and barras... bloody good eating, and we've got the best mud crabs in the world.'

N.T. STANDS FOR NORTHERN TERRITORY OR NOT TODAY, NOT TOMORROW OR NEVER..!

Then the conversation turns to drinking and driving. 'Wrecks everywhere,' I'm told. 'Used to be you never went anywhere without a slab of beer – now three pints and you're dead meat, mate. Every coppo's got a breathy. But NT is more relaxed than anywhere else is: outside the city limits you can go as fast as you bloody well like. Just don't drive at night, mate, or even in the early morning or late afternoon – bad time for hitting roos.'

'And remember,' says Robbo, 'a big red king roo's bigger than *you*, Kingsley! Hit him and you're history. Some bloody Germans hit one – dented their bushbar right into the radiator. And there it was, lying dead, or so they thought. They propped it up and dressed it in a jacket, hat and sunnies; hung a spare camera round its neck. Then they posed for pictures next to the roo. Can you believe it – the thing suddenly leapt up, bounced over the fence and hopped off into the bush with all their stuff, and in the jacket pocket was their passports. The coppers in Alice Springs just laughed and only believed them when they developed their photos. True story, mate!'

The stories get worse as the night wears on: box jellyfish, spiders and snakes all have their turn. 'And whatever you do, mate,' says Tommo, 'don't try to eat a koala bear: one bite and you're dead.' Tommo, with his shaved head and pale skin, doesn't look the Outback type, but nevertheless we all nod in drunken agreement.

Day 235: In Darwin you wait, mate!

Still we wait for parts from down south. By this time the managers of the Leprechaun Motel feel so sorry for us that they let us stay for free. Glennis Kerr, the workshop forewoman, is really sweet and doing her best. 'Please understand, this is Darwin,' she keeps telling us. And so we wait, wandering around to pass the time. It's quite refreshing to see how patriotic most Australians are: signs and labels read 'Real Australian', 'Made in Australia with Australian ingredients', and 'Buy Australian'.

Sport is also a big part of Australian life. Aussies are great gamblers and things are hotting up for the Darwin Cup horse race, which takes place this weekend. A lot of people come up to Darwin for the event and the superb winter weather. I've never seen so many 4x4s, all with radio aerials, extra spare tyres, canvas swags and jerry cans. It's an invasion of the Northern Territory, and Aussie hats and sunnies are all you can see behind the tinted windows of their fully rigged vehicles. A number of them are travelling pensioners, called 'grey nomads', who spend years touring their own country. They're linked to their mates by radio and meet up with them at their favourite campsites. There're some wonderful old characters, some in giant camper vans, others pulling caravans, and one less fortunate fellow simply living out of the back of his ute – his only belongings are a swag, a billy, a few plates and a knife, fork and spoon, which he just licks clean after use.

Day 236: And wait...

The Land Rover parts still haven't arrived, so we'll be here for another day at least. I suppose we just have to remember that Sydney is over 4 000 kilometres away, but sometimes I can't help wondering if we'll ever reach Australia's Capricorn line. We wander down to the docks, where yachts cruise past on the evening breeze and a full moon rises over the Arafura Sea. We eat barramundi and have a few drinks to the sounds of a two-man band

23°27'

playing old Beatles numbers. It's all so civilised, the quayside full of English tourists eating their fish and chips, but this is not what we've come to Australia for.

Day 237: And wait...

Still we wait.... Now they've lost all the freight to Darwin! We're getting desperate, as tomorrow (Friday) is a public holiday, which means we could be stuck here for the long weekend. To kill time we go to a local museum. In a darkened cubicle we put on headphones and listen to the roaring of the wind, the sigh of the rain and the scraping of thousands of sheets of corrugated iron. It was on Christmas Day 1974 that Cyclone Tracey ripped through Darwin, causing mass destruction and the largest evacuation of people by air in Australia's history.

Midday, and it's back to the Land Rover garage and Glennis Kerr. The electronics box (to replace the old one that was 'drowned' in East Timor) has arrived – they've found the freight after all. But what good is the new ECU (electronic control unit) box when the mechanic doesn't know how to fit it? He stares worriedly at the computer he's plugged into *Chuma*. We're desperate to get the vehicle fixed, so we call Umhlanga Land Rover on the satellite phone and the mechanic in South Africa talks him through the computer procedures. Success at last – *Chuma* starts with a roar, and at last we have an expedition!

Days 238–241: Road trains and roos and Rockhampton

The drone of Land Rover engines is music to our ears. It feels great to be moving again as we make the long journey from Darwin to Rockhampton. Alongside the road lie hundreds of dead kangaroos and scores of cattle – the 50-metre-long road trains seem to stop for nothing. Taking a break at the roadside, we meet Greg, a road train driver. 'Once you're barrelling along, mate, it takes 200 metres to stop. Cattle, roos and goats – we just go straight through them. Bullbar takes out everything,' he says. 'We travel at about 90 kilometres per hour and some days we cover 1 000 kilometres. There are some road trains that have travelled 30 million kilometres in their time. Great life – only see the missus once a week! The new railway line from Alice to Darwin? Ha! They'll never compete with us,' he asserts.

We find driving difficult once it gets dark. Our spotlights may be blazing, but our eyes are glazing over. Still, we press on – we want to reach the Capricorn line as soon as we can. Mashozi sits on the edge of her seat on full

LINDA SPARROW – A TOUGH LITTLE AUSSIE SHEILA! WE FIRST MET IN EAST AFRICA – SEARCHING FOR GORILLAS IN THE CONGO – YEARS LATER SHE JOINED US ON A MOUTH TO SOURCE ZAMBEZI RIVER JOURNEY – WHEN SHE HEARD WE WERE COMING TO AUSTRALIA – WELL! THAT WAS THAT AND SHE SIGNED ON IMMEDIATELY – IT'LL BE GOOD TO HAVE A TRUE BLUE AUSSIE ON BOARD – SHE CAN TRANSLATE!! – JOKES ASIDE IT WILL BE GOOD FOR MASHOZI TO HAVE FEMALE COMPANY – A WELCOME CHANGE FROM US BLOKES!

roo and cattle alert. We sleep rough on the roadside in our new canvas swags, with the road trains roaring past us. Then we're up early and foot flat on the accelerator again. The sheer scale of the country is overwhelming – most of it flat and monotonous.

Finally, after three nights and four days, our long journey brings us to the Tropic of Capricorn and Rockhampton, beef capital of Australia. At O'Dowd's Irish Pub we meet Linda Sparrow, an old friend from previous expeditions. With her is Luke Cormack, the Capricorn Expedition cameraman, who has flown from London to meet us. The mood in the pub is tense: over 600 local people have been laid off with the recent closing of the meat works, due to labour disputes. A fight breaks out, and soon there are fists flying all over the pub. A drover (Australian cowboy), wearing a battered cowboy hat, just rolls another cigarette – not even looking up from his Bundy rum and coke. It's like a scene out of an old Western. The pub closes at 9 pm and we move upstairs, where we're staying, to sit outside our rooms on the wide, balustraded verandah overlooking the street. There is much laughter and excitement, as we catch up with Linda and Luke and make expedition plans. Tomorrow we fill the Capricorn calabash!

Day 242: On the sea bed of the Great Barrier Reef

Ross and I, dressed in scuba gear, my beard waving about like an out-of-control sea anemone, lie on the ocean floor where the Tropic of Capricorn passes through Australia's Great Barrier Reef. We suck in air and blow out bubbles as the Capricorn Expedition calabash fills with sea-water. Against a backdrop of ancient coral and colourful fish, we shake hands, Zulu style. Then father and son fin slowly to the surface. The Australian leg of our Capricorn journey around the world has begun! Mashozi, Linda and Luke, in *Chuma* and *Susi*, meet us on the beach on 23° 27'. It's a beautiful day and we make camp above the highwater mark on a stretch of deserted beach that runs south, down to the mouth of the Fitzroy River.

Day 243: On two wheels to the Fitzroy

From the Great Barrier Reef to Longreach – that's our challenge over the next two days and the only way to do it is by bicycle. With all the hassles we've had it feels as if we've already completed an entire expedition. But, here we are, only at the beginning. When I think of the journey ahead my mind boggles: over 4 000 kilometres to go, across some of the toughest country in the world!

Thumbs up from the Capricorn section of the Great Barrier Reef.

CORAL SEA
CAPRICORN CHANNEL
BY BICYCLE ◁□▽ FITZROY
FITZROY RIVER VALE CATTLE STATION
ROCKHAMPTON
AUSTRALIA'S BEEF CAPITAL
CAPRICORN MONUMENT
CAPRICORN HIGHWAY WEST TO LONGREACH
QUEENSLAND GEMFIELDS
23°27' LONGREACH GATEWAY TO THE OUTBACK
DIAMANTINA GATES NATIONAL PARK
CARLO CATTLE STATION QUEENSLAND
BOUNDARY NORTHERN TERRITORY
SIMPSON DESERT LARGEST PARALLEL SAND-RIDGE DESERT IN THE WORLD – BLOODY NIGHTMARE!
EAST MACDONNELLS
ALICE SPRINGS FOR R&R

We learn that the large cattle station called Fitzroy Vale, some 50 000 acres along the Tropic of Capricorn between the sea and the Fitzroy River, belongs to a Greek shipping magnate. Fortunately, Frank, the manager, saw us on local TV last night and is only too happy to guide us down to the beach and 23° 27'. He looks like a storybook Australian: Stockman's hat, collared shirt, denim jeans, boots and a Land Cruiser 4x4 ute with a dog in the back. 'Great cattle country,' says Frank, 'but wet as hell in the rainy season. In 1991 I crossed from my house here to the Fitzroy River by boat, over the tops of the fences. We're in a bad drought, but still this place has got grass and a month ago we had some fluke rain.'

From a cliff we view the lands he manages and the coral sea beyond, dotted with Curtis Island, Capricorn Point, Great Keppel and a little island that Franks calls 'The Nipple' because of its distinctive shape. It'll be impossible to follow Capricorn from the beach to the Fitzroy by Land Rover – too much swampland and thick scrub, plus a rocky wooded hill and a number of fences. So, it's Ross and me on the mountain bikes, with an arrangement to meet Mashozi, Linda and Luke at Frank's homestead.

It's a tough ride and we're unfit after all the hanging around in Darwin. We push though thick mud, stinking swamps and heavy bush, and over thousands of cattle divets set in the hardened grey mud, which shake rider and bicycle to pieces. The joy of the ride, though, is seeing kangaroos and wallabies in the wild, and the birdlife is plentiful. By the time the sun sets red behind the Great Dividing Range, we're lifting our bikes over the final cattle fence. We see Frank outside his house – he cracks his whip and swears at the dogs. We meet Frank's son, who was laid off from the meat packing plant and now uses his dogs to hunt down wild pigs. He exports the meat and says he can make up to AU$700 a night. Good money, but one of his dogs was ripped open in the hunt last night and might not survive. Then we see *Chuma* and *Susi*'s lights coming up the road – Mashozi, Linda and Luke were worried about us. It's taken us most of the day to do our first 13 kilometres, following the GPS to stick to Capricorn, and by now the 'Capricorn 23° 27' that I wrote in the sand on the beach when we set off will have been washed away by the hightide. Tomorrow we've got the ride from Frank's house to the Fitzroy River. But how to cross the Fitzroy? We'll worry about that in the morning.

Day 244: Living with crocodiles

Down in the mangroves on the Fitzroy flats lives croc farmer John Lever with his giant saltwater crocodiles known here as 'salties'. They're larger than our Nile crocodiles. He's really chuffed with the Nile crocodile skull we've brought him from South Africa. 'Be warned!' he says. 'There're still some massive salties that live in the Fitzroy.'

Although we don't have to cover a great distance, the bicycle journey from Frank's place becomes an uncomfortable challenge. Thousands of hard, dry cattle divets, as well as mounds and cracks in the clay that can break a leg, make it almost impossible to ride over the terrain, and most of the time Ross and I walk. There're also the countless fences, over which we have to lift the bicycles; then we climb through and move on again. Earlier this morning Frank signed the Capricorn Scroll on the steps of the old homestead, built in the late 1800s. His father was born in the house and now Frank manages the place for Gregory Hadjielefthesiadis, who, when he visits a few times a year, flies the flags of his native Greece, his cattle company and Australia. On arrival, and again when he leaves, he rings the old ship's bell that stands in the garden overlooking this vast tract of land we are now crossing.

We wade through a deep, cold pool – slimy at the bottom. My skin tingles and the hairs on the back of my neck rise – I hope there're no salties! We arrive at the Fitzroy River dead on sunset: a massive red-orange orb sets over the water; we've survived the coastal plains of Capricorn. Here we meet up with the rest of the team again, and we all pile into the Landies to head through the dust and the cattle to Rockhampton.

Day 245: Rockhampton – Australia's beef capital

Good natured Matthew Williams heads up Capricorn Tourism (in fact, the area is known as the Capricorn Coast). We meet at the Capricorn Monument outside his offices – he's invited the local press and TV, and he gives us contacts that will assist us down the Capricorn Highway that heads west out of Rockhampton to Longreach: 'Gateway to the Outback'. Our first lesson, of course, is to learn to speak 'Stralian'. In the Outback, words are abbreviated and drawled through a closed mouth, so as to keep the flies out. Rockhampton is 'Rocky', a smoke break is a 'smoko', and the town of Barcaldine along the Capricorn line is simply called 'Barky'. Why, even our expedition member Linda Sparrow's name is shortened to 'Spaz'.

Terry O'Hannigan, an ex-cattle rancher, has restored the Old Great Western Hotel in Rockhampton, and pictures of stockmen and cattle hang from the walls. But what makes it really unusual is that you walk through the pub into a real live bullring. Terry explains: 'This is the stockman's home from home. When they come into Rocky, this is where they head for to ride bulls, meet women and drink their wages away. They roll out their swags on the verandah upstairs or bunk down in the old hotel rooms – no charge for that; we don't want them driving their utes drunk. There's one fella that comes in here every few months – doesn't touch a drop in the Outback, but when he walks through these doors he's already pissed on adrenaline, from all the excitement of coming to the bright lights. Last time he was here he took all his clothes off and swung from the chandelier. Bloody thing ripped out of the ceiling and he landed on his back, in the middle of a table full of women diners from Brisbane. They loved it and bought him supper!'

23°27'

Day 246: Sapphires, rubies and emeralds

We're moving west again, with our bicycles and swags tied to the roofrack. Shame about the dead roos on the roadside. We travel past thousands of gum trees and the Great Divide mountain range. Our destination is the Queensland gem fields of Sapphire, Rubyvale and Emerald.

In Rubyvale we meet Peter Brown, who arrived here penniless in the early seventies with a VW Beetle, tent and a dog called Dingo. It's been a tough life, he tells us, 'I dug most of the sapphires the hard way, with a pick, jackhammer, wheelbarrow and windlass. It kept me fit and I won the first wheelbarrow race from Anakie to Rubyvale – easiest AU$1 000 I ever made. It was like the Wild West in the old days: we lived on the edge and when you dug something out you could stick it into your mouth to clean off the dirt, hold it up to the sun to admire it and go down the street and sell it to any one of the Thai buyers for cash. They'd come from Bangkok, suitcases bulging with dollars. But, let me tell you, there were times I was "off stone" (out of luck) and struggled for a loaf of bread.'

While we are sitting around a log fire Peter tells me, with a wild glint in his eyes, the story of 'the big one': 'Size of a bloody goose egg it was – found by a kid. His stepfather gave him a pushbike for it, then hocked the gem to the Anakie pub for booze. Years later it sold for a million bucks in New York! Yeah, the old Anakie pub was quite a place: stockmen with their hats, miners with their sapphires. They talked cattle, dirt fortunes were made and the place never closed.' But not everybody has made it as 'good' as Peter, and the area is littered with old, rust-red Bedford trucks and dilapidated mining machinery. Some failed, others drifted off to the gold, diamond and opal mines, but some 600 are still certified hand-miners.

Peter Brown - the Sapphire miner

Day 247: West to Barky

Outside Sapphire, and following the GPS, we come across an old rusty ute, a derelict caravan, piles of litter, barking dogs and a herd of white goats. As we draw close all hell breaks loose. A strange apparition comes running towards us, one hand raised, and with a maniacal scream she shouts, 'F... off! You're scaring my bloody goats!' We stop the Landies and I do the normal, 'We're from Africa travelling the world along Capricorn' bit, and fortunately she calms down. She's about 50 years old and dressed as a man – in men's trousers, an old sweater and men's shoes – her long, thick hair is tucked under her tattered cap and bits of rags are tied around her hands. Bless her, but she stinks to high heaven of sweat and urine. We all quickly move upwind. Her name is Col and she lives alone with her herd of milk goats. Imagine living alone in the dry scrub country, with its searing summer temperatures and cold winter nights. 'Found a few sapphires in my life,' she says with a laugh, 'but never a really big one. I leave that to the others, and now I have my goats.' Mashozi gives her a Zulu beaded bangle, which she pulls

Here in Australia's beef capital they have to bolt on the bull's "nuts" - the university students nick them as mementos!

WE TRY AND LEARN A BIT OF `STRALIAN',
AT TIMES IT'S LIKE A FOREIGN LANGUAGE!

ARSIE/TINARSE – VERY LUCKY

ARVO – AFTERNOON

BANANABENDERS – QUEENSLANDERS

BANJO – A SHOULDER OF MUTTON, A SHOVEL OR FRYING PAN

BILLABONG – A WATERHOLE IN A RIVERBED OR CREEK

BILLY – A ROUND METAL CONTAINER WITH A LID & WIRE HANDLE

BLACK STUMP – THE BACK-OF-BEYOND

BLIND FREDDY – A VERY UNPERCEPTIVE PERSON

BLUE – AN ARGUMENT OR FIGHT, ALSO A NAME FOR REDHEADS

BOTTLE'O – OR PUB IN THE SCRUB! A DRIVE-IN BOTTLE STORE

BUSHWHACKER – OUTBACK RESIDENTS (SLIGHTLY DEROGATORY)

COCKY – A FARM BOSS OR FARM OWNER

CLEANSKIN – THE NAME GIVEN TO UNBRANDED CATTLE

DAMPER – UNLEAVENED BUSH BREAD

DUNNY – AN OUTSIDE TOILET

SHEILA – A YOUNG GIRL OR WOMAN

STOCKMAN OR DROVER – AN AUSSIE COWBOY

SWAG – A TYPICAL AUSSIE CANVAS BEDROLL

SWAGMAN – A TRAMP OR BUSH WANDERER – WHO CARRIES HIS SWAG OR 'BLUEY' ON HIS BACK –

over her wrist. She slowly writes in the Capricorn Scroll, struggling to form the words and mouthing them as she does so. As we move off she waves – a tiny, lonely figure in the dust. Was she born crazy, I wonder, or did some misfortune in her tough life make her this way? But, then again, who's crazy: old Col the sapphire-hunting goat herder or this mad bunch of Capricornians attempting to circumnavigate the world along an imaginary line?

Still following the GPS through old mine dumps and scrub, we come across the first bottle-o or 'pub in the scrub', as the locals call it. Yes, a drive-in bottlestore, right on the Tropic of Capricorn – only Down Under! We buy a 'slab of VB stubbies' (a pack of VB dumpies; VB's a popular brand of beer) – no worries, mate! The next town along the line is Barcaldine

23°27'

(pronounced 'bar-called-in'), or just Barky. It's dark by the time we arrive and it's been the normal 'eyes out on stalks' routine – scanning the road for roos, emus and cattle. It's too late to camp, so we book into the Shakespeare Hotel. These old Outback hotels with their giant rooms, wide verandahs, corrugated iron roofs, pokies (game machines), sticks (pool) and great pub meals are excellent value. A 'drover's special' has chops, steak, sausages, bacon, six fried eggs and half a loaf of bread, served with Bundy rum or beer. For a couple of dollars you can place the palm of your hand on a machine that registers how sexy you are. Mashozi get an eight, but Luke is pissed off to find he only scores one! 'What the f...,' says the bargirl. 'There're no available men here. Most of the good-looking drovers and shearers – well, they're already married. What about you, sweetness?' She says looking across at either Ross or Luke; I can't tell which. Her name is Roy and she tells us how she shoots roos and shears sheep; they breed them tough in the Outback.

Later, when we get to bed, I have troubled sleep – full of nightmares from too much meat and the deafening roar of cattle- and sheep-filled road trains driving down the main road past the hotel. Plus, the old bedsprings in the huge bed have obviously been punished over the years.

Day 248: Sorry, cocky!

We're up early, and Roy the sheep-shearing Sheila we met last night offers to take us out to a cocky's (farmer's) farm, where a gang of her mates are shearing sheep. Kangaroos hop across the vast Mitchel Plains here, hundreds of them. The entire area is settling in for a long drought and we come across hundreds of cattle on the move. This is common practice in Australia when things get dry: drovers on horseback, with a back-up vehicle and a cook, take to the old stock routes, moving the massive herds of cattle in search of grazing. The fortunate sold their cattle for excellent prices before the drought. At the moment up to 25 000 head of cattle per week are being trucked out from Longreach to the meat markets on the coast.

At the sheep station a line of men, electric sheep-shearing clippers in hand, work tirelessly, clipping the fleeces from giant Merino sheep. Women work at the sorting table, and others work the wool press – turning the fleeces into bales for export. Australia is the largest exporter of wool in the world. An enthusiastic, yapping sheep dog runs along behind the sheep, urging them forward into the pens. Outside, some of the sheep are being de-tailed, castrated and de-wormed by the cocky, a rather aggressive freckle-faced man in an Aussie hat, who turns round to us and says, 'Why don't you f... off, you bloody South Africans, I've got enough bloody problems today without you buggers being here!' I apologise for not wanting to be de-tailed or castrated. He's obviously having a bad day, and I presume Roy didn't make the proper arrangements for us to be here. During a smoko I chat to the shearers: they earn a good living and enjoy their work, but one young fellow says, 'I hope my kids will be able to have an easier life.'

We return to Barky and say goodbye to Roy. Mashozi leaves a note for the angry cocky explaining that we meant no harm. 'Ours is a peace and goodwill journey,' she writes, 'so please don't take Roy to task – sorry, cocky!'

Day 249: Longreach - 'Gateway to the Outback'

Chuma and Susi growl along merrily through the village of Ilfracombe and on to Longreach, home to the legendary Stockman's Hall of Fame – part-funded from the sale of cattle in what was Australia's last great cattle drive.

Like most places in Queensland, Longreach makes us truly welcome, and ABC radio, who first picked up our story in Rockhampton, continues to broadcast details of our Capricorn adventure. I readily agree to a live interview in Longreach, seeing it as an excellent opportunity to make cattle station owners along Capricorn aware of our journey – apart from which, the radio presenter is a really pretty, bubbly character (you can ask young Luke – I think he would tell you that beautiful girls are something of a rarity in the Outback). And so I tell a few Capricorn yarns over the air, including that of our journey down the Jompa Jozz trail in Mozambique and how, at the time of our crossing, an unfortunate immigrant was found clinging to the branches of a tree, crazy with fear – below him the remains of his four companions, who were eaten by a pride of lions. Some time later, while we are still in Longreach, a yellow V8 Holden ute roars to a halt alongside us. 'How ya goin', mate?' asks the occupant. 'You must be the blokes travelling the Tropic of Capricorn – heard ya on the radio. Pity the lion didn't get the black fella up the tree.' Linda is infuriated. 'Racist bastard,' she mutters.

Day 250: You'll never make it, mate!

The Aussies love a great adventure, and wherever we stop they gather round to ask questions. There's also a lot of pub talk: 'Watch out for the big brown snake. It's as thick as your arm!' someone warns us. 'You'll never make it through the Simpson Desert. The dunes run north to south and you're going from east to west against the dunes.' 'You'll die out there and the crows will peck out your eyes,' says one alarmist soul. 'Check your boots each morning, mate. You never know what's crawled into them during the night,' is one of the more sensible comments.

From Longreach we travel west, across Queensland, through the Diamantina Channel country – thousands of dry river courses run like veins and arteries across Capricorn here. It would be impassable during a flood and even in the dry it's extremely hard work for *Chuma* and *Susi*. Then it's on to Carlo, the last Capricorn cattle station in western Queensland, which is owned by brothers Dallas and Gary Hill. We meet them at their homestead after they've just come in from mustering cattle using helicopters, 4x4s and motorbikes. They're down on supplies at the moment, so we cook up a stew and share our Captain Morgan with them. They recently bought the 500 000-acre ranch we're on for just over a dollar an acre. We learn that the price per acre generally includes everything on the land as well (cattle, buildings, etc.). The living here is rough: the 'house' consists of two mobile homes connected with corrugated iron. Out back is a shed and a dunny (an outhouse). They bought this station with an estimated 3 000 head of cattle on it, but now, after the muster, they find they've actually got an additional 1 100 'cleanskins' – unbranded wild cattle, which have probably never been seen by a human being before. How's that for a bargain?

23°27'

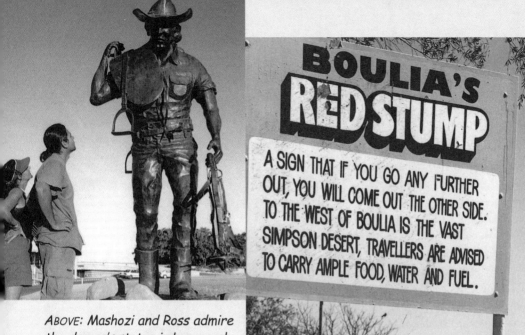

BOULIA'S RED STUMP

A SIGN THAT IF YOU GO ANY FURTHER OUT, YOU WILL COME OUT THE OTHER SIDE. TO THE WEST OF BOULIA IS THE VAST SIMPSON DESERT, TRAVELLERS ARE ADVISED TO CARRY AMPLE FOOD, WATER AND FUEL.

ABOVE: Mashozi and Ross admire the drover's statue in Longreach. RIGHT: We re-supply at Boulia, where there is this sign as a warning to travellers. We have to do the Simpson along a GPS line way to the south.

As with so many cattle station owners, Dallas and Gary are concerned at what is happening to cattle ranchers in Zimbabwe. Obviously the news has been full of President Mugabe's land grab. We swap yarns and have a great evening, during which Damian, the station's drover, appears to be falling in love with Linda! As usual we all sleep under the stars in our swags. Not even in Africa are there such starlit skies – it looks as if you could just reach up and touch them, so it's no wonder that most Aussie bush poets mention the stars. What we miss, though, is the distant roar of a lion or the cackle of a hyaena. There's so little wildlife in this great expanse, and after Africa it feels strange and empty.

Day 251: **If you don't live on the edge you're taking up too much room**

The Outback Aussies love their one-liners. When Ross is fixing a puncture, Drover Damian, dressed in jeans, collared shirt, Aussie boots, wide-brimmed hat and sunnies, notices the bank of spotlights that run in a line above the Landies' windscreens. He takes a drag of his hand-rolled smoke and mumbles, 'Afraid of the dark then, mate?' Ross laughs. Gary writes these words in our Expedition Scroll of Peace and Goodwill: 'If you don't live on the edge you're taking up too much room. Good luck for the Simpson!' The Aussies call journeying into the unexplored, 'To travel beyond the black stump,' as the old colonial surveyors used black stumps as markers.

Before we plunge into the Simpson Desert we make sure we have the correct emergency numbers, including those of the Royal Flying Doctor Service. Dallas draws us a mud map (an Aussie term for drawing a map in the ground) to the edge of the Simpson, and then, finally, we're off again – travelling 'beyond the black stump'. The Land Rovers need to be as light as possible – we've learnt that from the Namib – so we've rationed ourselves to two litres of water per person per day (with some extra for emergencies). Our main and reserve diesel tanks we've had to fill to the brim, and we each have an extra 175 litres in jerry cans, but food supplies have also been kept to a minimum. We also have extra tyres, tubes, puncture repair kits, a hand pump, high-lift jacks, sand ladders, a spade and, yes, a few bottles of Captain Morgan rum for those cold desert nights. We're all really nervous about crossing this great desert, and we've certainly been warned about it – should something go badly wrong out there in the middle of the Simpson it could well mean the end for us. There are no air strips there, so it would be difficult for the Flying Doctor Service to reach us, and should we break down and lose satellite communications – well, I guess we would last as long as our water and supplies.

I make the decision to dedicate our crossing of the Simpson Desert to Dr Cecil Madigan, who, with a party of nine men and nineteen camels, first crossed what was then loosely known as the Arunta Desert, in 1939. But that was further south and to our knowledge no vehicle has ever crossed the world's largest parallel sand-ridge desert along the Tropic of Capricorn. It was Madigan who later renamed it the Simpson Desert, after Mr AA Simpson, an Adelaide indus-trialist who sponsored his expedition – and that's how one of the greatest deserts in the world came to be named after a manufacturer of washing machines!

Our 1:250 000 survey maps, sponsored by Geoscience Australia, are on hand, Ross has the GPS attached to the *Susi*'s dashboard and, for emergencies, we have our African Satellite Corporation sat-phone. To cope with the soft sand dunes we drop our tyre pressure to one bar. The feeling of extreme remoteness here reminds me of our Capricorn crossing of the Namib and Atacama deserts. Once again we are on our own without another human being anywhere around.

We roll out our swags and make a fire at the edge of the Simpson. We discover that the old, dry, gidgee branches make excellent firewood. Mashozi knocks up a stew, the sparks from the fire leap into the night sky and there's an occasional lonely cry from a dingo. I play 'Waltzing Matilda', which I've just taught myself, on the harmonica, we all drink some renoster coffee and then, warmly dressed, we creep into our swags for our first night in the Simpson.

Day 252: Red dust and spinifex

Prior to setting off in 1939, Cecil Madigan wrote these words: 'I am convinced that there is still one patch of Australia where the white man's foot has never trodden and that is the sand-ridge desert in the south-eastern corner of the Northern Territory. The sand ridges make the use of motor transport impossible, while the lack of feed and water has prevented penetration by pack horse or even camel.' And here we are, trying our luck.

The desert night was freezing cold. We start the day with filling our waterbottles and siphoning some diesel from the jerry cans on the roof into the main tanks. We check the maps and the GPS points – then we're off into the great unknown. By midday we reach the Northern Territory boundary, close to the point where the famous Australian explorer John McDougall Stuart was turned back by the vast expanse of the Simpson. Not before he'd written these words, though: 'It is remarkable that these sand ridges extend in parallel into the very heart of the interior, as if they absolutely were never to terminate!' Another adven-turer named Bryce Russell boasted that he could cross the Simpson alone. He left from Oodnadatta in the winter of 1937 and hasn't been heard of since.

23°27'

For us it's like being at sea, as we charge into the oncoming swell of hundreds and hundreds of sand dunes. With a black pen Gill marks off each one we get over, on the Land Rover's sunvisor. Some dunes we make first time; others defeat us, and with engines roaring we charge them again, bouncing over giant tussocks of prickly spinifex grass, the spinning wheels throwing up sheets of red dust. It is absolute murder for man and machine (and the Sheilas don't much like it either!). When we stop for the night we have to wash our eyes out with an eye bath. Then comes the bitterly cold wind again, and the tyre mending around the fire.

Days 253–260: Ridges and spinifex

Many of the Queensland Aussies told us that what would make our journey impossible was getting the Land Rovers over all the sand ridges, but as it turns out our main problem is actually the giant tussocks of spinifex, or porcupine grass, that grow on and in between the dunes. Some of these spinifex mounds are over two metres in diameter and are laden with wind-blown red sand, which has been caught up in the weave of spiky grass. Sometimes it's impossible to find a clear route through all the spinifex mounds, so we simply have to bounce over them. This causes the vehicles to lose their momentum, which, as we attempt to race up the dunes, is absolute hell. The porcupine quill-like spikes of the spinifex grass dig into our legs and hands, causing septic sores. This happens while we are walking around camp or digging out and winching the vehicles – you can't avoid it; it's everywhere.

The days, which have quickly become painfully repetitive, start to run into one another, as we push and winch our way through the desert. To cope with the dunes we are forced to keep our tyres at very low pressures and punctures become a real problem – we've had sixteen already. We have to be very careful to avoid the small, spiky hardwood bushes that go through the tyres like a hot knife through butter. Today we only make 28 kilometres along 23° 27', and it's taken us ten hours. The wind howls and there's red dust everywhere. I'm glad my forefather landed in Africa and not Down Under.

Day 261: Flies and spinifex

Another bitterly cold night, but at least it helps us to save on drinking water. If it were mid-summer this journey would be impossible. Our lives seem to consist of a uniform monotony of spinifex and sand ridges. Between each sand ridge is a valley that stretches for a kilometre or two; then we have to tackle yet another ridge. The vehicles lurch from side to side as we bounce

THE SIMPSON – LARGEST PARALLEL SAND RIDGED DESERT IN THE WORLD.

over the spinifex mounds. It's murder on their suspension and there's always the danger of one of the Landies rolling, especially when we're driving them sideways up a dune. The red dust gets in everywhere: into our ears and eyes, into our mouths, and, to make it worse, there are the flies. Yes, even here in the middle of nowhere!

We camp alongside a giant red ant heap, which glows in the firelight. Despite everything, we've actually had a good day – we're learning to handle the conditions better, getting over the sand ridges with less winching and digging. We throw some lamb chops on the fire and rig up the satellite phone to check in with our sponsors and friends. Making contact with the outside world relieves a little of the loneliness of the Simpson.

Day 262: Gum trees and wild camels

Ross keeps us dead on course and we cross the Hay River at midday. The western bank is steep and crumbly, but the Landies make it up with the help of the winches and a nearby gum tree. It's wonderful to see gum trees growing next to the dry riverbed (there must be underground water), and there is a big herd of wild camels here, but the flies are terrible.

We push on up the next sand ridge, forever following the GPS. We're monitoring our water and fuel supplies carefully and, thankfully, are doing better than expected. Still, Linda is concerned that we're falling well behind on our schedule. She's just started her own business called 'Two Dogs Media', and might have to fly out from Alice Springs to go back to work. She originally hoped to complete all of Australia, but it's slow going. The tougher it gets, the more Ross enjoys himself – he always loves a physical challenge and has a never-say-die attitude. He's doing a great job of navigating us along the Capricorn line. Luke, the cameraman, is usually cheerful, but today he's got a slightly serious look: on last night's sat-phone call he learnt from his girlfriend in London that he is about to become a dad. He's thrilled at the news, but it's tough for him being so far away. Luke is proving to be a fantastic expedition member – not only as a cameraman, but also for his willingness to get involved in all aspects of expedition life, especially when it comes to 'opening the bar'!

Mashozi is doing a great job of keeping us well fed from her diminishing supplies. Cecil Madigan's rations had to last nine men for six weeks. Their food supplies consisted of five 50 lb bags of flour, 250 lb of salted meat, several cases of Imperial-brand assorted canned meats, as well as onions, potatoes, dried fruits, bacon, honey, golden syrup, rice, condensed milk, tea, coffee, cocoa, sugar, jam, cornflour, curry power, herbs, sauces and even 24 lb of fresh butter – plus Albert, a professional cook!

The rocking and rolling of the vehicles makes me feel almost seasick at times, so I've learned to wedge myself against the door and hold onto the bottom of the roofrack with my right hand. My lower back takes strain, as do my eyes from the constant glare and red dust. Sometimes I envy Madigan – it must have been a more relaxing trip by camel. It's late afternoon and I walk up a sand ridge to look out over the desert. It's as if we're alone in the world: not a vehicle track, not a footprint, not a single sign of human beings. Most likely no-one has ever before stood where I'm now standing. We drive on and soon reach the Plenty River, where we camp under the spreading branches of a ghost gum. At least there are no flies at night. Tonight we've found plenty of firewood and Mashozi cooks up a pot of deep-fried potato chips – absolute luxury! And, as always, there are the amazing stars of the Outback.

WE'RE GETTING THERE!

Day 263: Success at last – we fly the Aussie flag

We attach the Australian flag to a straggly gum pole and plant it in the red sand. We've crossed the Plenty River and have climbed the final dune! Now the largest parallel sand ridge desert in the world lies behind us. It has been an awesome and humbling experience. The Land Rovers and the Capricorn team have all made it, but, believe me, this is the sort of thing you do only once in a lifetime!

There's no time to waste, so we carry on through the beautiful East MacDonnells mountain ranges. What a treat; no more sand ridges and bloody spinifex. Alice Springs, here we come! Suddenly, Susi's breaklights come on and Ross shouts to us over the radio to be careful. Unfortunately, he's run smack into a kangaroo and it lies dead on the side of the road. A few kilometres further on I have to swerve violently to prevent a leaping kangaroo from hurtling right through the windscreen! It's extremely dangerous to drive at night here, so we slow right down with our spots on full. Hot showers, clean sheets, good tucker and beer as cold as a mother-in-law's kiss await us in the paradise of Alice Springs....

Ross's navigational skills have kept us perfectly on track and we meet the Stuart Highway at the Tropic of Capricorn beacon. The team perks up and with engines roaring we race down the highway, south, into a town called Alice. We find a motel at nearby Heavitree Gap, where rock wallabies wander into our rooms. We enjoy a night of didgeridoos, country-and-western music and mountains of meat – after all those punctures, we're having a 'blowout' of a different kind for a change. As I step out of Todd's Tavern, a rather inebriated Aboriginal prostitute shouts out to me, 'Come over here, you great big bearded slut!' It's nice to feel wanted, but a shame to find a once-great hunter-gatherer people so affected by the white man's liquor! The Capricorn team loves the taunt and I'm referred to as 'the slut' for the remainder of our journey across Australia.

Days 264–265: A town called Alice

Originally founded as a telegraph station, today Alice is the hub of central Australia, and the closest town to this section of the Tropic of Capricorn. These days it's full of motels and tourist shops selling didgeridoos, and is no longer the remote outpost it used to be. We visit the School of the Air, known as 'the world's largest classroom', which broadcasts lessons to Outback kids and covers an area of 1.3 million square kilometres. On HF (high frequency) radio I give the little children of the remote cattle stations a talk on the Tropic of Capricorn.

I'm enjoying Alice Springs – it's got a nice, laid-back feel to it. Steven Byrnes of the Royal Flying Doctor Service shows us around his operational headquarters and offers his support for our next Capricorn challenge – the Gibson Desert.

We are fully aware of the danger of snakebites, especially as it is getting warmer. We visit Rex Neindorf at Alice Springs's Reptile Park and he gives us advice on Australia's many venomous snakes. It seems that the greatest danger is the brown snake, and we are warned to be careful when gathering firewood.

'All you'll feel is a slight scratch, but you could be dead in two days,' says Rex. 'Don't remove the venom from the bite – this way a doctor can identify the snake. Just bind the area tightly with an elasticized bandage and call the Flying Doctor Service immediately. No worries, mate!'

I was hoping that visiting the town would give me the opportunity to meet Aborigines, but I'm bitterly disappointed. Many of the Aborigines that roam the streets of Alice Springs are booze-ridden dropouts, who hang around the liquor stores begging or just waiting for them to open. At night the police trucks cruise the area picking up the vagrants and breaking up fights. It is a great sadness that the indigenous people of Australia have been ruined by a type of colonial dependency that allows them to exist without dignity. But it's never all bad, and we meet Gural Wakarn (that's his Aboriginal name, which means 'black crow flying' – his English name is Tommy Crow), who has his own little Aboriginal cultural centre just north of Alice, closer to the Capricorn line.

What a fine man. He teaches Ross to play the didge and on the side of my Land Rover he paints a sacred serpent and small footprints that lead from waterhole to waterhole. On the door he paints three people sitting around a fire.

'It's your family,' he says, 'Kingsley, Ross and Gill, and the snake and the footprints will guide you to water in the Gibson Desert.'

Sitting on some large boulders overlooking Alice Springs, Gural Wakarn talks about the plight of the Aborigines and the need for them as a people to not lose touch with their ancient ways. He signs our Scroll of Peace and Goodwill and, with renewed hope, we part ways.

Day 257: Ancient Uluru

We leave the Tropic of Capricorn for a day or two, as we want to visit the famous Uluru (Ayers Rock) and the Olgas. How could we come to Central Australia and not experience The Rock? This ancient Aboriginal spiritual place is spoilt somewhat by the thousands of tourists, but it's a mind-boggling experience seeing these monoliths glow red in the setting sun. Later, we make our way back to Alice.

23°27'

Days 258–259: Thieving mongrels!

Having survived Africa and South America, who would have thought that we'd get ripped off in Alice Springs? They break into our motel room at Heavitree Gap, just south of Alice. Fortunately the 'thieving mongrels' (an Aussie term) miss the case of exposed video material and the video cameras, but they take off with a long-lens Cannon and the digital camera, with its stored images of our crossing of the Simpson Desert! It is a huge blow for us, and I wish the fleas of a thousand camels upon them.

We check out of the motel and unroll our swags under some drooping desert oaks at the base of a giant red sand dune. We must be crazy – here we are back in the Simpson; haven't we had enough? The truth of the matter is that, even after a few days in Alice, we miss the freedom and isola- tion of the unspoilt Outback, where the sparks from our fire seem to leap up and join the stars. It turns out to be a bit of a farewell party for Linda Sparrow. It's a shame that she has to fly back to her job in Sydney. We'll miss her cheer- ful face around the fire, and who'll teach us to speak 'Stralian' now?

Days 260–261: The West MacDonnells

As we slide off the old corrugated Ghan track in a cloud of red dust, the Quantas flight from Sydney passes overhead. We make it to the Alice Springs airport just in time for Linda to catch her flight – there's no chance for tears as we hurriedly bundle her onto the Sydney flight. Tonight she'll be in a bubble bath and we'll be camping under the stars somewhere in the West MacDonnells.

We say goodbye to Alice Springs, load our trusty 4x4s with enough diesel and supplies for 1 500 kilometres, and head out west through the sculptured gorges and waterholes of the rugged West MacDonnell range. Beyond them lies the challenge of the massive Gibson Dessert, with its vast Aboriginal lands.

We are now heading into the second half of our Capricorn Expedition across Australia, and the West MacDonnells make for a lovely change from the dry, red Outback. Here there are woodlands and clear, icy mountain pools; giant gorges and gaps in the mountains that have been carved out of the solid red rock over millions of years; dry, sandy rivers and white-trunked ghost gums; blue skies and a full moon. West of Glen Helen, we camp in a small, dry creek just as the last of the red sun fans out over the horizon. There's plenty of firewood, freedom and fun. Luke and I find the last bottle of Captain Morgan that Ross hid behind the seat, in an attempt to save it for the finish of the Australian leg of the Expedition.

But, despite the change of scenery, the team is tired and somewhat irritable, myself included. I know what the problem is with Ross and Luke: they're missing their families. Ross's little Tristan has just started playschool, and I know Ross would have liked to be there on his first day. Luke's girlfriend has just emailed a sonogram to him, which he got in Alice, so he's also been a bit on edge. Mashozi's missing home, and we three Holgates are all a bit tense about our current financial situation. We are way, way over budget, and will have to face the music and the bank manager when we get home. But there's more to it than that. The truth of the matter is that the huge distances and effort of crossing Australia along an invisible line are wearing us down.

Unlike Africa and South America, with their fascinating mixtures of countries and languages, Australia's Tropic of Capricorn has so far been mainly an endless sameness of red rock, red sand, spinifex, gum trees, scrub and constant deserts – although the more pleasant scenery here has lifted our spirirts a bit. But, it's not just that it's tough going; it was the endless monotony that was the Simpson Desert – and knowing that what lay ahead of us was simply more of the same. The only difference is that, in the Gibson Desert, the dunes run east to west. So, while in the Simpson we had to climb each dune, in the Gibson we can, we hope, run between them. What we really need to do is climb the mental obstacle.

tral Australia has an estimated 40 000 wild
els, humpbacked descendants from the time
t they were introduced by the early explorers.

'THE DREAMING'

Being an Aborigine is not only a matter of identifying with boomerangs, spears and bark paintings. It is identifying with a cultural heritage and a belief in the dreaming that gives our spirit a special relationship with this land, and sharing an historical experience that makes us unique to this country. It gives us a set of value judgments that guide our conduct. It decides our relationship with people, attitudes to possessions, to time, family and death. It could be described as a way of thinking and relating in common to different groups of people. Aboriginality is not the colour of one's skin and not only that we are of Aboriginal descent - being Aboriginal is a state of mind.
- Gural Wakarn

Day 262: Ancestral lands - what they've become

We carry on west, to the Aboriginal settlements of Haasts Bluff and Papunya, from where, fortunately, there's a track leading to the Gibson. Nothing could have prepared us for this, our first Aboriginal settlement: dirty, littered, smashed buildings, broken windows, wrecks of burnt-out cars, a sign that forbids alcohol and a fine of AU$1 000 if grog is found in your car, as well as one forbidding you to leave the road and another reminding you that you need a permit from the Aboriginal Land Council in Alice to enter the settlements.

We tried to apply for a permit six months ago, but each time we called we were told that the men of Haasts Bluff were away on men's business or that the relevant authority had left, or there was simply no reply. We were fobbed off and got the feeling that no-one wanted us here, least of all the Northern Territory Authorities who really gave us the cold shoulder. What did they want with some crazies who were attempting to follow the Tropic of Capricorn? So we were ignored, in the hope that we'd give up and go away. But here we are in Papunya, where the diesel pump is locked away in a steel shelter to protect it from vandals. The community store, full of every Western commodity, is run by a New Zealand family who genuinely seem to have empathy with the Aborigines, apart from which, 'It's good money and we love the desert,' they tell us. And all around are dishevelled, dejected Aborigines: on the dole and living off the government.

It reminds me strongly of South Africa's old 'Bantustan' or 'Homeland' policy – foreigners not welcome, permits only. It seems that here, even though a huge amount of guilt money is being spent, most Aborigines still live on the dole, and glue-sniffing, alcoholism, suicide and crime are all on the increase. What a sad plight for the indigenous people of Australia. And, while it's easy to criticise, we don't know the answer. In Alice, too, there were vagrants, beggars and alcoholism, sad souls sleeping in the dry Todd River, and we had the experience of being shut out by grunts and downcast stares. For many, their dignity has gone; killed by hand-outs, alcohol and drugs. Where is the laughter and dignity that we've found in other indigenous peoples along the Tropic of Capricorn? Here there's the great sadness of a people caught up in a way of life far removed from their ancient roots.

We make camp on a burnt patch of ground, under a burnt-out tree, near a burnt-out car, with black wood heating our kettle. Black crows cry mournfully around us and, as the full moon rises, a dingo howls in the distance. Tomorrow we head for Kintore/ Walungurru, where we hope to find diesel.

Day 263: A shame

More burnt-out cars line the road to Kintore. We turn left at a brightly-painted Aboriginal signboard, which leads us into the settlement. Once again, as in Papunya, it's like a war zone. Smashed and burnt cars lie everywhere and the government-funded settlement is in tatters. The small but modern homes have smashed windows, some have no doors, litter lies everywhere and mangy dogs and their unkempt owners look at us with dark suspicion and, in some cases, open hostility. Greg, the white Aussie who runs the shop here, pumps diesel for us at AU$1.40 a litre, which is a lot, even by Australian standards. Aborigines drive past in already-battered new Land Cruisers – there's obviously no shortage of cash here, and, as Greg explains, 'Those people in the cities haven't got a clue what's happening out here. The government just pours

ANCIENT WAYS - DESTROYED BY KINDNES

in the money. This is supposed to be a "dry" area, because of the problems with alcoholism, but the people are still killing themselves on booze and drugs. They are being killed by kindness.' He looks up at me through his dark black sunglasses; I notice he wears an earring.

Aborigines shuffle in and out of the litter surrounding the shop. Some look drugged and dazed. Greg, who's lived here for four years, shouts to a white Aussie mate, 'Take the blokes to the house so they can fill up their water containers. They're going around the world along the Tropic of Capricorn.' And so we follow Pete to the house – first waiting for him to finish his Mars Bar and plastic bottle of water, and then toss the wrapper and empty bottle out on the street. Why be different?

Pete is an art dealer who ships out local art from Kintore to overseas buyers. Packing cases are everywhere, as are paints and brushes. He walks over a large completed canvas that's lying on the floor, the red dust on his feet giving the layers of ochre dots more authenticity, I suppose. 'I'm married to an Aboriginal woman,' he says roughly, 'and speak a bit of the local lingo. I'm in partnership with Greg at the store. I'm just up here for a couple of weeks to buy art.' Earlier, Greg explained that some of the artists make up to AU$300 000 a year from their art. I asked the obvious question: 'What do they do with the money?' 'They just give it away or piss it up, or buy drugs,' he replied. 'And all the burnt-out cars?' I asked. 'Well, sometimes someone dies in the accident, so they just burn the car. Other times they break down and just get so angry with the bloody thing that they burn it in a temper.' 'It's a fairly recent thing,' said Pete. 'It all started over at Hermansburg a few years ago – this burning of cars.'

Pete shows us the tap, swears at the dog and shouts to some dishevelled Aboriginal women leaning over the fence, who want to 'come in and use the bloody phone!' says Pete. Pointing to the large painting he's just walked over, I ask how much a piece like that would go for.

'Are you a buyer, mate? If you're not, I'm not f...ing telling you!' Rather lamely I explain that all our expedition budget allows for is fuel and supplies. Then I explain to Pete about the Capricorn Scroll of Peace and Goodwill we are carrying around the world. Could he steer us towards one of the Aboriginal elders for it to be endorsed here in the settlement?

And so we find ourselves at Walperry's place, last house on the left. Litter and dogs are everywhere, two women and a baby sit under a tree, there are red hand prints all over the wall and a big, red, painted canvas is spread out on a paint-splattered verandah. We find another white art dealer here and he looks up suspiciously at us. 'F...ing carpet baggers,' mumbles Pete. He jumps out of his vehicle and throws the canvas angrily aside. Getting the message, the other fellow soon moves off, and we are free to chat to Walperry. He only speaks one or two words of English, but Pete interprets for us. Walperry endorses the Scroll with an illegible scribble. According to Pete, he came out of the desert in 1985. 'How many people still live in the desert?' I ask. 'Maybe two, maybe three,' he replies. We shake hands with him. He has a proud face and a thick black beard, and wears a big black cowboy hat. 'Do the people still hunt traditionally?' I ask Pete on our way out. 'Some can, but rarely do. Nowadays they use a rifle or, mostly, they just kill them with this,' he taps the large bullbar of his Land Cruiser.

As we drive out of the settlement we ask an Aboriginal woman for directions. Over her shoulder she carries several long, fat, snake-like Kangaroo tails – a local delicacy. Outside Kintore we stop alongside the road for our usual bully beef sandwiches. We hold our breath as a police van goes past, remembering that while we were filling up with diesel an

23°27'

DENTED
ENAMEL
MUG -

Aboriginal man there asked, 'You got a permit, mate?' Ross nodded confidently. Then he
added, 'Just stick to the road, mate. You no go Lake MacDonnell; that's our country.'

It's mid-afternoon by the time we turn off the Sandy Blight track and head west, following
the Tropic of Capricorn through the burnt bush towards Lake MacDonnell.

There has been good rain and the desert is flowering. As expected, we don't come across a
single Aborigine. They are all in the run-down settlement, where the government put them, and
where there are government schools, health clinics, a shop and state hand-outs – a place where
they can sniff petrol and glue, where food is guaranteed and if you get sick the Flying Doctor
takes you to the city. In Kintore you can sit and dream of the past as you paint dreamtime dots
on canvas for the wealthy white man. The money, the booze and the drugs are good. It makes
you forget. But in your heart, and all around you, the dreamtime lives on in the red desert,
amongst the birds, insects and wild animals, in the wind, the sun and the stars, in the stories
around the fires at night and in the eyes of Walperry, the last man to come out of the desert.

Here in the middle of nowhere we have four tyre-destroying punctures in less than five
minutes. Short, burnt, hardwood bushes snap beneath the tyres and turn into nail-like spikes
that pierce the sidewalls. Ahead of us, towards Lake MacDonnell, the 'puncture bushes'
spread out like a minefield; we only have one good tube left and are now short of patches.
Mashozi clears away some of the sharp spinifex with a spade and we lay out our swags
beneath the stars. In the yellow beam of the Land Rover lights Ross mends tubes and tyres.
Suddenly the tyre lever snaps up and smashes into his nose. Blood pours and Mashozi runs
with antiseptic cream and cotton wool. As I lie awake in my swag, I think of the Aboriginal
words spoken to us in Kintore: 'You no go Lake MacDonnell; that's our country.'

Day 264: Lake MacDonnell – will Ross make it?

It is impossible for us to continue west through the bush to Lake MacDonnell at this point.
We'd need a lorry-load of tyres and tubes. Either we detour or come up with a plan. Father
and son toss a coin: I catch it heads up, so the task to walk to Lake MacDonnell falls on
Ross's shoulders. It's a 30- to 40-kilometre round-trip. He takes a radio, water, an emergency
medical kit, a sleeping bag and supplies. His objective is clear: to place one of our Capricorn
Expedition signs where the Tropic of Capricorn meets Lake MacDonnell. Luke will go with
him to document the moment. Ross promises to radio us on the hour every hour and, if he's
not back by 3 pm tomorrow, we will contact the Flying Doctor Service and call for help. I
shudder at the thought – what if a brown snake gets him out there or if something goes
wrong? Mashozi cries at the sight of her only son disappearing west, leaving the two of us
amongst a pile of punctured tyres in this desolate, empty place. No sign of people anywhere.

We wait anxiously for each radio call. Just before sunset, we get some static and a
broken call from Ross: 'There's a luxury holiday resort here. You won't believe it – I'm
sipping an ice-cold gin and tonic!' I admire his sense of humour. I ask him how much
water he's got left and for a true description of the place. The static comes through again
and I imagine him out there, his aerial probably up a tree. 'It's beautiful,' he says. 'No
water, just a big orange sun setting over a massive empty salt pan, in the middle of which
is our Capricorn sign. We're pretty buggered, so we'll be turning in early. Over and out
till 7 am tomorrow.' When night falls Mashozi and I sit around a lonely fire, thinking of

YOU NO GO LAKE MAC DONNELL

our only son, also sleeping next to a little fire under the same stars, on distant Lake MacDonnell. I'll only relax once he is safely back in camp.

Day 265: An oasis, flying bugs and good news

Right on time, at 7 am, we get the radio call – all is well, and Ross and Luke are on their way back. Unfortunately, today is one of the hottest days we've yet had. Soon the sun's up – it's absolutely boiling and the flies are out in full force. We get another call from Ross; he's feeling the heat and the water is running low. When he and Luke finally get back they say, 'We thought of girls all the way there and water all the way back!'

'I lay awake dreaming about water,' says Luke. 'I even hoped that our tin of tuna fish was in brine and not oil; anything for moisture!'

Thank God they made it safely – no brown snakes. I still think of Rex Neindorf's chilling words: 'All you'll feel is a slight scratch, but you could be dead in two days.' We make our way back to the Sandy Blight Road, and now Mount Leisler is on our left as we drive the corrugated track back to Kintore. We put in some more expensive diesel and then head west again. While we are filling up, the same Aborigine who asked for the permit calls out to Ross, 'Hey you! Mr Round-the-World!' It seems as if we've been accepted. An old Ford with no windscreen, and full of long-haired Aboriginal teenagers, comes flying through the settlement in a cloud of red dust and with the thump, thump of loud music. I give a cheerful wave and they wave back. In a country as controlled as Australia there's a sort of wild freedom out here that's very refreshing. We head out across the Kiwirrkurra Aboriginal lands, west, between the dunes of the Gibson.

We can't believe it – in the middle of a desert! It's like a mirage: ducks skim the surface of a massive stretch of blue water, which soon turns golden in the setting sun. There are lots of bugs, but it's still an unbelievable paradise. This is the result of the massive flooding we were told about; the worst in the last hundred years. Here we are, like desert nomads who have found an oasis. From this beautiful place we make the most important satellite phone call of the expedition, to Matthew Frank, our friend and documentary distributor in London. Ross talks to him in hushed and expectant tones, and then comes the incredibly good news. National Geographic in Washington has agreed to purchase the rights to our Capricorn adventure! The looks of relief on Mashozi and Ross's faces say it all. The cash crisis is over and we celebrate in paradise. Who ever thought that we'd find a lake in the Gibson Desert?

Day 266: Floods at Kiwirrkurra

We winch the Landies through the deep, clear water. If the electronics got wet... well, we'd be truly buggered! A technician

ROSS GOES ON BY FOOT – DETERMINED TO PLACE A CAPRICORN SIGN ON LAKE MACDONNELL – WE'LL MAKE RADIO CONTACT EVERY HOUR BUT WHAT IF SOMETHING GOES WRONG?

WATER

5L

would have to be flown in from Alice with a computer, and we don't even know if that would have to be possible – so the winching is done with a degree of apprehension, but we get through the water all right. A bit further on we call in at the Kiwirrkurra settlement for diesel. The sign demands that we report to the Aboriginal Council Office. Unlike Kintore, it's reasonably clean here and has a friendly atmosphere. We meet Mike, the white administrator, who reports to the Aboriginal leaders and is employed by the federal government. He has a no-nonsense attitude, and knows about our journey (thankfully, Linda managed to arrange some of the necessary permits for us before our arrival in Australia).

Henry, another white Aussie, runs the store here, and there are two white teachers at the school. 'Why no Aboriginal teachers?' I ask one of them – a pretty, tomboyish young girl who's just arrived from Perth. 'I don't know,' she replies, 'but I get paid a fortune and the kids are lovely. You come school tomorrow?' she asks of a tattered little ginger-haired girl, who looks away shyly and jumps into an old Ford full of kids and turns up the music. 'Looks like a great trip,' says the teacher from Perth, eyeing the national flags of the ten Capricorn countries on the sides of our Land Rovers. Her eyes stick on Brazil. 'That's where I'm going next,' she says wistfully.

I meet the local chief, a tall, strong-looking man wearing a broad-brimmed Aussie hat. He speaks only pigdin English and we have a colourful interview with lots of smiles and hand-shakes, but we hardly understand a word he says. He endorses our Capricorn Scroll of Peace and Goodwill. 'You come back. Eat him bush turkey – him very good,' he says, pointing to a little naked kid who is sharing a large turkey bone with a stray dog. 'You African man, why not black?' he asks and laughs, pumping my hand up and down. He makes me feel there is some hope.

We see a middle-aged Aborigine, with dirty dreadlocks and a T-shirt shiny with age, sweat, fat and dirt, spend a fortune in Henry's store, buying Fray Bentos, tinned meat, pies, chocolate-chip cookies, imported tinned soups, chocolate bars, sweets and bottles of fresh orange juice. The only traditional item he buys is a shiny silver billycan for AU$10. 'You won't believe it,' says Mike. 'We must have the highest per capita amount of money spent on services, care and handouts in the world. Millions have been spent since the floods. Sugar diabetes is a big problem here. They'll rather drink a bucket of Coca-Cola than a bucket of water. We're also trying to stop them chewing gum, but we need to keep it going for the meantime, to help lure the people back. You won't believe the amount of money that's spent.'

Driving west into the sun, dust and heat we see some dingoes and loads of wild camel tracks. We spend the night at Jupiter Well, where a red, metal hand-pump produces clear, clean borehole water from a black plastic pipe. Believe me, the Australian Outback really makes you appreciate water. We bathe, wash clothes and shampoo the red dust from our hair.

We are surrounded by hundreds of tall desert oaks and the night wind sighs through them. The yellow-white spinifex grass shines in the moonlight and there are dingo tracks everywhere. But we're almost too tired to enjoy it all. The journey is killing, and tedium has set in. Luke smokes and tries to be cheerful, but he's losing some of his youthful enthusiasm as the expedition begins to wear him down. These days we sit on our rolled up swags around the fire – only rolling them out at the last moment, to make sure no brown snake or other creature has slithered into them for the night. Sadly, the Captain Morgan is finished,

THE LOCAL CHIEF SPEAKS ONLY PIDGIN ENGLISH.

I SOMETIMES THINK WE SHOULD CHANGE THE LTDR. AT 6TO1 WE'RE HURTING BAD!

but we rustle up some *catembe*: red box wine and Coke. It reminds me of Mozambique.

Days 267–276: Forever west

What a long, long journey... Sometimes it feels as if we're travelling along ancient Aborigine, dreamtime travel lines. Days run into weeks. We're like a camel caravan of old. Over and over again we inspan, outspan, gather fire-wood, sleep under the stars, think constantly of water and, because we are in our modern Land Rover 'ships of the desert', we worry about diesel and tyres. We've been on the go for a long time and know every creak, groan and shudder of tired old *Chuma* and *Susi*. It's absolutely incredible how they have coped. Never in my life have I been forced to punish 4x4s to such an extent – we've taken them through swamps, deserts, mountains and now the great Gibson Desert, with its red sand dunes running east to west. We find some new-born dingo pups in an old disused well. Mashozi is ecstatic and spends time photo-graphing them. It's getting a lot warmer now and we see a biggish snake; everyone's being a bit more careful, checking their boots, as well as their swags. We sleep between the red sand dunes, and our camp is criss-crossed by dingo and wild camel tracks.

Red dunes: they go on forever. Will we ever make it? It's still over 1 000 kilometres to Ningaloo Reef and the west coast. Our short-term objective is to reach Lake Disappointment, which is dead on the Tropic of Capricorn. Everybody's worn out by the size and the sameness of the place, but, still, the Gibson Desert is easier than the Simpson – we're able to travel down the valleys between the high parallel red dunes, rather than having to climb them all, as in the Simpson. At least here the rains and flooding have brought life: beautiful desert flowers, made even more beautiful by their dry, red sand surroundings. It's hard going for the Capricorn Expedition's vehicles and people alike, but what an adventure! The only problem is that we've run out of bloody grog, and you can be sure there will be none at Lake Disappointment! We

23°27'

DINGO — IT MAKES PUPPIES. MASHOZI'S DAY

come across a huge rocky outcrop alongside the old Canning Stock Route. We climb to the top of it and sit like baboons on the edge of the high red cliff, looking out over the desert.

We battle on through the heat and the sheer isolation, and we are hit by a massive sand storm that's so strong it forces us to stop the vehicles. Visibility is down to almost zero. We push on into the night, desperately trying to make up a bit of time. Mashozi is not a dry country person, and she's also taking strain with the constant lurching from side to side in the Landies, the bloody kit falling all over the place, the rattling of the kettle, the heat, the dust and the flies. We are trying to reach Lake Disappointment today, but finally, well into the night, we throw our swags out at Georgia Well. The wind is howling and everybody's absolutely dog tired. We struggle to find firewood and blunder around in the dark grabbing at branches by torchlight, worrying about snakes. A few spiders visit our swags, but we don't get bitten, and the cold wind continues to blow through the night.

Day 277: All alone on Lake Disappointment

We get up early in the morning, as always, but today we really struggle to get going. We simply can't resist the attraction of the borehole pump here, and everybody lines up to wash their clothes and bodies. What a treat! Ross even shaves, and birds gather around to drink from the pool that we leave behind.

We really push it now, travelling as fast as we can. I'm carrying all the kit in *Chuma*, so I can't go quite as fast as Ross in *Susi*. I also have to hang back because of the choking dust thrown up from the Landy in front. Ross is a bit moody today; he gets like that at times, especially when he is missing home. Finally, at about midday, we are rewarded with a magnificent sight: blue, blue sky and red dunes falling into a snow white salt lake – Lake Disappointment. Our plan is to cross it by Land Rover. Ross edges *Susi* onto the white, salty crust, but he only goes out a few metres before the crust breaks and the vehicle sinks down to its axles in deep mud. We walk out across the lake for a few hundred metres, but it just gets softer still. It would be useless even to try – the vehicles could get stuck here for weeks, so we winch *Susi* back onto hard ground.

Ross did the Lake MacDonnell walk; now – bad luck! – it's my turn. 'Come on, you old slut!' laughs Mashozi. I load up one of the mountain bikes with supplies and enough water, and take just a thin sleeping bag, despite Mashozi's warning: 'You're gonna freeze.' My supplies include a tin of bully, some baked beans, biscuits, peanut butter, jam and an energy bar.

No tea, coffee or juice, just water, and, as I mentioned before, no bloody grog! It all reminds me so much of Lake Atacama, but that feels like a hundred years ago. I think of the big salt pans in the western Kalahari, but those too seem to belong to a different time. Now the challenge is to cross Lake Disappointment. It all starts off well enough, but the crust of the lake, which looks to me like a giant apple strudel, gets softer and softer as I go further out, and the surface crumbles and breaks to reveal the goo beneath. I find a little thorny devil out here, right in the middle of bloody nowhere. I can't believe he is still alive. There's not a fly or insect in sight, and certainly no water. Just how is he surviving?

As always, I feel humbled by my awe-inspiring surroundings. Here I am, just a little speck in the midst of this emptiness. The sinking sun leaves behind a layer of orange and light blue along the horizon that soon fades. Then I'm alone under the stars, and still I can't believe how full and bright they are – close enough to touch – with the Milky Way a white band of millions of lights. The salt of the lake glows softly white. It's an exquisite scene, but what a terrible night – I've got no fire and the ice-cold water of the lake seeps up through the cracks in the salt crust and into my sleeping bag. I don't sleep a bloody wink; just lie here looking at my lonely black footprints around the camp, disturbing the snow-like whiteness of Lake Disappointment.

I wake up early and place a Capricorn marker, which I've brought with me all the way from South Africa, right on 23° 27'. I need to beat the heat, so I load up my inadequate sleeping bag, the remaining supplies and my drinking water (life itself out here) onto the bicycle, which for most of the time I have to push rather than ride. I'm like a tiny figure on the moon, and all that connects me to Mashozi, Ross and Luke is a small two-way radio that beeps – low battery.

Then, to my delight, I catch sight of the two Land Rovers glinting in the sun. As a bit of a joke I throw the bike down and run screaming towards them as if I've lost my marbles out here on Lake Disappointment (which probably is the case anyway!). But the laugh is on me, as both my thighs cramp up and I fall to the ground in pain. All the sitting in the Land Rover, followed by the push and ride across Lake Disappointment, has just been too much.

Day 278: Jiggalong ... along ... along

We are now leaving the Gibson Desert and pushing hard down the Tanamani track to the Aboriginal settlement of Jiggalong. Until one has been to Australia one doesn't really have a true feeling of distance – and that's coming from a man of Africa! The corrugated track is horrific; the scenery beautiful. We stop only to siphon some more diesel from the jerry cans and have a hurried meal. *Chuma* and *Susi*, with their constant four-wheel-drive, do very well on the narrow, sandy, bumpy road that twists and turns for hundreds of kilometres. The Kalahari cowbell jingles from the bullbar of *Chuma* and the koala bear mascot swings from the rear-view mirror as we race west to Jiggalong. After all these months on the road I feels a sense of oneness with *Chuma* – its squeaks, the twisting and creaking of the chassis and the comforting low growl of the engine and transmission. We're like snails travelling with our homes.

The old Aboriginal mission of Jiggalong is now a new community, run by whites who

23°27'

live in mobile homes with satellite dishes and new 4x4s parked outside. We stop outside the shop, which is clean. We find the white administrator here; he's a tubby little fellow, dressed in Bermuda shorts and a baseball cap. 'You're supposed to have a permit,' he says to us. I nod confidently, knowing that this is one of the places for which we were able to get a permit. I'm just about to produce it when he says, 'Don't worry, mate. The Aborigines here won't have anything to do with permits. It's only the buggers in Perth that want all this paperwork.' *Now* we find this out, after all the anxious moments of struggling to sort out our permits! We push on west.

Our Capricorn journey is all about GPS lines and dots on a map, and the next dot we're headed for is called the Capricorn Roadhouse. It's situated on the highway that leads from Perth to Newman, just a short distance south of the mining town of Newman. Before we leave, the administrator of Jiggalong tells us about a short cut and we roar off into the sunset, down the red dust track. As usual Ross drives in front, navigating, and Mashozi and I suck the dust. We picture the Capricorn Roadhouse in our minds: for Mashozi it means a hot bath and a chance to wash clothes, for Ross and me it means (we hope) a mixed grill and a cold Captain Morgan, not to mention a comfortable bed and, that great British invention, the porcelain throne! It'll also give us the chance to re-supply in nearby Newman.

But, despite our determination, and the fact that we've managed to cross both the great Simpson and Gibson deserts, we're now lost in the darkness of the Jiggalong Aboriginal lands, confused by the numerous mining and cattle tracks on this seldom-used road that keeps losing itself in dongas and river beds. We eventually find an old roadsign, but it's been burnt black in a bush fire and we can't read it. So it is that a sad little team of Capricornians once again find themselves huddling around a small fire, eating two-minute noodles, rolling out their swags and thinking of the elusive Capricorn Roadhouse.

Days 279–280: Capricorn Roadhouse at last!

We're still lost, and we come to a cattle station owned by a couple called Ben and Helen. Ben and his daughters are busy mustering cattle. Helen refers to her husband as 'the oldest teenager in the district. He uses a gyrocopter to round up the cattle and we've just had quite a social time at the local Newman Rodeo. It's a good life for us out here. When there are good rains we buy new motorcars and go on holiday, and when the drought comes... well, we just have to lock up the cheque book!' Helen signs our Capricorn Scroll, and we drink tea, eat fresh cookies and play with the dogs. It is all so homely, and we are so unkempt and dirty. Helen asks us if we'd like to have a shower, but we're hell-bent on getting to the Capricorn Roadhouse. 'Just an hour away on an excellent road. Watch out for road trains; they're transporting a lot of cattle at the moment.' And so we're off.

A little later we arrive at a dusty Outback affair, spread out on the right-hand side of the Newman road. 'Capricorn Roadhouse' is printed in large yellow lettering on the wall. The roadhouse has fuel pumps, a tavern, shops and a basic truckers' restaurant with some rooms out at the back, which the pretty waitress Chris refers to as 'the dongas'. There's a jukebox and the cold beers run freely. Their steak, egg, chips, chops, sausage, bacon and tomato, served with fresh white bread, beat even the contents of Mashozi's grub box! Old mobile homes with flush toilets and hot showers serve as our rooms. After the Gibson Desert, it's bliss.

Now it's just 1 000 kilometres to the Indian Ocean. Cousin Fish is travelling all the way up from Perth to meet us at Lynden Station and escort us to Ningaloo Reef for the end of the expedition. After we've spoken to him on the phone we go and stock up on supplies at Newman, a modern supermarket, and some delightfully drunk Aborigines are sitting behind the bottlestore singing hymns. They, too, have probably travelled from Jiggalong Mission.

Days 281–283: Almost there!

These cattle station owners seem to have all the mod cons: new 4x4s, an aircraft in the hangar, a tutor for their children and a cook for the drovers. One station owner notices Mashozi looking up at a picture of a group of girls dressed in full Aussie cowboy gear. 'Two bloody marriages,' he says, 'and all I got was daughters. Now every mongrel son of a bitch is chasing their pants off, wanting my station for bugger all!' They're a tough bunch and we soon learn to play down our expedition by poking fun at ourselves: 'We're the stupid buggers following this imaginary line around the world,' we say. 'Come in for a beer, mate. Roll out your swags on the verandah,' is the general response.

This part of Western Australia's Tropic of Capricorn is known as Pilbara and the scenery here is more dramatic, with rocky outcrops and craggy mountains. The journey wears on – more gates, more fences, more red dust and more scrub. Will it never end?

We meet Cousin Fish and his family at Lynden Station, owned by John and his son Sean. They cook up a wonderful seafood barbie and we drink up a storm – they're fantastic hosts. Fish is a great comic and he entertains us well into the night. We're very grateful to him; without his help in getting *Chuma* and *Susi* cleaned in East Timor, the Australian leg of the Capricorn Expedition would never even have got off the ground.

23°27'

Day 284: Ningaloo Reef, 23°27' – we've made it!

Dusty boots, bush jackets, scratched sunglasses and hats go flying, as, with an immense feeling of jubilation, we race down the soft, icing sugar-white sand dunes and plunge into the cool, blue waters of the Indian Ocean, on the southern tip of Australia's Ningaloo Reef. Are the spinifex grass, red dust, endless desert heat and innumerable punctures really finally behind us, or are we still travelling through Aboriginal dreamtime? Have we, like so many before us, simply gone 'bush', driven crazy by the far horizons, the shimmering mirages and the endless open expanses? We've been travelling so long and so hard that it's difficult to believe the Australian section is finally over!

We pour out the seawater from the Zulu calabash, carried all the way from the Great Barrier Reef over 4 000 kilometres to the east. The wind blows from the south, but not hard enough to keep the bloody flies away. We dive and swim, shake hands, laugh and hug each other with delight. The sea washes the cinnamon-red bulldust from our crumpled clothes and travel-weary bodies. A reef shark swims lazily through the shallows. I glance at Gill and Ross – what an amazing privilege to be able to adventure like this as a family. We've crossed Australia from coast to coast through some of its widest areas, very often following only the GPS. At times the journey seemed near impossible, but here we are at last emptying the calabash. Looking down on us from the top of a dune are the other two brave members of our Capricorn team – *Chuma* and *Susi*, the two battered Landies that have become our second home. The Tropic of Capricorn has thrown everything at them: the flooded swamp-lands and landmines of Mozambique, the high Andes of South America and the Capricorn deserts of the Kalahari, Namib, Atacama, Simpson and Gibson. Should they have failed us, at times it could have cost us our lives. *Chuma* and *Susi*, we salute you – and Luke, without whom this leg of our crazy adventure across Australia would never have been documented on video – now to be shared by many around the world.

This area is part of a massive sheep station, and the owner, Lee Burkett, has given us permission to camp at the base of a dune. We light a fire and, joined by cousin Fish and his lovely family, we empty Mashozi's Capricorn Expedition grub box. Steak and chops sizzle on the coals and ice tinkles in large enamel mugs. To my immense delight, I find that Fish has brought some Captain Morgan rum! We recount our Australian experiences: the tough Aussie characters we met along the way and the Aussie humour that we've so enjoyed. We talk about snakes, cattle, crocodiles, kangaroos and the sad Aboriginal settlements we've travelled through. Particularly sad when you think that the Outback has played host to the oldest surviving human culture for at least 50 000 years. But then I think of Gural Wakarn (black crow flying) who we met in Alice. We exchanged Zulu beads for Aboriginal rhythm sticks and he painted the side of our Land Rover with a sacred serpent, footprints and water-holes. He said it would bring us luck and carry us through the desert, and so it has. I thought of him often along the way, especially when, camped in some strange and deserted place, out of the blue the quiet was interrupted by the raucous cry of a black crow.

I gaze out west over Ningaloo Reef. The tide is coming in, there isn't another human being in sight, nor a single footprint on the white beach. The others are all in camp, a little back from the beach. I realise how emotionally attached I've become to this imaginary line called Capricorn. Out there across the Indian Ocean lies Madagascar, our final Capricorn challenge – that mystical island lost in time. The inside of my swag is still coated with red dust. I pull my old Masai blanket over my shoulders and gaze up into the stars. As always in Australia they seem lower and brighter. I know that in the future, when I think back to our journey along Capricorn, it'll be the beauty of Australia's starlit evenings that I'll remember forever.

Day 285–297: Madagascar - a window of opportunity

We ship the Land Rovers from Perth back to South Africa, and make arrangements through our friends at Flight Centre to fly to Antananarivo from Jo'burg. On the telephone I speak to the Madagascan Consul. The civil unrest is quietening down and there seems to be a window of opportunity for our journey across the island. If we survive Madagascar, we'll return to the Tropic of Capricorn just north of the ancient city of Inhambane on the coast of Mozambique, to the very place where we set off from over a year ago. Finally, the end is in sight and it looks as if we just might complete this crazy Capricorn odyssey around the world!

ABORIGINAL SIGNS

BLOOD OR WATER.

WATER HOLE.

CAMPSITE -

EMU - EARTH MOTHER

LIGHTNING.

EXPEDITION - RUM - CAPTAIN MORGAN -

RAIN

DREAMING TRACK WITH EMU -

Madagascar

Madagascar the world's fourth-largest island is a mystical place, lost in time. The civil unrest has eased and there seems to be a window of opportunity for this, our final Capricorn challenge. We aim to follow the Tropic from Vangaindrano in the east to St Augustine in the West. We expect rivers, swamps, rainforests, mountains and Zebu cattle carcass – the Madagascan Consul believes it's impossible.

Day 311: Antananarivo here we come!

We find ourselves winging our way over the Mozambique Channel to Madagascar, our final Capricorn country – thanks to the friendly support of Barry Robinson-Butler from Flight Centre. The flight is full of gold and gem dealers, journalists, politicians, businesspeople and returning Malagasy nationals. The pretty airhostesses speak in broken French and accented English. Another great adventure is about to begin, as we set out to complete the last leg of our Capricorn Expedition around the globe.

I always thought that Madagascar would prove our greatest Capricorn challenge and, of late, the news from this Indian Ocean island has just got worse and worse. The normally peaceful and laid-back country of Madagascar is being shattered by civil unrest. It all started with the presidential elections ten months ago, in which the old, corrupt President Didier Ratsirake was democratically outvoted by the ex-Mayor of the capital Antananarivo, charming businessman Marc Ravalomanana. Ratsirake and his supporters had too much to lose, so they refused to accept the outcome and decided to battle it out against forces loyal to the newly sworn-in President, causing a split in the armed forces. Bridges were blown up, people killed and Antananarivo was virtually cut off from the outside world for eight months. A pessimistic Madagascan Embassy worker told me, 'Old Ratsirake is holed up in the east coast port of Tamatave. Kingsley, you'd better be careful. He's got Algerian-trained palace guards who are twitchy and shoot straight. Better you don't go!'

But recently we learnt that things have quietened down, as Ratsirake's fled the country and the new President is firmly in control. Flying east, I look down over the coast of Mozambique and the 400-kilometre stretch of water that separates Madagascar from Africa. I sense a window of opportunity and wonder: Can we make it? Gill's fear is not civil unrest – surprisingly for someone who is not afraid of lions, snakes or elephants, her great fear has always been rats. Unfortunately, she recently chanced on an article in the latest *Royal Geographical* magazine, in which the author warns travellers to Madagascar of a return of the Black Death: bubonic plague carried by rats.

THE ISLAND OF MADAGASCAR – AT TANA WE MEET THE NEW PRESIDENT – WHO ENDORSES OUR CAPRICORN SCROLL OF PEACE & GOODWILL

INDIAN OCEAN – WE DIP THE CALABASH AT VANGAINDRANO ON THE EAST COAST –

WITH JEAN BAPTISTE'S TRACTOR INTO THE RAIN FOREST –

THE INCREDIBLY TOUGH, LONG WALK WITH PORTERS – VILLAGES MOUNTAINS

HARD GOING!!

RAIN-FOREST

VAST SEMI ARID PLAINS – ZEBU CATTLE

MANGOKY RIVER

DRY SPINY FOREST ZEBU CART MISSION STATION ST AUGUSTINE'S BELAMOTY BAY

PAINTED TOMBS!

TULEAR

MOZAMBIQUE CHANNEL

Day 312: You must be bloody crazy - it's impossible

David Fox, South Africa's Consul to Madagascar, is a delightfully eccentric old chap whose link to Madagascar goes back many years to when he was the first to send South African-bred racehorses to the island in the '60s. Mashozi, Ross, our good friend Tim Chevallier (the National Geographic cameraman) and I take an old Citroën taxi to meet David at the Hilton Hotel in Tana. He hands over our 1:250 000 survey maps and a letter of introduction in French. Then, in his very English accent, over a Three Horses beer, he says, 'Just look at these maps – you must be bloody crazy. If you look at the terrain, the rainforests, mountains and semi-deserts and the lack of roads and infrastructure... well, to be honest, I don't think you've got a chance in hell.' We laugh and raise our glasses; such is the nature of our journey.

Day 313: The Capricorn team meets the President

Using David Fox's letter, and after exercising a great deal of Third-World patience, we get an appointment to see Mr Marc Ravalomanana, the new President. There's a bit of a scare on at the moment. It's been rumoured that foreign mercenaries, hired by the deposed President, are about to fly to the island. Bearing this in mind, I have my beard trimmed in the market and put on my new green, checked Land Rover shirt, long trousers and polished boots. With luck my grey beard and the fact that we are travelling as a family will dispel any fear of us being mercenaries, but you never know how jittery the military and police will be.

The red, green and white Republic of Madagascar flag flutters over the grand French colonial-style, red brick Presidential Headquarters. Here we're greeted with red berets, camouflage outfits, automatic weapons and full body searches. Mashozi, Ross and I smile a lot and shake hands with all and sundry. The Presidential guards seem watchful and edgy as Tim Chevallier unzips the long, black tripod bag, (to the uninitiated it probably looks like a rocket launcher!), and two serious fellows ease their automatics into firing position. From the old leather Capricorn Expedition journal bag I produce David Fox's 'French letter', and the Capricorn Scroll of Peace and Goodwill, which has by now become dog-eared from being carried all around the world. A tough-looking red beret talks Malagasy into his two-way radio. We are told to wait. Finally, relief comes in the form of a smiling Presidential secretary, who ushers us into a grand, high-ceilinged waiting room. Outside are a helicopter pad and a clear view of the capital city.

Antananarivo is a city of umbrella-clad markets, narrow mud and brick double-storey houses, with carved wooden balconies, winding cobbled streets, rice paddies and colourful old Citroën taxis. Set amidst a dozen hills, the city is overlooked by the now-gutted Rova (queen's palace), designed by Scottish missionary James Cameron and built in 1867 for Queen Ranavalona. Its central support was made from a 39-metre rosewood tree trunk. The story goes that it took ten thousand slaves to drag the giant log up from the eastern rainforests and that one thousand men succumbed to exhaustion along the way. At least we will have only ourselves and our expedition supplies to drag along. Still, I suspect we will be in for a tough time.

Armed guards stand to attention as we are escorted into the Presidential chambers. The President greets us warmly. He is pro-South Africa and wants to improve ties with our country. We pose for photographs and he endorses the Capricorn Scroll with a goodwill message and his signature. Let's hope this will give us safe passage across the island.

MARK RAVALOMANANA - THESE MALAGASY NAM ARE QUITE A MOUTHFUL

In the market I'm offered white chalk balls to ward off evil spirits; a mixture of honey, rum and aloe leaf for stomach ache; and a long, thin tuber – a Madagascan form of Viagra. In the lounge of the Hotel de France we interview local hopefuls who are keen to act as interpreters on our journey. But, when they hear of our route, they say it is impossible. There are no roads, they tell us, and they ask how we'll get through the rainforests and mountains. A local company specialising in putting together expeditions assures us that the only way to succeed is by light aircraft! To make matters worse we are warned about the danger of armed and dangerous Zebu cattle bandits, who are said to operate in the southern Capricorn region of Madagascar.

ANTANANARIVO

Ross, who is in charge of navigation, works out from the survey maps that the journey will be impossible by Land Rover. We'll have to travel on foot, and by bicycle and *pirogue* (dugout canoe). We'll meet our Land Rovers again across the Mozambique Channel on 23° 27', just north of Inhambane, where the Capricorn journey started 18 months ago. That is, of course, if we make it across Madagascar.

Day 314: Cinq-cent-cinq and pousse-pousse

With our rucksacks, tents, raingear, boots, bicycles, maps, GPS unit, Zulu calabash and Capricorn Scroll of Peace and Goodwill, we set off. We're heading for Fianarantsoa, on our way to Vangaindrano and the commencement of our Capricorn journey from east to west across Madagascar. The east coast town of Vangaindrano lies near the 23° 27' line, approximately 1 000 kilometres south of Antananarivo.

Why is there always so much damned kit? How we miss *Chuma* and *Susi* – our second homes, with a place for everything. But we have to be practical. We can't cut a road through the rainforest with our vehicles – man has done enough damage already – so we'll need porters. We pack and repack, trying to lighten the load. It's going to be tough going, so I squeeze in a few bottles of Captain Morgan for the renoster coffee. We load up an old Peugeot 505 taxi (cinq-cent-cinq), driven by a man named Mammy. He used to drive government officials but now freelances for the owner of the Peugeot. He sucks his teeth continually and has got a slightly nervous manner, but he seems willing and has travelled the route before.

Ross, Mashozi, Tim and I have now been joined by Bakoly Razanamiarantsoa, a tough young Madagascan girl with a mane of long black hair. After word got out that we were looking for an interpreter, she arrived at the Hotel de France looking for us. Her English is good and she has trekked the rainforests before. I like the fact that she has her own rucksack and well-worn hiking boots. She understands the dialects of the south and is a bit of a GI Jane-type character. Although she admits to being afraid of what lies ahead, especially the danger of Zebu cattle bandits, she agrees to be our brand new expedition member. She's prepared to take up the challenge, and we like her for it. It will also be

23°27'

BAKOLY RAZANAMIARANTSOA
SHE'S GOT QUITE A SURNAME HASN'T SHE –
BAKOLY IS AN EXPERIENCED TRANSLATOR
AND GUIDE AND HAS EXPERIENCE IN
'TREKKING' THE MADAGASCAN RAIN FOREST
SHE'S ONE OF 10 CHILDREN AND UNDERSTANDS
THE DIALECTS OF THE SOUTH – SHE ADMITS TO
BEING AFRAID OF WHAT LIES AHEAD ESPECIALLY
ZEBU CATTLE BANDITS – WE LIKE HER AND
HIRE HER FOR THE MADAGASCAN LEG –

B – WITH HER
MANE OF BLACK
HAIR AND THE
CAPRICORN
CALABASH –.

good for Gill to have a female companion and, what's even better, she says she's a good cook. We nickname her 'B'.

Travelling south, I can see Madagascar's diversity in the people's faces: a unique blend of south-east Asian, African, Indian and Chinese, not to mention Portuguese, British, Dutch, and pirates of many nations – all of whom attempted to settle here. After these peoples came the French, and now a team of 'odd bods' trying to follow the Capricorn line.

As the taxi makes its way to the starting point of the expedition we discover that Mammy is a terrible driver. He switches off the engine and freewheels down the hills at a furious rate, dodging Zebu carts, hand-pulled trolleys, cattle and sheep, ancient lorries and pedestrians carrying goods to market. We reach our overnight stop thankful to be alive!

The town of Antsirabe lies 169 kilometres south of Antananarivo and was founded in 1872 by Norwegian missionaries, who were attracted by the cool climate and the healing properties of the thermal springs here. For Mashozi and B it's the best place to buy basic supplies for the journey ahead. We choose some inexpensive, Third-World lodgings for the night and the two women take off by *pousse-pousse*, the Malagasy version of a rickshaw. Brightly painted and often with amusing names, several hundred *pousse-pousses* fill the town streets. This is the main form of transport and it provides tough employment for the barefoot athletes who spend a lifetime pulling goods and people around Antsirabe. The old Imperial Hotel serves us the best Chinese meal I have ever tasted, which we wash down with the local Three Horses beer. We get a few shy smiles from the 'working girls' in the foyer when we leave, and get back to our lodgings by *pousse-pousse* pulled by friendly operators Joseph and Jean-Claude.

Day 315: Bed springs and rice paddies

After negotiating with the hotel staff and agreeing on a price, we are proudly escorted upstairs to our hotel room. The porter finally gets the key to fit the lock, and we settle in, our mountain of rucksacks and expedition gear piled up on the floor. A little fellow armed with a pair of scissors comes running into the room. With a flourish he cuts a cotton thread joining the sheets to the well-used bedspread. Beaming with pleasure he holds up the thread – proof that no one else could have slept in the bed – so we presume the sheets are clean.

Third-World hotels in Africa, parts of South America and Madagascar seem to follow the same few basic rules. Plumbing and sewage should never work properly and must have that characteristic smell of rotten cabbage, bed springs have to be squeaky and sag to the floor, and there must always be a spaghetti-like jumble of electrical wires, not to mention lights that flicker or simply give up the ghost. The sound of traffic, livestock, early morning roosters, giggles and bumping and grinding from the room next door make up the generally acceptable cacophony of night sounds. Tonight these also include Joseph, Jean-Claude and a group of other *pousse-pousse* operators, who wait patiently outside our room in the hope of further business.

Day 316: The Dash to Fianarantsoa

After an indifferent night's sleep we're back in Mammy's Peugeot taxi, racing across the highlands. We are in the country of the Merina, of Malaya-Polynesian origin, whose double-storey houses are built mostly of brick or mud. We stop to buy bananas and bread in the colourful town of Ambositra. Some claim it means 'place of eunuchs', a reference to a battle during which the Merina destroyed the village of the neighbouring Betsileo people, after which there was a sacrifice and mass castration of the Betsileo. We don't stick around here; our destination is Fianarantsoa, home to the Betsileo, who are renowned throughout Madagascar for their rice cultivation techniques.

We hold on for dear life, as the taxi careers along the narrow road that takes us through a vista of terraced rice paddies in vivid shades of green. Some of the bridges on the way were blown up during the recent civil unrest and we are forced to detour over makeshift causeways. Roadblocks abound and there is a strong police and military presence. Obviously our party is quite out of the ordinary and invites suspicion, but this turns to salutes, smiles and handshakes when we produce the Capricorn Scroll of Peace and Goodwill – now signed by the President.

THE GREYBEARD RESTING ON A POUSSE- POUSSE

It's dark by the time Mammy's taxi roars into Fianarantsoa.

Day 317: By antique train through the rainforests

We're up at first light, but get off to a bad start. Ross has a kidney infection. He's had it for some days now and is treating himself with antibiotics. I've got the squits from an underdone Zebu steak I ate last night. We say goodbye to Mammy. Secretly I'm glad to see the last of him and his Peugeot taxi, but I'm not sure if the old train to the coast will be any safer.

The decaying French colonial railway station at Fianarantsoa is packed, and travellers loaded with goods push forward onto the narrow platform. There is great excitement, as this is the only rail link to the east coast. Our first-class tickets don't guarantee us a seat; people clamber aboard, the departure whistle sounds and flags are waved, but nothing happens and no-one seems to care. A mere two hours later we set off through the rainforest. The antique carriages

23°27'

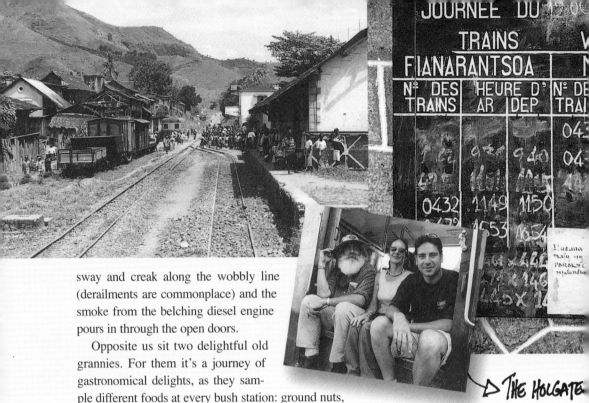

D THE HOLGATE

sway and creak along the wobbly line (derailments are commonplace) and the smoke from the belching diesel engine pours in through the open doors.

Opposite us sit two delightful old grannies. For them it's a journey of gastronomical delights, as they sample different foods at every bush station: ground nuts, smoked fruit bat, freshwater prawns, boiled cassava in banana leaves, bananas, brochettes of Zebu meat stabbed onto wooden sticks and pieces of boiled pork.

I get special permission from the train driver to ride up front on the cowcatcher, as the locomotive sways, screeches and groans round the corners, and roars through countless narrow, stone-walled tunnels. It's a rollercoaster ride through some of the most fascinating scenery I've ever seen, with hills and valleys shrouded in misty rainforests that seem to go on forever. David Fox's words echo through my mind, 'You must be bloody crazy. I don't think you've got a chance in hell.'

The outline of countless rainforest mountains to the south, where the Capricorn line is, looks beautiful but frightening. Is this the type of terrain we'll have to cross? I get a sick feeling. If we can't get porters who know the area, we'll be in trouble.

The ramshackle stations and this antique train are the forest dwellers' only link to the outside world and today our Capricorn party is the latest attraction. At Mahabako Station kids come forward to feel my beard, others just to stare. A pretty little girl carries a flat winnowing basket full of yellow bananas on her head, others offer duck eggs, trays of cooked liver and fried strips of Zebu. A leper approaches with hands outstretched. One of his legs is a matchstick, the other a knobbly pink and red mass of huge, leprous growths. I give him some money; he smiles and moves off into the crowd. It's dark by the time we get to Manakara, on the Indian Ocean, where, amidst huge confusion and much good humour, we're carted off by *poussepousse* to some palm-thatched bungalows on the beach. The civil unrest in Madagascar kept foreign visitors away for months, and I think our arrival is seen as a return to peace on the island. During the night, a strong wind blows off the Indian Ocean, the palm trees whistle and sigh and a tropical rainstorm cools the night air and keeps the mozzies at bay. We've made it to the east coast and are a step closer to reaching 23° 27'.

192

Day 318: Nymphets and dugouts

I've lived most of my life on the east coast of Africa, so it's good to walk barefoot in the sand and smell the tropical vegetation again. Over a breakfast of pawpaws, bananas, French bread, honey and coffee, Tim tells us how, as he was entering his hut last night, a young nymphet with a sparkling gem in her nose suddenly appeared from beneath the palm trees. 'Her intentions,' says Tim (who really is quite a gentleman, born in Malawi of colonial stock), 'were very obvious, and there was no doubt she fancied a night with me under the old mozzie net! She was a real sweetie, and even got as far as putting her foot in the door. In broken French I tried to get across my firm refusal. She was shocked! How could I refuse a night of pleasure? In desperation I said, "Not t'night Josephine, please come back tomorrow evening," knowing full well we'd be gone by then. So she smiled sweetly and asked for money for *pousse-pousse*.' B is amazed: 'Why didn't you let her in?' Yes, indeed, many of the Malagasy girls are beautiful and willing – it's a pretty island.

The Canal des Pangalanes is a string of natural rivers and artificial lakes, which stretches for approximately 600 kilometres from Toamasina to Farafangana, on the east coast. Huge, green elephant ear plants skirt the waters. It's absolutely beautiful, and we do a section by *pirogue*. One could spend weeks here, but our destination remains Vangaindrano, the closest town to the Tropic of Capricorn. We find digs at the Tropic Hotel, run by Félicité and Jeanine. Helped by B, they cook up a feast of tough Zebu stew, wild spinach and sweet potatoes for us. In this little hotel the letter 'R' is carved into the wooden pelmets above the doors, and into the bed headboards and diningroom chairs. We're told it stands for Robson

The two old ducks on the train attempt to teach me Malagasy, a language with its origins in Indonesia. Malagasy words and phrases can be very poetic, I learn. The Malagasy term for 'dusk' is 'maizim-bava vilany', which, literally translated, means 'darken the mouth of the cooking pot'. 'Two or three o'clock in the morning' is 'misafo heilika ny kary', which means 'when the wild cat washes itself'.

Place names may have up to 14 or 15 letters, and are difficult to pronounce. We've got the London Missionary Society to thank for the fact that Malagasy is no longer written in the Arabic script with which it was originally transcribed, but the pronunciation does make it difficult to recognise written words when you hear them spoken. When words end in a vowel the final syllable is pronounced so lightly that it is often just a stressed last consonant. For example – and this I learn from Bradt's informative Guide to Madagascar – the Sifaka lemur is pronounced (rude, but memorable) as 'she-fuck', but words derived from English like 'banky' and 'hotely' are pronounced much the same as in English. Difficult, isn't it? My favourite phrase becomes 'hona no vaovao' – 'What's news?' or 'How're things going?'

MASHOZI & THE GASTRONOMICS!

Ronaldo, the former President's representative in the nearby market town Vangaindrano. Now he's nowhere to be seen, and I understand that many of the past President's people have been jailed or are in hiding.

Day 319: At the ocean on 23°27'

We make our way on foot down to the beach on 23° 27'. It is with great emotion that Mashozi, Ross and I dip the calabash into the Indian Ocean, south-east of Vangaindrano. Ahead of us lies our journey along Madagascar's Tropic of Capricorn.

Rain clouds gather and the humidity is so high that the air feels as thick as golden syrup. Local fishermen are amazed to come across this little family going though a strange ritual of filling a beaded Zulu calabash with seawater. But, after all, Madagascar is an island of strange taboos, beliefs and rituals (known as *fady*). Most Madagascans share a belief in the power of ancestors, known as *Razana*. Zebu cattle are sacrificed to the ancestors and, in the highlands, *Famadihana* (the turning of the bones) is still practised. This is a ceremony of great rejoicing, during which the corpse of a dead relative is exhumed, wrapped in new shrouds and paraded around the village, before being returned to the family tomb. The corpse is treated as though it were alive – it is spoken to, shown new developments in the village, involved in the feasting and generally given a good outing. B explains to me: 'Here on this great island we never forget our dead relatives. We are forever together, dead or alive.' Wouldn't it be great, I think, if after I'm dead my old bones could be taken down to the local for a booze-up!

Days 320–322: Jean Baptiste's tractor

Walking through the coastal forest we come across a giant chameleon. Madagascar's natural wealth includes half the world's chameleons, some reaching 70 centimetres in length, B tells us. She goes on to explain that seeing a chameleon means good *fady* or good luck. We laugh and push on. She says that for some clans chameleons are taboo and considered bad luck. Others believe that the Malagasy people are like chameleons, one eye on their ancestral past, the other looking into the future. Rain drips off the banana leaves and we duck under the thatched eaves of a village hut on the outskirts of Vangaindrano.

B's heard a government tractor and trailer are stationed

IT WOULD BE IMPOSSIB.
WITHOUT THE PORTERS –
ESPECIALLY BARTO THE
BRAVE .

here for general road maintenance and for transporting government supplies. We negotiate with Jean Baptiste, the tractor's driver, to take us up the mud track to the village of Bekofafa. We sign a little contract with Jean Baptiste: 750 000 FMG (Malagasy francs) – half now to buy diesel, the other half on safe delivery to our destination. He'll pick us up in the morning.

Never in my life have I had such an uncomfortable ride. How we miss the Land Rovers! It takes us two days to do 48 kilometres. At anything over 10 kilometres per hour the tractor and trailer go into a frenzied epileptic fit that pulverises our backsides and loosens our teeth. One wrong move of the steering wheel and we'll slide over the edge, hundreds of metres into the deep gorges below. It's really dangerous, and we slip and slide through deep, red mud. As the track climbs steeply up towards the peaks of the coastal rainforest, my mind goes back to our crossing of Brazil through the tropical forests and mountains of the Serra do Mar.

The local Barra people are poor but friendly, and we buy groundnuts, bananas and sweet potatoes from them as we pass through their villages. At the village of Ranomena we hire porters for the long journey ahead. We will need them to guide us, find food and assist with the carrying of our expedition kit and supplies. We understand there are absolutely no roads ahead and that we will have to rely on the porters to show us the way along a small track that leads to the village of Ampihamy. From there we will either have to find new porters or rely on these ones to continue through to a dot on the map called Ivahona, which is approximately 250 kilometres from here. The porters tell us that this is a route seldom travelled and that along the way there are mountains, rainforests and, in the drier areas beyond, the danger of Zebu cattle bandits. A number of young men in this area regularly hire out their services as porters to carry food crops (mostly rice) to village markets in the outlying areas. As my personal porter I choose Barto (short for Bartholomew), a man of 28 with large, cracked feet and a wide, toothy grin. He's a simple rice farmer of the Antisaka people, and is married with two children and another on the way. He soon teaches me a few words of Malagasy. No foreigners come this way and this is the very first time he will be making the journey west.

Jean Baptiste's tractor finally brings us and our porters to the Itomampi River. Hell, are we glad to see the last of his metal monster! B is concerned about crocodiles, explaining

INDIAN OCEAN
DIP CALABASH
VANGAINDRANO
JEAN BAPTISTE'S TRACTOR
RANOMENA PORTERS
BEKOFAFA VILLAGE
CROCS!!
ITOMAMPI RIVER
WE CROSS BY DUG OUT
SAKATAVY VILLAGE
RAIN FOREST MTS
CAPRICORN 23°27
FOREST CAPRICORN CAIRN
TO PROTECT THE FOREST
TOUGH GOING!
SWAMPS
BEGOGO VILLAGE BARRA TRIBE – SOME OF THE CHILDREN HAVE NOT SEEN WHITE PEOPLE BEFORE!
STEEP HARD GOING
ANTANDROI CHANT IN THE NIGHT!
AMPIHAMY VILLAGE
BEAUTIFUL WATERFALLS
IVAHONA – WE SAY GOODBYE TO THE PORTERS

that many Malagasy people fear crocodiles and snakes, believing they are reincarnated people, but we're too tired to worry, and we camp on a sand bank. Soon we have a fire going and the nine porters dip into a huge pot of rice and vegetable sauce, using banana leaves as spoons. We pour some Captain Morgan into a boiling pot of ground coffee and add condensed milk and sugar. It tastes delicious. I only know a few tunes on the harmonica; these include a rugby version of 'Gallway Bay', 'Waltzing Matilda', 'We are Marching to Pretoria' and the Swahili favourite 'Maleaka'. Still, the porters enjoy the diversion and it takes our minds off what we believe will be a very tough journey ahead. Ross goes through the survey maps and plots GPS points. Only one of the porters, a tough-looking youngster by the name of Gobi, has been as far as the village of Ampihamy. That was two months ago, to sell rice. Let's hope he remembers the way. It rains during the night and the porters quickly erect a bivouac of banana leaves supported with sticks.

Days 323–332: Ten days of hell

Madagascans have an almost mystical attachment to rice. King Andrianampoinimerina (how's that for a name?) declared in the 18th century: 'Rice and I are one.' Loyalty to the King was even symbolised by time spent in the rice paddies. The Malagasy eat rice three times a day and the annual consumption is estimated at 135 kilograms per person. Watching the porters at breakfast I realise it might be twice that, or perhaps they were simply starving for a good meal. Part of the contract with the porters is that we will supply them with food. Rice, I learn, is the measure of all things. The traditional Malagasy calendar is constructed in terms of the different stages in rice cultivation and a journey such as ours is measured not in days but in the number of pots of rice that will need to be cooked in the span of time it will take to walk the journey. We even use *ranovola* (rice water), obtained by boiling water in the pan in which the rice was cooked, as a thirst quencher.

I realise that our journey can only succeed if we have enough rice, and so we send a few of the porters off to purchase some more from the village of Bekofafa. We add sweet potatoes, and the promise of village chickens if all goes well. All this negotiation with the porters is done through B. She rations the food and distributes the loads that they bear, carried on either end of a pole supported over the shoulder. It is mid-morning by the time we've all crossed the Itomampi River by *pirogue*.

In these mountain rainforests there are no pack donkeys or oxen. Everything is carried by porters and, whilst our mountain bikes are helpful for the first few kilometres, we soon realise what a mistake it was to bring them. The rainforests are so thick and the paths so steep and narrow that it is impossible to use them and they become handicaps of branch-catching metal that have to be carried through the forest. The villages are far apart now and the forests exceptionally beautiful. There is the constant sound of lemurs and birds, and the mountain streams are clear and fresh. The going gets harder and harder, as we make our way along steep, narrow paths, through thick rainforests and the occasional reeded swamp, where we sink up to our knees in stinking black mud. The porters are extremely tough, balancing their loads over stepping-stones and single-pole bridges. The sweat streams from my brow and off the tip of my nose. The path zig-zags through high mountains and thick forests. One day we walk 38 kilometres, but according to the GPS it's only 8.9 kilometres as the crow flies. Still, it's the only way forward through this rough country. Tim and Mashozi begin to suffer badly with blisters, and my old knee injury forces me to wear an uncomfortable knee brace. Soon I'm dissolving painkillers in my waterbottle and I once again start to resent this body that I'm forced to live in.

Boots and socks on, boots and socks off – the river crossings are endless. Our evening camp locations are wonderfully picturesque, but we are forever in search of more food and long-necked village chickens for the porters. Mashozi continues to hate this killing of live-stock, especially when the chickens are tied squawking to the porter's baggage and marched alive towards a supper destination, where B will cook them up with rice. The porters can't believe her complaints and the fact that she makes sure the trussed-up fowls are given water at each stream or stop. Needless to say, she sticks to rice and veggies as part of her anti-chicken campaign, which means a little more protein for us and the porters. The purchase of village chickens is a huge incentive for the porters, who are happy to push hard for the next village in the hope of adding chicken to their rice. Barto the Brave's few English words now include 'cheekin', uttered with a huge, toothy grin and a thumbs-up sign.

For a day now, B has been rather grumpy and uncommunicative, complaining of a headache, fever and sore kidneys. During the night the fever gets worse and we hear her groaning from her tent. Fortunately, she recognises the symptoms of malaria, treats herself and sweats it out.

In the morning she's up and about. We offer to rest up for the day but she's having none of it. She gives a few crisp commands to the porters and soon has her rucksack on her back. She really is a tough cookie. Our road across Madagascar is a thin, red, eroded path that clings to the contours of the long mountain range that runs like a spine down the length of Madagascar. I constantly have to stop and gasp for breath. The views are endless, and one day runs into the next. In the villages woven mats are spread out for us in the shade of the eaves of the mud-walled huts. It is so much like mainland Africa, but so different. The physical features of the people's faces betray a distant Malaysian/ Polynesian origin, and the soft tones of their language are very different from the Swahili of East Africa, from which Madagascar broke away in the separation of the Gondwanaland super-continent some 160 million years ago.

'At each village we come to, wide-eyed, snotty-nosed children come up to shake our hands. They stare at my beard in disbelief. Many of them have not seen white people before, and here I limp into camp, wild looking and sweat-stained – not exactly the ideal exam-ple of the European race. Eggs, rice and chick-ens are brought to our camp. The village girls dance shyly and sing a song about a lovers' quarrel. Most of them are beautiful, and when they dance they use delicate hand movements, much like those practised in the East. After each village the endless walk carries on.

THE CALABASH IS CAREFULLY
WRAPPED IN A RUCKSACK —
THE SCROLL GETS SIGNED
BY VILLAGE HEADMEN —

One night we camp in a pristine rainforest clearing, and with the help of the porters we erect a Capricorn cairn of stones, topped with a Capricorn sign. I tell the porters it's a *fady* to protect the rainforest and, as if on cue, the birds call from the forest and a family of brown lemurs come swinging through the tall trees. I'll remember the beauty of this place forever. As we exit from a patch of dark, steaming rainforest, B smears honey on a forest altar of tall stones that marks an old grave. We all go quiet as she mumbles a prayer in Malagasy. Later she tells me that her heartfelt prayer was for us not to be attacked by Zebu cattle bandits. She seems really concerned about this and constantly questions the porters about our safety.

There's a certain loneliness to our journey. Travelling with our porters we're like a small trickle of ants attempting to cross a giant landscape. After a cold, wet night we awake to immense solitude. Our satellite phone batteries are dead and there isn't a person on earth who knows where we are. 'Barto the Brave' points to my knee with his stick, 'Kingsley's knee, big f... up,' he says, and laughs. I have been teaching him some English! He has become a great friend, helping me cross rivers and narrow pole bridges and forever darting off to fill our waterbottles upstream where the water is cleaner. He helps Mashozi and me with camp duties and has great strength and determination.

In the middle of the night, whilst camped in a dry river bed, we are disturbed by the mournful singing and chanting of what sounds like a large group of men on the move. Are these the dangerous Zebu cattle thieves, I wonder? They walk through our camp but don't stop, and we hear their singing and chanting echoing from way up in the mists of the rainforest. Next morning we learn from B that they were a group of Antandroi men who have made their way from the arid western plains to the rainforest. They have come to cut down a big tree, with which to make a coffin for a dead man from their village. This they will carry back on their shoulders for 100 kilometres or more. The sound of their singing and chanting is very similar to that of the Nilotic Samburu and Masai, and we wonder at the connections between these people and those of East Africa, from where some Madagascans originally came.

Finally, after zig-zagging for some 250 kilometres along the Tropic of Capricorn, we reach the village of Ivahona. It has a school, a Catholic church, a row or two of thatched mud-brick huts and a weekly village market. The entire population of about a thousand people turns out to see us limping down the dusty main street. We clear the little trading store out of Cokes and Fantas and devour a plastic bag full of rock-hard biscuits.

There is a track from Ivahona, which we are hoping to follow to the Mangoky River by vehicle. Then we plan to continue from here down the river by *pirogue*, so this is the end of the road for our friendly porters. We pay them more than the agreed amount, then empty our rucksacks of everything we can give away. Barto is quite emotional. I gave him a cycling shirt, Captain Morgan raincoat and a Land Rover cap. The porters all take time to sign the Capricorn Scroll. Some, like the Bushmen in the Kalahari, the Topnaars in the Namib and the South American Guaranese, can only endorse the page with a shaky cross. Still, they are men of men, with a true warrior ethic – without them we'd never have made it. We've reached the halfway mark; they'll have to return all the way home. They ask us to sign the

THINGS GO BAD!

notebooks from their village, a sort of passport or *carnet de passage* to prove that they've been porters with us and are not returning with money and goods from the proceeds of stolen Zebu cattle. We wish them *veloma* (goodbye) and *bon voyage*. 'Barto the Brave' waves until he is out of sight down the dusty path. I'll miss him.

Days 333–340: At an all-time low...

An old Peugeot pick-up and a commandeered foreign-aid Land Rover carry us across wide Serengeti-type plains to our next destination, the village of Ianakafy on the Mangoky River. From here we hope to use *pirogues* for the next leg of the journey. To our great disappointment, we learn this isn't going to be possible. We are out of the mountains and rainforests now – here it's hot and dry. There's been no rain and the river is too low for dugouts. We've got a difficult decision to make: do we take the long detour around by road or do we stick to the Capricorn Line and walk it? We are absolutely dog tired and fatigued. Mashozi has blood blisters on blood blisters and she's so exhausted that we're concerned she won't make it. My knee's swollen and extremely painful, Tim, the old campaigner, is able to soldier on although he's having trouble with his feet, but Ross is pale and bilious. If he's not okay by tonight we'll treat him for malaria. B is over her bout of malaria and is keen to give it a go.

I miss my good friend Barto – I came to rely on him. The situation now is a very different kettle of fish. Most of the porters here are drunk and slovenly, a dodgy lot from an area where the people trade in stolen cattle and sapphires. The vibe is not good. They take one look at us and double the normal rate: 100 000 FMG or they are not interested. To be honest, I don't blame them. We look such a sorry sight and they know they've got us between a rock and a hard place. B says we must be careful, and gets the local *gendarme* (a hard-bitten character) to write down the names and details of all the porters in case there is an incident. And so, despite our condition, we decide to move on. We've completed nine of the ten Capricorn countries around the world. How can we give it up now? Mashozi is unsure about her ability to go on. Ross sits in the shade with his head in his hands; he now has a fever. Tim is worried about getting to the west coast in time to get back to Tana and then on to Kenya, where he is committed as cameraman on an important wildlife shoot. All I know is that there is no turning back, despite the fact that we're at an all-time low, huddled in the shade in this rather unfriendly village.

It takes hours to organise our new porters. I understand better now how it must have been for the early explorers who, like ourselves, were totally reliant upon the goodwill of porters. B does a fantastic job, strutting around organising the loads and chatting to the men. With her massive mane of black hair and her little khaki shorts struggling to contain her energetic bottom, our girl from Tana totally confuses the porters.

By the time we reach the Mangoky River, Ross is too weak even to put up a tent. He's vomiting and has diarrhoea. I treat him for dysentery and, as it happens, Mashozi, whom we were most worried about, ends up nursing us both, as I develop an intense fever, severe headache and sore kidneys – the first signs of malaria. She immediately treats me with Artesan and Doxycyline. It's a bad night all round, but still we rise at 4 am to try to beat the heat. For Ross and me it is the worst day of our journey, as we struggle on past rocks and baobabs in

23°27'

the intense heat. Here there are no crystal clear rainforest streams, so the porters dig holes in the river sand and suck the brak water, using their shirts as filters. We use purification pills and hope for the best. We buy village chickens, which we eat with rice, and drink Bovril in hot water. I spend my days thinking about putting one foot in front of the other and water, cool, cool water, not to mention a long glass of Captain Morgan, Coke and ice!

Tim and B are okay, and Ross and I are growing stronger, but poor Mashozi is now absolutely whacked. I find her sitting on an anthill refusing to go another step, tears streaming down her cheeks. I think how tough all this is for her small frame, but I know dynamite comes in small packages. Tim and I urge her on, explaining that we will camp on the banks of the nearby Imaloto River. The map indicates it's about four kilometres away. Like a Comrades Marathon runner, she draws on her inner strength and we move on: her small frame wobbling along, her legs sticking out from her faded khaki shorts, her dusty brown boots plodding forward – who would guess that she's a granny! Tim, who is doing a great job of recording our journey, asks her to do a piece to camera. She gets toughly emotional and delivers a firm message. 'I want you to know,' she says, 'should anything happen to me out here, I don't want my bones to be buried in Madagascar. I demand to go back to Africa!' Although born in England, Mashozi regards Africa as her home. We've been married for 35 years and I love her to bits.

At the riverbank a soldier with an AK 47 tells us to wade across the Imaloto River. Too dangerous to camp here, he says, as we're surrounded by rough and tough miners who are scratching sapphires from the riverbank. It's nearly dark, the river is deep and swift-running, and we're concerned about crocs, but in we go, wading up to our waists.

Mashozi is desperately tired and running solely on adrenaline now. We're almost across when Tim slips backwards on a sloping shelf of rock and the video camera goes under. There is a shocked silence. He should have had it in a plastic bag, but, like the rest of us, he was just too exhausted. When he reaches the opposite bank he tries to dry it out, but it's gone on the blink with a used tape stuck inside. What a disaster! What will happen to our National Geographic documentary, without which we've got no way to pay for this crazy adventure? To get another camera flown out from SA would be an expedition in itself: we're in the middle of nowhere.

We camp for the night and B cooks up some rice, but we are all too tired and dehydrated to eat. We boil some sweet tea, but, sadly, the rum is finished. Sapphire bandits nearby or not, we sleep like the dead. Next morning poor Tim is as down as his dead camera. We boil up some dirty water and drink it with Bovril. I dream of fried eggs, sunny side up, baked beans, bacon, marmalade and toast. We trudge on into the heat. The rocky outcrops look like Zimbabwe's Matopos and the giant baobabs remind us of home. By midday Mashozi is walking in a trance. Too tired to drink, she needs to be stopped every few minutes and forced to swallow from her waterbottle. The path becomes sandy as we stumble through thick dryland bush and scrub. The constant ringing of the cicadas (Christmas beetles) is deafening.

In the distance I hear Ross calling, 'Nondwayiza!' my Zulu name. I answer him, but hear no reply. Then his call comes again and we change direction to find Tim and Ross seated in a village stuffing bright yellow mangos, skin and all, into their mouths, their chins and shirts yellow with mango juice. Soon Mashozi and I, and the remaining porters (most have gone ahead to the village of Benenitra with B, as our food has run out and they were determined to push ahead) are biting hungrily into the soft, yellow, succulent flesh. Mashozi eats eight and Tim, Ross and I something like ten each. Instantly our strength returns and we begin to laugh at our predicament, and how ridiculous it is to be following this bloody imaginary line.

A pretty, smiling girl with gold in her teeth feels my swollen back and ankles, and shakes her head. A tall sapphire miner, who looks like a pirate and is armed with a long knife, eyes us up and down, then shares a mango with us. There is a cart track leading out of the village towards Benenitra. I draw a picture in my notebook of humped Zebu oxen pulling a cart, then point at Mashozi's feet and go through a bit of a charade. A smiling villager scribbles 25 000 FMG. I shake hands with him; we have a deal. Soon two tame, silk-skinned Zebu are being led to the yoke. We throw our rucksacks into the cart and help Mashozi climb aboard the cart, with iron-rimmed, wooden-spoked wheels, chauffeured by a bare-chested young Barra man. Tim, Ross and I walk behind the cart, happy to be free of our rucksacks and strengthened by the mango feast. Mashozi lies, uncomplaining, like a corpse amongst the luggage; her boots are off and her blistered toes point up towards the sun.

The country east of the market town of Benenitra is breathtaking: far pavilions of blue mountains feed clear streams and bright green rice paddies. We swim in a shallow stream. The views are all too much for Tim, who decides to try resurrecting his deceased camera. I sit in the shade of a tree and wait. Ross works some technical wizardry with a screwdriver and everyone is delighted when the old tape ejects. Tim inserts a new one and the camera, although noisy, starts rolling. What a relief!

WATER BOTTLES

DOG TIRED AND WORN OUT

We find it's market day when we hobble into town and literally hundreds of villagers surge forward to see a white woman being carried into Benenitra on a Zebu cart. B, the porters and all the kit are there to meet us. The administrator allows us to use his humble office. We call for drinks and the villagers cram every door and window to get a better view of the strange Capricorn foreigners. Soon the heavens open and the tropical rain comes down in torrents. I hear people screaming and shouting as an out-of-control Zebu cart comes tearing though the village, the oxen at full gallop. The wooden cart bounces off a verandah post and tips onto one wheel as it rounds the corner. The cart driver whoops and shouts with glee; Madagascan rum is cheap and drunk driving is not limited to motor vehicles. We pay off the porters and shake hands warmly, there's something about sharing a difficult journey that binds people together.

I think B has pushed herself too hard; she is now exhausted. Nevertheless, we push on to Belamoty. Packed like sardines in the back in of an old orange diesel truck, we share the journey with mothers and babies, sapphire traders and merchants returning from the market. A jolly band of local musicians with homemade guitars and drums livens up the journey, and the passengers howl with delight as Ross and I stand up and wobble our weary bodies to the rhythmic music. The narrow, sandy track crosses river beds and rice paddies, and we stop at every village to load and off-load passengers and goods. Sure, my body aches and my mind is numb with fatigue, but somehow for the first time I can taste victory. It's dark by the time we reach the village of Belamoty, where once again we are mobbed by hundreds of locals who come running out of their reed huts when they catch sight of us. It's obviously been a long time since foreigners came this way. Tim rolls the camera with a grin. To be a cameraman on expedition requires an enormous amount of extra effort and he is always ready with a smile or a joke. Mashozi laughingly calls him the vicar, because of his colonial upbringing and his proper English ways. The owner of the lorry signs our Capricorn Scroll with a flourish. The 50-kilometre journey has taken us a bone-jarring three hours.

Day 341: Sister Mary and the nuns of Belamoty

At Belamoty we meet our first white person along Madagasar's Tropic of Capricorn. Her name is Sister Mary Raphael, and she came out to this village from Brighton some 20 years ago. She stayed to help heal the sick and teach in the school. Once the chief of the village agrees that we can stay, Sister Mary and the Malagasy sisters simply can't do enough for us. Two old, high-ceilinged rooms are swept out, candles are lit and water for bathing is drawn from the well. The mozzies buzz furiously. 'Yes,' say the sisters, 'malaria is very bad here.' We are called to supper; they must have opened up the pantry and used all their supplies. The table is beautifully prepared and, after our days in the bush and rainforests, everything looks so neat and clean. Sister Mary says grace in Malagasy, and a feast of chicken, rice, soup and eggs appears, followed by tea, coffee, biscuits, fruit salad and condensed milk. We can't believe our good fortune.

Sister Mary struggles at first with her English; she hasn't spoken it for so long. But once she gets started she talks and talks, telling us of her struggle here, the lack of drugs and supplies, the days of French colonialism and then the socialist period when she was forced to attend Marxist indoctrination classes. But now, after the recent civil unrest, things are back to

IT'S GETTING CLOSER - I CAN ALMOST SMEL
THE INDIAN OCEAN & THE END OF MADAGASCA

normal and she hopes for the best. 'Armed Zebu cattle thieves do roam the area, but if caught they are publicly burnt to death in the village and, recently, a minor offender had his hands chopped off. These were paraded around the village on a stick. But you must understand,' she says with a smile, 'cattle rustling is a way of life. How else can a young man pay for a bride?'

Next morning we are taken around the small hospital. Zebu carts packed with straw serve as ambulances. There is a little girl there, paralysed down one side and they don't think she will make it. One young man in the hospital was gored by a bull. The refrigerator motor has packed up and there is no way of keeping their limited drug supply cool enough. Still, Sister Mary remains hopeful. We will try to send her parts from South Africa when we get back. Finally, we wave goodbye; the mission pickup truck is giving us a lift to the coast. In the Capricorn journal Sister

ROSS AND THE SISTERS OF BELAMOTY MISSION

Mary writes, 'Courage, the end is in sight – you must have accumulated an enormous store of beauty to take home with you.' Our journey will soon be over and we'll return to our home comforts; it's Sister Mary who has the courage.

Day 342: Pirates, tombs and slave traders

Our Capricorn journey takes us through spiny forests, ancient baobabs and decorated tombs. Our destination is the northern end of the Bay of St Augustine, one of the early trading sites for 16th- and 17th-century European pirates, slavers and spice traders. A Zebu cart carries our kit out to sea, the oxen neck deep in water. The wind fills the square sail of a lightweight *pirogue*, hand-crafted from dry forest trees. Ferdinand and Pamdakara, our skipper and crew member, are rugged, nomadic Vezo fishermen, guardians of ancient maritime sailing skills that brought the first immigrants to Madagascar. We sail out into the azure blue of the Mozambique Channel. The wind picks up and Ferdinand, looking like a tough, weathered pirate, rides the outrigger. Ross checks the GPS. Dead on 23° 27' we turn into the wind to empty the Zulu calabash of seawater that we've carried across Madagascar.

I pass Ross the calabash and push him overboard. We all hug and shake hands. Mashozi has tears in her eyes – there've been no rats! Tim smiles with relief. I wonder how he's managed to find the extra energy to film this whole journey. He is one of South Africa's greatest adventure cameramen, and unfailingly good humoured. B dives overboard: what a girl. Ross's eyes are sunken – he has lost a great deal of weight. The sun sets over the Mozambique Channel. I must admit there have been times when I thought that we wouldn't make it, but we have!

Day 343–354: Mama Africa welcomes us home

We've flown back here to South Africa, but our journey's not entirely finished yet. Our Capricorn Expedition is a circle, and to complete our circumnavigation of the globe by land along the Tropic of Capricorn we must head back to the Limpopo River and then on to 23° 27', just north of the ancient city of Inhambane.

Day 355: Back on 23° 27'

When we last followed this track through the coconut palms and down to the beach, there was nothing here. Now some South Africans with a Mozambican partner are building a small palm-thatched lodge, virtually on Capricorn. We make our way down to the exact point on 23° 27'. It's humid and overcast; old friends Ann and Don Balmer have joined us, as have Ross's girlfriend Geraldine and their son Tristan Kingsley, who is now two years old and dances like a Zulu champion.

We swim in the warm Indian Ocean, pitch our tents, throw meat on the coals and have a party sitting around a blazing driftwood fire. Then the rain hits us: it's the tail of a cyclone, and soon our tents are blown flat and we're running around in the rain trying to tie them down. The wind and rain are ferocious and everyone is quickly drenched to the skin, as the elements howl and whistles around us. Ann and Don's tent starts to flood and they are forced to stab holes through their groundsheet to let the water out. It seems as if the Tropic of Capricorn wishes to be remembered to the last.

Day 356–357: Bringing the Capricorn calabash home

We take the Zulu calabash that has travelled around the world on the Tropic of Capricorn, and fill it with Indian Ocean seawater. This is a symbolic end to the expedition. Outside the Governor's Headquarters in Inhambane, Señor Aires Ali signs off the Capricorn Scroll of Peace and Goodwill. Colourful local resident and owner of Barra Lodge, Dave Law is also there to congratulate us, as is our old friend Erwin Jakes from Maxixe.

From Inhambane we head south across the Limpopo River. It's been a great adventure and it seems as if the water in the calabash has connected our African Cradle of Humankind to the other Capricorn countries around the globe. The Capricorn Scroll of Peace and Goodwill is full of messages, signatures and simple crosses. It's been endorsed by friends, village headmen, governors, chiefs, old wizened Bushmen, South American Guaranese Indians, central Australian Aboriginals, mayors, the new President of Madagascar, barefoot porters, Vezo fishermen and now, finally, the Governor of Inhambane.

Day 358: Capricorn - The End

It's late afternoon by the time we drive the travel-weary Land Rovers into the cattle kraal at Shakaland from where

WELCOME HOME SMILES! FROM GRANDSON TRISTAN AND THE ZULUS AT SHAKALAND —

we left some 18 months ago. It feels like a dream. Friends, media and sponsors are all there to meet us. It's wonderful to be back home, as water from the calabash is sprinkled onto the floor of the great hut.

The dust rises as the Zulus stamp their feet to ancient warrior dances and the *ingungu* rhythm drum drones on throughout the night. Captain Morgan flows like water, and *Chuma* and *Susi* seem to sigh with relief. The press badgers us for expedition anecdotes. This, I suppose, is our moment of triumph, but what this family journey has really taught us is that it's humankind that makes the world go round. Although we might come from all walks of life, creeds and races, it's that basic sense of humanness (*ubuntu*) that binds us all together along this imaginary line called Capricorn.

ON 23°27' WE TURN THE PIROGUE INTO THE WIND AND EMPTY THE CAPRICORN CALABASH INTO THE MOZAMBIQUE CHANNEL —

AND SO THE CAPRICORN SCROLL AND CALABASH ARE BROUGHT HOME SAFELY! WE'VE MADE IT!

CAPRICORN SCROLL OF PEACE & GOODWILL

CAPRICORN CALABASH.

VICTORY AT LAST!

Cooking with the Captain

Kingsley doesn't go anywhere without a bottle or two of Captain Morgan Rum. It's great as a mosquito repellent, kick starts instant parties and can even be drunk warm in an enamel mug, not to mention renoster coffee. 'We even cook with it,' says Kingsley, 'and I don't mind sharing a recipe or two with you.'

The Captain's Steak à la Fosholo - (Steak à la Spade)

This is the best when everyone's tired and hungry and you have been late getting into camp. The wind's howling and you are all too bloody lazy to open up the grub box. Don't forget that the first thing you always do – and it's a golden rule when on safari – is light the fire, unfold the old camp chairs, put on the camp kettle and break open the Captain Morgan.

In no time at all everyone's relaxed and it's time for instant nourishment. That's when you unscrew the old spade from the side of the roof rack. The same spade that you go to the toilet with and use to dig the vehicle out of holes. So do yourself a favour, push it in and out of the sand a few times to clean it up, rub it with an old rag and put it over the hot fire. soon it's red hot, that's when you throw on that massive piece of rump that's just starting to go off. In seconds it's sizzling away. Sometimes you don't even have to get off your chair; just lean over and pour the Captain straight from the neck of the bottle over the steak. Careful, the flames are high, so watch your beard! Turn the steak over and do it again; then throw the sizzling protein onto wooden Zulu meat platter (*ugqoko*), cut it into thin strips, pour coarse salt and hot chilli onto the side of the platter and get the team to eat Zulu style: each person coming forward one at a time to dip the long slivers of blood-oozing, succulent steak into the salt. Immediately start digging into the cool box for the next piece of steak, pour more Captain's and continue with Steak à la Fosholo.

Renoster Coffee

So often there is no pudding in camp and you'd like to end the evening with something sweet. Take the old cotton bag of cheap ground coffee, complete with string attached, and let it boil away in the dented camp kettle. Pour a big tot of Captain into an enamel mug and add the strong black coffee. Make two holes in the condensed milk tin (have a big suck whilst no-one is looking), then blow through one hole and the condensed milk will squirt out of the opposite hole straight into the coffee mug. Ask one of the thinner members of the party to squeeze into the back of the Land Rover and haul out Ouma's rusks – happy dunking!

N.B. On cold desert mornings renoster coffee is also a great breakfast brew that generally adds to one's navigational skills.

ENAMEL MUG A BIG ONE FOR SPECIAL OCCASIONS AND RENOSTER COFFEE -

Glossary of Capricorn words and phrases

adeus – 'goodbye' in Portuguese
Alrededo põr Tierra del Mundo – 'around the world by land' in Spanish
animitas – an Andean cactus
bakkie – South African term for a utility vehicle
bienvenidos – 'welcome' in Spanish
billabong – Australian term for a pool in a creek
billycan – Australian term for a round, tin cooking vessel
biltong – sundried meat
boa noite – 'good night' in Portuguese
boa tarde – 'good day' in Portuguese
boerewors – type of South African sausage
bom dia – 'good morning' in Portuguese
bon jour – 'good day' in French
bon voyage – 'have a good journey' in French
braai(vleis) – South African term for a barbecue
buenos dias – 'good day' in Spanish
buitepos – 'border post' in Afrikaans
buraco – the hole left from an explosion
bushmeat – meat such as duiker, impala, venison and warthog
cachimbo – herbal tea
Caipirinhas – brand of Brazilian alcoholic drink
carioca – an inhabitant of Rio
carpet bagger – an Australian term for a thief
cerveja – 'beer' in Spanish
Chaco – dry, semi-desert area in Brazil and Paraguay
chuascaria – barbeque-style Brazilian restaurant
cinq-cent-cinq – Peugeot 505
cleanskins – Australian term for unbranded cattle
coppo – Australian term for a police officer
didgeridoo (didge) – an Aboriginal wind instrument
difflock – mechanism used to improve 4x4s' traction
domba – type of Venda dance
donga – gulley
dreamtime – Aboriginal history
dumelang – greeting in North Sotho (Pedi)
dunny – Australian term for an longdrop toilet
estancia – Argentinean cattle station
fady – Madagascan taboo or luck
farofa – type of Brazilian dish
favela – Brazilian term for a shanty town
fazenda – Brazilian term for a cattle station
fossas – type of little mammal
freshies – Australian term for freshwater crocodiles
g'day cobber – Australian greeting
gaucho – South American cowboy
gendarmerie – military police
giya – frenetic Zulu personal dance to one's ancestors
(muchas) gracias – '(many) thanks' in Spanish
gringos – Spanish term for foreigners
hacienda – South American homestead
halala – 'hurrah' in Zulu
hambani kahle – farewell greeting in Zulu
icece – Zulu coming-of-age ceremony
imphephu – type of wild heather burnt to call up ancestral spirits

induna – Zulu headman
ingungu – Zulu rhythm drum
inselberg – very large rocky outcrop
inspan – to decamp
ishaka –intestinal beetle
isigenyana – Zulu hunting dance
izingqoko – traditional Zulu wooden meat platter
ja boet – South African expression of affirmation
Jompa Jozz – To jump the fence to Johannesburg
kaptein – 'captain' in Afrikaans
katembe – red wine and Coke
kraal – an enclosed group of huts
Laurentina – brand of Mozambican beer
lekker – 'great' or 'tasty' in Afrikaans
mampoer – homemade alcoholic drink
mealies – maize
mlungus – Zulu term for white people
mtethu – established traditional practice
muthi – African Medicine
mvalalisa – Zulu farewell ceremony
nada – 'nothing' in Spanish
njomani – ilala palm wine
(munto) obrigado – '(many) thanks' in Portuguese
off stone – Australian term meaning 'unlucky'
okes – South African term for men
outspan – to make camp
pantanal – 'swamp' or 'marsh' in Portuguese
pão – Portuguese bread
pousada – 'guesthouse' in Portuguese
pousse-pousse – Madagascan riksha
ranovola – 'rice water' in Malagasy
renoster coffee – Captain Morgan rum and coffee
salaama – Madagascan greeting
salties – Australian term for saltwater crocodiles
sangoma – Zulu diviner
sawubona – Zulu greeting
siyabonga – 'thank you' in Zulu
slab of stubbies – Australian term for a case of beers
slap chips – soft French fries
slipface – steep side of a desert sand dune
sunnies – Australian term for sunglasses
tenrecs – type of tiny rodent
tereré – South American herbal tea
Terra da Boa Gente – 'land of good people' in Portuguese
thamala elanga – 'to sit in the early morning sun' in Zulu
ubuntu – sense of humanness and togetherness
umfanyan – young Zulu boy
ute – Australian term for a utility vehicle
vasbyt – Afrikaans term meaning 'bite the bullet'
veloma – 'goodbye' in Malagasy
velskoene – South African handmade leather boots
Voorktrekkers – South African Afrikaaner colonists
xau xung – Bushman greeting
yerba maté – South American herbal tea

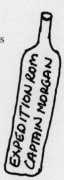

Siyabongas, thanks and obrigados

It's been a fascinating journey, made possible by a wonderful mix of human beings. Thanks, Roger Gaisford, for sowing the seeds of this crazy Capricorn idea in the first place. Thanks to Moira Moses, Paul Melhuish, Erwin Rencken and Lesley Sutton of Land Rover South Africa: without Land Rovers *Chuma* and *Susi* we'd still be travelling along Capricorn on foot! Good old Captain Morgan's spirit of adventure kept us going through thick and thin – a special thanks to Carl Reinders and his Captain Morgan team. African Satellite Corporation: thanks, Ernst Spaans, you were our lifeline. Barry Robinson-Butler of Flight Centre: you gave us wings. Duncan Davies of Phoenix Shipping and Eddie Cairns of Polaris: *siyabonga*! To Aart van der Heijden, Charl van Wyk, Barry Leitch and all at Shakaland: thanks for a great send-off and welcome-home party, and thanks to all the friends who attended.

Thanks, in Mozambique, to: Paul, Liz and Nigel Hallowes; Erwin and Sylvia Jakes; Dave and Gill Law of Barra Lodge; Custodio Manhica, our friend and translator; Mateus Ngonyama; and to the Governor of Inhambane Señor Aires Ali – *munto obrigado*! In South Africa: Chris and Betty Morris; Sgt Morné Carelsen; Johann (Mabarule) and Jocelyn Oelofse of the Kruger National Park; Arrie Horn and Klaas Boonzaaier of Limpopo Province's Ivory Trail; the Shangaan people of the ancient salt works at eSoutini; Chief Madzivhandila; Chris Olivier and the Gilfillans at the Lalapanzi Hotel; and old friend Tom Shearer at The Ranch. In Botswana: Oom Doep at Parrs Halt; the Kalahari cattle station owners; the rangers at Khutse Game Reserve and the small Bushman community near Ukwi. In Namibia: Kaptein John McNab of the Rehobath Basters; Ben Beytell, and especially Kobus Alberts of the Ministry of Environment and Tourism; Chief Reuben of the Topnaars; Heine Schlushe, the crazy microlight pilot from Swakopmund; Martin Reimann of Walvis Bay Protea Hotel; and Don and Ann Balmer, who joined us at Inhambane.

In South America: Alexandré Mirande, the friendly Carioca from Rio who introduced us to the fantasy world of Brazil; Chief Auwa, sons Donezetti and Diago, and Albino the hunter, not to mention the kindness of Nhandaru, god of the forest; Maude Motto of Isle la Grande and the friendly revellers of Porto Figuera; the hospitable *fazenda* owners of the Mato Grosso; Salia, who guided us across Paraguay; Señor Ramon of Estancia Santa Maria and the Nivaclé Indian community of Escalante; Major Nikolini of the Argentinian *gendarmerie*; Martin Escudero, the young Spanish translator; and Manuelle Morena the *gaucho* of Casa San Antonio.

In Australia: old friends, Vic and Carmel Hall, and cousin Ian Fisher – bless you, Fish, we'd never have made it without you; Karen Byron from Land Rover Australia; Andrew Harper, one of Australia's greatest modern-day explorers – thanks, mate, for all the advice; Geoscience Australia, for the excellent survey maps, and the Royal Australian Flying Doctor Service in Alice Springs for being on standby to assist us; a special thanks to the Stockman's Hall of Fame in Longreach and all the colourful and hospitable station owners of Australia's Outback, in particular Gary and Dallas Hill of Carlo Station, Tim and Sean D'Arcey at Lyndon Station and the Horricks at Warroora; the Aboriginal people of Central Australia, especially to Gural Wakarn (Tommy Crow) – Tommy, your paintings on our Land Rover proved to be our lucky talisman across the Gibson.

In Madagascar: crossing the island would not have been possible without the support and friendship of David Fox, the Durban-based South African Consul to Madagascar; Mark Ravalomanana, the new President, we thank you for your hospitality and wish you well. As you take your island paradise along a difficult road into the future we implore you and your government to preserve your beautiful rainforests. Bakoly Razanamiarantsoa ('B'), for interpreting and guiding us along our difficult Capricorn journey across Madagascar – and please thank all the porters for us, especially my friend Barto.

Thanks to the team at Struik Publishers who stuck with us through everything and have been bold enough to turn the Capricorn Expedition journal into this book. A special thanks to Steve Connolly, Dominique le Roux, Monique Whitaker, Alison Day, Lesley Hay-Whitton and Janet Larsen.

To dear friend Taryn Stoddart, whose penalty for holding the fort whilst we were on expedition was tirelessly to type out the manuscript taken from the scribblings in my journal. To Matthew Frank at RDF Media in London, thanks for hanging in there and succeeding in turning our journey into a television series with National Geographic.

To all those wonderful people we met along the Tropic of Capricorn: I am sorry that I am not able to mention you each by name, but thanks for your kindness and hospitality. To expedition members Troy Wade, Nicola Balcomb and Linda Sparrow, and to cameramen Mike Yelseth, Tim Chevallier and Luke Cormack: thanks for the shared friendship of the Capricorn journey. To Mashozi and Ross, we did it as a family – the memories of our crazy Capricorn journey will, I know, remain with us forever.

Kingsley Holgate

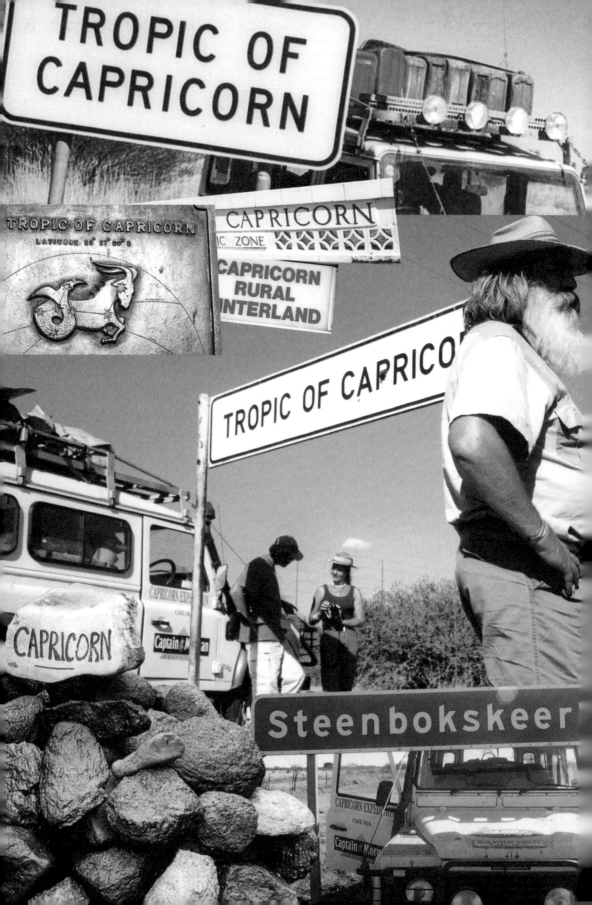